ST. THOMAS AND THE PROBLEM OF THE SOUL
IN THE THIRTEENTH CENTURY

ST. THOMAS

AND

THE PROBLEM OF THE SOUL IN THE THIRTEENTH CENTURY

By

Anton Charles Pegis, Ph.D.

PONTIFICAL INSTITUTE OF MEDIAEVAL STUDIES

Toronto, Canada

1934

ISBN 0-88844-406-0

Copyright by

PONTIFICAL INSTITUTE OF MEDIAEVAL STUDIES

Published 1934
Reprinted 1976

UNIVERSA PRESS, WETTEREN (BELGIUM)

FOREWORD

The following work was originally presented to the University of Toronto as a thesis in the spring of 1931. Since then, it has been changed and, in part, rewritten, though the substance of the work is still the same. The changes include the addition of an introductory chapter and the complete revision of the chapter devoted to St. Bonaventure. Other changes introduced in the thesis include such minor corrections in language, etc., as are ordinarily involved in the revision of a manuscript.

I must express here my indebtedness to Professor Etienne Gilson for his kind assistance and patience in the choice and completion of the subject; to Father Gerald B. Phelan, for many delightful conversations on the significance of Thomistic ideas; to Father Henry Carr, for his help in reading the texts of Plato, Aristotle and Nemesius; and to Father John F. McCormick, now of Loyola University, whose friendship and encouragement and guidance are more pervasive than acknowledgment can equal or measure.

A. C. Pegis.

November 11, 1933,
Marquette University,
Milwaukee, Wisconsin.

CONTENTS

Contents

ST. THOMAS AND THE
PROBLEM OF THE SOUL IN THE
THIRTEENTH CENTURY

I. INTRODUCTION.

The transformation of Aristotle the logician into Aristotle the philosopher, which took place during the quarter of a century preceding the famous condemnation of 1210, is important not only because of the significance of Aristotle in the thirteenth century, but also because of the circumstances surrounding his entrance into the west as a philosopher. Aristotle came into the Latin world neither alone nor unheralded, for his works were accompanied, and even preceded, by treatises which reveal the depth of his influence and the universality of his philosophical vocabulary. His own treatises were accompanied by numerous and important commentaries, Greek and Arabic in origin, which were intended to explain his text, but which often succeeded in pressing or otherwise altering the meaning of his ideas. While a great variety of interpretation thus grew up,[1] that of Averroes became the most famous,

---

1. The obscurities to be found in the text of Aristotle are notorious. In the twelfth century, John of Salisbury could write as follows of the *Posterior Analytics*: "Ad hec, liber quo demonstratiua traditur disciplina, ceteris longe turbatior est, et transpositione sermonum, traiectione litterarum, desuetudine exemplorum, que a diversis disciplinis mutuata sunt, et postremo, quod non contingit auctorem, adeo scriptorum deprauatus est uitio, ut fere quot capita tot obstacula habeat. Et bene quidem ubi non sunt obstacula, capitibus plura. Unde a plerisque in interpretem difficultatis culpa refunditur, asserentibus librum ad nos non recte translatum" (*Metalogicon*, iv, 6; ed. C. C. J. Webb, Oxford, Clarendon Press, 1929, p. 171). Thus, according to John of Salis-

and if Aristotle entered the west as the Philosopher, Averroes followed him as his Commentator.

Averroes is a remarkable and, in view of later events, very significant example of the influence which Aristotle exercised before his entrance into the Christian world. For him Aristotle is not only a great philosopher, he is also a prodigy of nature, embodying the highest perfection of which man is capable. Thus, according to him, Aristotle is the founder of logic, physics and metaphysics, and after fifteen hundred years no one has found any serious errors in his works; he is a man apart, more worthy to be divine

---

bury, a Latinized Aristotle presented not only difficulty of style, but also corrupt manuscript readings, and this was so generally recognized that many thought that the *Posterior Analytics* was badly translated.   Similar remarks are to be found in Roger Bacon.   Later on, during the Renaissance, one of the many objections to Aristotle was the obscurity of his language. Vivès, for example, considers that one of the causes of the decay of the liberal arts in his day was the obscurity of the ancient authors, especially Aristotle. In the quotation from the first book of *De Causis Corruptarum Artium* which Iohannes Launoius gives, we read: "Themistius quodam loco furori simile esse dicit, si quid speret, se ex Aristotelis scriptis sententiam eius penitus assecuturum. Idem ipse Aristoletes ad Alexandrum scripsit neminem commentarios illos, quos Rex doleret in vulgum missos, intellecturum, nisi qui abs se domi audiuisset. Nec solum obscuritas fuit in rebus sensorum sed etiam in uerbis. Affectavit enim quoddam dicendi genus pressum et adstrictum." Vivès there notes that the translators have made matters worse because now "clarmores, tumultus, tragoediae, quae de intelligentia dicti cuiusquam Aristotelis excitarentur, non de illius essent, sed interpretis sensu." Add to this the history of Aristotle's works down to the time of their publication by Andronicus of Rhodes (c. 50 A.D.) and the controversies which arose as to the authenticity of some of them, and Vivès is then ready with his conclusion: "Quis posset bene sequi ducem tam obscure admonentem?" Cf. Ioannes Launoius, *De Varia Aristotelis in Academia Parisiensi Fortuna*, cap. xiv; ed. Io. Hermannus ab Elswich, Vitembergae apud Saxones . . . Typis Samuelis Creusigii, 1720, p. 263-267.

than human: *dignus est esse divinus magis, quam humanus.*
"I believe," he writes elsewhere, "that this man is the very
norm of nature, the exemplar that nature found to reveal
the highest perfection that man could reach in this world."
And again: "The teaching of Aristotle is the highest truth,
because his intellect was the culminating point of the human
intellect; hence we may say quite appropriately that he was
created and given to us by divine Providence that we might
learn all that could be learned: *Aristotelis doctrina est summa
veritas quoniam eius intellectus fuit finis humani intellectus,
quare bene dicitur, quod fuit creatus et datus nobis divina
Providentia, ut sciremus quidquid potest sciri*".[2] To
Averroes, therefore, the name of Aristotle was synonymous
with philosophy itself, with a sort of incarnation of all human
wisdom; so that it is not surprising to find that he became
the prophet of Aristotle, much as Lucretius had become the
prophet of Epicurus.

While it is extremely difficult to determine whether Averroes is as successful an interpreter as he is an enthusiastic
disciple,[3] it is fortunately less difficult and more immediately

---

2. The necessary references will be found in P. Mandonnet,
Siger de Brabant et l'Avérroisme latin au xiiie siècle, 2nd ed. *(Les
philosophes belges,* vi-vii), Part I, Louvain, 1911, p. 153-154.

3. P. Mandonnet *(op. cit.,* p. 155-156) would answer the question
by an almost unqualified affirmative. The *almost* adds that Averroes simply carried some Aristotelian doctrines to their logical
conclusion, while Aristotle had left them undeveloped; but "dans
leur grandes lignes, les doctrines d'Averroès sont contenues soit
explicitement, soit implicitement, dans celles d'Aristote" (p. 155).
That is why Siger of Brabant can be considered an authentic disciple of a consistently developed Aristotelianism: "A ce point de
vue, et c'était celui de Siger de Brabant, l'Avérroisme n'est autre
chose que l'aristotélisme poussé à ses conséquences" (p. 156).—
For the opinion of St. Thomas Aquinas on this question, cf. *infra,*
ch. iv. B. For Duns Scotus it is Avicenna who appears to be the
correct interpreter of Aristotle: cf. E. Gilson, *Avicenne et le point
de départ de Duns Scot (Archives d'hist. doctr. et litt. du moyen*

pertinent to determine the attitude of the thinkers of the thirteenth century toward Aristotle and his prophet. Now, it is abundantly clear that they shared neither the enthusiasm nor the interpretation of Averroes. Even such individuals as Siger of Brabant and Boethius of Dacia, who appear as the chief protagonists of Averroism, are careful to make their *intentions* clear: they intend merely to report such doctrines, not to accept them as true.[4] But if, apart from the enigmatic position of the Averroists, there was general and decided opposition to Averroes, there was no agreement with respect to the philosophy of Aristotle. The disagreement, indeed, extended not only to the meaning of his texts, but also, where they were agreed upon his meaning, to the compatibility of his ideas with Christian doctrine. The problem which thus faced the thirteenth century was a fundamental one, and the positions adopted by the various thinkers marked decisively the different mentalities of the age; for in their attempt to express to themselves and to others their attitude towards the philosophy of Aristotle, the theologians of the thirteenth century were called upon to formulate in an explicit way their own philosophical decisions. As a result, the different reactions which this problem of evaluating and interpreting Aristotle brought into existence are one of the principal means that we have of distinguishing the various doctrinal currents of the thirteenth century. More particularly, these reactions to the philosophy of Aristotle came

---

âge, II) Paris, J. Vrin, 1927, p. 93, n. 1. As we shall see, St. Thomas will accept neither an Averroistic nor an Avicennian interpretation of Aristotle, although in particular problems he will side with one or the other as the question demands.

4. Cf. Siger of Brabant, *Quaestiones de Anima Intellectiva*, qu. iii, ed. P. Mandonnet, *op. cit.* Part ii, Louvain, 1908, p. 153-154; qu. vi, p. 163; qu. vii, p. 164, 169. Some recently discovered texts of Siger seem even to suggest the hypothesis that his own position became later more closely similar to that of St. Thomas Aquinas. See F. Van Steenberghen, *op. cit. infra*, p. 19, note 17.

to mean the extent, if any, to which a Christian tradition, whose speculations were deeply Augustinian, could and did yield to the influence of Aristotle.

If we recall, in a general way, the influence of the Platonic tradition on St. Augustine, it will become clear that the problem of the reception of Aristotle in the thirteenth century was equivalent, in its bare outlines, to the renewal of the ancient quarrel between Plato and his illustrious pupil. Nevertheless, the terms of the conflict were new, for something had happened to the doctrines of both thinkers before their transmission to the middle ages.   Briefly, what had happened was that Plato had been baptized by St. Augustine,[5] while Aristotle had been submitted by the Arabians to the influence of their religious beliefs. The result was that those doctrines of Plato which, as such, were unacceptable to Christianity, received a transformation distinctly favorable to their reception within the Christian world; while the doctrines of Aristotle, initially more suspect, were destined to be accentuated by the Arabians in precisely those points in which the possibility of conflict with Christianity was greatest. That Plato had taught, or appeared to teach, the doctrine of creation in the *Timaeus,* that he had upheld so passionately the immortality of the soul in the *Phaedo* and in the tenth book of the *Republic,* that he had championed, with such religious fervor, the existence and providence of God in the *Laws,* the work of his extreme old age, to say nothing of his famous theory of Ideas, were facts

---

5. An important and often-quoted text of St. Augustine, in which this transformation of Platonic doctrine takes place, is *Liber de Diversis Quaestionibus* 83, qu. 46; Migne, *Patrologia Latina*, vol. xl., col. 29-31. For an analysis of this text and a collection of references showing its later history, cf. M. Grabmann, *Des hl. Augustinus quaestio de ideis (De diversis quaestionibus lxxxiii, qu. 46) in ihrer inhaltlichen und geschichtlichen Bedeutung,* Philosophisches Jahrbuch, 43, 3 (Fulda, 1930), p. 297-307.

which tended spontaneously to insure his position in Christian thought.[6]

Aristotle, on the contrary, possessed no such credentials. The eternity of motion, the doctrine that the Prime Mover had no knowledge of the universe (and therefore no providence over it), the famous attack on the theory of Ideas, so serious an error in the eyes of a Christian theologian,[7] a

6. I do not imply, of course, that all these works were known to the middle ages. On the contrary, at the turn of the thirteenth century only a part of the *Timaeus*, the *Phaedo* and the *Meno* were apparently the only Platonic dialogues accessible directly to the Latin world. The *Phaedo* and *Meno*, translated in the twelfth century by Henricus Aristippus (cf. O. H. Haskins, *Studies in the History of Medieval Science*, Harvard U. Press, 1924, pp. 165 ff., do not seem to have had much circulation. Thus, Leopold Gaul has shown that of the many works of Plato to which St. Albert refers, only the *Timaeus* was known to him directly, while in the case of the *Phaedo* and *Meno*, which he knew in part, a "direkte Kenntnis der betr. lateinischen Uebersetzungen selbet ist aber äusserst unwahrscheinlich." Then, basing his judgment on Albert's extensive knowledge and great interest in Platonism, L. Gaul concludes that the twelfth century Sicilian translation of the *Phaedo* and the *Meno* "an den Stätten wissenschaftlicher Forschung in den genannten Gebieten, d.h. also in den meisten Zentren des damaligen geistigen Lebens, noch nicht bekannt geworden waren" (Leopold Gaul, *Alberts des Grossen Verhältnis zu Plato*, in *Beiträge zur Geschichte der Philosophie des Mittelalters*, xii, 1, Munster, i. W., 1913, p. 9-30, especially p. 29-30).—St. Thomas' reference to the *Republic* in the *De Unitate Intellectus* is taken from Themistius who uses the sun allegory in his commentary on Aristotle's *De Anima*: cf. *infra*, p. 189, n. 3.

7. For example, in the eyes of St. Bonaventure it is this denial of the Ideas and, consequently, the divine exemplarism, which has made Aristotle the leader of those philosophers who *tenebras secuti sunt*. Cf. the famous text of the *Collationes in Hexaemeron*, coll. vi; *Opera*, ed. Quaracchi (cf. *infra*, p. 26, n. 1), vol. v, p. 360-361. This text will be found also in P. Mandonnet, *Siger de Brabant*, I2, p. 156, n. 2. A comparison between this text and the list of propositions condemned by Stephen Tempier, Dec. 10, 1270 (*Chartularium Universitatis Parisiensis*, ed. Denifle-Chatelain,

psychology that appeared to endanger the immortality of
the soul:—here are ideas that are not calculated to appeal
to the Christian mind. But when these ideas are so formu-
lated and motivated that Aristotle is made to deny creation,
the providence of God and the possibility of individual immortality, then what might have remained simply a source
of prejudice against him really became a point of explicit
and radical opposition to him. It is not surprising, therefore, to find that Aristotle entered the thirteenth century
a man condemned.

In the long series of condemnations which followed,[8] we
must note two facts, namely, the official attitude of the papacy
towards Aristotle and the rôle of St. Thomas in the development of Aristotelianism. While the decision of the local
council of Paris in 1210,[9] confirmed by Robert de Courçon
in 1215,[10] had forbidden the teaching of Aristotle, Pope Gregory IX took a modified view on the question and opened
the way for the reception of Aristotle into the Christian
world. Thus, his reaffirmation of the decree of 1210 was
only a provisional measure until such time as the texts of
Aristotle were examined and freed from error: *quousque
examinati fuerint et ab omni, errorum suspicione purgati.*[11]
In accord with this attitude, he appointed a commission of

1889, vol. i, p. 486-487) will reveal clearly the close connection
which St. Bonaventure saw between Aristotle and Averroism.—
St. Thomas Aquinas himself, in commenting on Aristotle, considers it necessary to point out explicitly that Aristotle's criticism of
the theory of Ideas does not affect in any way the divine exemplarism: "Sciendum autem quod illa ratio, etsi destruat exem-
plaria a Platone posita, non tamen removet divinam scientiam esse
rerum omnium exemplarem" (*In Metaph. Aristotelis Comm.*, Lib.
I, lectio xv; ed. M.-R. Cathala, Taurini, 2nd ed., 1926, no. 233).

8. For a continuous history of the condemnation, cf. P. Mandonnet, *Siger de Brabant*, 1² p. 1-64, 90-112, 196-251.

9. *Chartularium*, vol. I, p. 70-71.

10. *Chartularium*, vol. I, p. 78-79.

11. *Chartularium*, vol. I, p. 138.

three men to undertake the work of revision, *ne utile per inutile vitietur* and *ut quae sunt suspecta remotis incunctanter ac inoffense in reliquis studeatur.*[12] The activity of Pope Gregory IX, therefore, is decisive in the reception of Aristotle. It forms, indeed, the immediate antecedent of St. Thomas' activity at the court of Pope Urban IV.[13] For just as it was Gregory IX who assumed the responsibility of putting the works of Aristotle at the disposal of Christian readers, so it was St. Thomas Aquinas who, through the long translating efforts of William of Moerbeke, brought this work to its completion. The immense amount of work that such a task required is well known. Ultimately it meant not only the complete reconstruction of the Latin text on the basis of Greek originals, but also a minute and literal commentary on the text for the purpose of insuring accuracy in the transmission of Aristotle's meaning.[14]

---

12. *Chartularium*, vol. I, p. 143-144.

13. During the interval, the faculty of arts at Paris, influenced, it may be, by the absence of any injunctions against the study of Aristotle at the University of Toulouse (*Chartularium*, vol. I, p. 131), seems to have understood the papal attitude towards Aristotle in a somewhat elastic way. Thus, among the regulations governing the English nation, passed early in 1252, the reading of the *De Anima* was made compulsory (*Chartularium*, vol. I, p. 228). Three years later (March 19, 1255) Aristotle made what has been called his official entrance into the faculty of arts, for in that year almost all of his works were made compulsory (*Chartularium*, vol. I, p. 278).

14. On St. Thomas' method as an interpreter of Aristotle, cf. M. Grabmann, *Mittelalterliches Geistesleben*, München, 1926, p. 281-289.

Between the decision of Pope Gregory IX and the historical reconstruction of Aristotle undertaken by St. Thomas, we must place the activity of St. Albert the Great. Cf. P. Mandonnet, *Siger de Brabant*, 1², p. 61-62; M. Grabmann, *Der hl. Albert der Grosse*, München, 1932, p. 13-15. As G. Théry has shown, one of the salient features of St. Albert's criticism of David of Dinant was the attempt to rehabilitate Aristotle by showing not only that David

Now, if it is quite clear that St. Thomas realized the ambitions of Pope Gregory IX, it is not clear why he should have undertaken a task that was to place him in a position acceptable neither to the faculty of theology nor to the faculty of arts. Let us suppose that he began his own direct study of Aristotle at the moment when he was writing the *Contra Gentiles,* or approximately in 1260.[15] What was it that

---

was confusing logic and metaphysics, but also that he was misusing and thereby compromising Aristotle. According to St. Albert, David's ideas, apart from being heretical and bad philosophy, are a *prava intelligentia dictorum Aristotelis (Summa Theologiae,* P. II, tr. xii, qu. 72, m. 4, a. 2; ed. Borgnet (cf. *infra,* p. 77, n. 1, vol. 33, p. 45.—Cf. G. Théry, *Autour du décret de* 1210 : *David de Dinant, Etude sur son panthéisme matérialiste* (Bibliothèque thomiste, VI), Le Saulchoir, 1925, especially p. 84-113.

In connection with the task of rehabilitating Aristotle as it was undertaken by St. Albert and St. Thomas, we may note the remark with which an anonymous translator of Philiponos' commentary on an extremely controverted part of the *De Anima* (III, c. 4-9) concludes his work: *Puto, qui haec legerit, ad intellectum litere Aristotelis plus quam ante lumen habebit.* Cf. M. Grabmann, *Mittelalterliche lateinische Uebersetzungen von Schriften der Aristoteles-Kommentatoren Johannes Philoponos, Alexander von Aphrodisias und Themistios* (Sitzungsberichte der Bayerischen Akademie der Wissenschaften, Phil.-hist. Abteilung, 1929, Heft 7) München, 1929, p. 12. Grabmann has argued at length that the translator of this commentary is not William of Moerbeke (*op. cit.,* p. 15-31).—As the translation of this commentary appeared about the middle of the century, it well represents the psychological difficulties which met the interpreters of Aristotle at that time and indicates an anxiety to determine, among the various interpretations of Aristotle which the Arabian commentators proposed, the meaning of Aristotle's original Greek text. The rôle of Philoponos, who was at once a Greek and a Christian, thus becomes significant: cf. Grabmann, *op. cit.,* p. 31-48.

15. Cf. M. Grabmann, *Mittelalterliches Geistesleben,* p. 295.— More recently, P. Synave has argued that the *terminus a quo* of the *Contra Gentiles* is March 13, 1258. Cf. P. Synave, *La révélation des vérités divines naturelles d'après s. Thomas,* in *Mélanges Man-*

caused him to concern himself with Aristotle just at the time
when one of the fundamental expressions of his thought was
taking form? At the time he was writing the *Contra Gentiles* Averroism had been growing in the faculty of arts for
about ten years[16]. Now, by espousing the cause of Aristotle
at precisely this time, St. Thomas was destined not only to depart from the traditional Augustinian doctrines of the faculty
of theology, but also to ally himself, at least in the eyes
of the theologians, with the Aristotelianism of the Averroists. St. Thomas' own procedure was some justification for
such an inference. The arguments which he uses in defense
of the soul as the substantial form of man could be found

---

donnet (*Bibliothèque thomiste*, xiii-xiv), Paris, 1930, vol. i, p. 362-
364. On some historical conditions out of which arose St. Thomas'
Contra Gentiles, cf. M.-M. Gorce, *La lutte "contra gentiles" à Paris
au xiiie siècle*, in *Mélanges Mandonnet*, vol. i, p. 223-243.

As we shall see, the second book of the *Contra Gentiles* is a long
and serious effort to separate Aristotle from his commentators. In
this work St. Thomas speaks as one who has studied the problems involved in Aristotle's psychology and who has come to definite conclusions of his own on their solution. As against this
definiteness of the *Contra Gentiles*, we may note the less positive
attitude of his commentary on the *De Trinitate* of Boethius: "Sed
quia verba Philosophi in III de Anima, *magis videntur sonare*,
quod intellectus agens sit potentia animae, et huic etiam auctoritas Scripturae consonat, quae lumine intellectuali nos insignitos
esse profitetur, cui Philosophus comparat intellectum agentem, ideo
in anima ponitur respectu operationis intelligibilis, quae est cog-
nitio veritatis, et potentia activa et passiva" *(In Boethium de Trinitate*, qu. i, a. 1; *Opuscula Omnia*, ed. P. Mandonnet, Paris, 1927,
vol. iii, p. 28). It thus appears that on more than one point the
thought of St. Thomas before the *Contra Gentiles* "est en travail":
cf. P. Synave, *loc. cit.*, vol. i, p. 353.

16. According to Mandonnet (*Siger de Brabant*, I[2], p. 59-63),
the rise of Averroism is to be placed shortly after 1250. Siger of
Brabant himself, however, does not appear in history until the
following decade. Thus far, the first fact that we know concerning
him belongs to the year 1266: *Chartularium*, vol. I, p. 450, 456;
Mandonnet, *op. cit.*, p. 80ff.

in Siger of Brabant,[17] and were capable of receiving in Pomponatius, however unjustly, a completely materialistic interpretation.[18]. Nevertheless, in spite of the apparent affinities

---

17. Cf. Siger of Brabant, *Quaestiones in Aristotelis Libros de Anima*, Lib. II, qu. 5, 6, 7; ed. F. Van Steenberghen, *Siger de Brabant d'après ses oeuvres inédits, I. Les oeuvres inédits (Philosophes belges*, xii), Louvain, 1931, p. 62-63, 64, 65. Cp. St. Thomas, *Summa Theologica*, I, 76, 3; *Quaes. disp. de Anima*, a. 11.

18. Cf. *Petri Pomponatii Mantuani Tractatus de Immortalitate Animae* . . . edidit . . . Christ. Godofr. Bardili, Tubingae, 1791, Sumptibus Joh. Georg. Cotta. Bardili used three seventeenth century editions for his text (cf. *op. cit.*, p. xxiii-xxiv). The treatise itself, which was published by Pomponatius in Bologna, in 1516, arose out of a remark that he made while lecturing on the *De Coelo* of Aristotle, namely, *Divi Thomae Aquinatis positionem de animorum immortalitate, quamquam veram et in se firmissimam* . . . , *Aristotelis tamen dictis minime consonare* . . . (*Tractatus de Immortalitate Animae*, Prooemium; *ed. cit.*, p. 1). Hence the following questions from his young Dominican pupil: "Primum scilicet, quid, revelationibus et miraculis semotis, persistendoque pure infra limites naturales, hac in re sentis, alterum vero, quamnam sententiam Aristotelis in eadem materia fuisse censes?" (*ibid.*; *ed. cit.*, p. 1-2).

The common ground between Pomponatius and St. Thomas is the rejection of the doctrine of the plurality of forms and, consequently, the rejection of the *motor-mobile* union between soul and body. Pomponatius' treatment of Plato in this connection is noteworthy: "Quidam enim ipsorum posuerunt, animam magis se habere ad hominem, ut motor ad motum, quam ut forma ad materiam. Et haec videtur fuisse mens Platonis, in principio Alcibiadis dicentis, hominem esse animam utentem corpore . . ." (*Tractatus*, cap. v; *ed. cit.*, p. 22). (The reference to Plato is *Alcibiades* I, p. 129e-131a.) Against this position, however, is the criticism of St. Thomas: "Hic autem modus . . . a Divo Thoma, in prima parte Summae, et in multis aliis locis impugnatur, et, mea sententia, abunde et manifeste" (*Tractatus*, cap. vi; *ed. cit.*, p. 22). Hence, by way of St. Thomas' criticism of the doctrine of plurality of forms, we arrive at the unity of the substantial form in man. It is here that the question of immortality arises. Let us note, at this point, Pompanatius' summary of the Thomistic position: " . . . quia tamen mihi videtur, quod D. Thomas copiosius et magis lucide

between St. Thomas and Averroism, the long polemic against
Averroes and his thirteenth century disciples that we find
in St. Thomas is clear proof of his intention to separate his
conception of Aristotle from an interpretation which, on

---

ipsum (i.e., this position) posuit, ideo ejus dicta solum referam,
utque ordinate intelligatur, ejus opinionem in quinque dictis col-
ligam. Primum itaque est, quod intellectivum et sensitivum in
homine sint idem re. Secundum, quod tale vere et simpliciter est
immortale, secundum quid vero mortale. Tertium, quod talis anima
vere est forma hominis, et non solum, ut motor. Quartum, quod
eadem anima est numerata ad numerationem individuorum. Quintum, quod hujusmodi anima incipit esse cum corpore, verum, quod
venit deforis, atque a solo Deo producitur, non quidem per gene-
rationem, sed per creationem, haec tamen non desinit esse cum
corpore, verum a parte post est perpetua" (*Tractatus*, cap. vii;
ed. cit., p. 24-25). Pomponatius has every intention of accepting
this tradition, not only because of Scriptural authority, but also
because of the authority of St. Thomas: "De veritate quidem hujus
positionis apud me nulla prorsus est ambiguitas, cum Scriptura
canonica, quae cuilibet rationi et experimento humano praeferenda
est, cum a Deo data sit, hanc propositionem sanciat . . . cum tanti
doctoris autoritas apud me summa est, nedum in divinis, verum in
ipsa via Aristotelis, non ausim contra eum aliquid affirmare . . . ."
(*Tractatus*, cap. viii; *ed. cit.*, p. 28). What he doubts, however, is
the ability of the natural reason to reach such a position: "Sed,
quod apud me vertitur in dubium, est, an ista dicta excedant
limites naturales, sic, quod aliquid vel creditum, vel revelatum,
praesupponant, et conformia sint dictis Aristotelis, sicut ipse Divus
Thomas enuntiat . . . In primo igitur ejus dicto non ambigo,
scilicet, quod re in homine idem sit sensitivum et intellectivum,
sed cetera quatuor sunt mihi valde ambigua" (*ibid.*). Now, the
union that is established between soul and body requires that the
intellect be the form of the body, for otherwise, "anima intellectiva non esset anima, cum, ut sic, non esset actus corporis physici
organici, quod est contra Aristotelem, ponentem illam esse definitionem communem omni animae, immo, per ipsum Thomam dictam univoce de omnibus animabus" (*ibid.; ed. cit.*, p. 32). But the
only condition under which Pomponatius will grant that such a
union is possible is the following: "Huic quidem dicto ego consentio, si ponitur materialis (sc. anima), verumtamen, si ponitur
immaterialis, ut ipse dicit, non videtur esse notum" (*ibid.; ed. cit.*,

certain fundamental points, he considered absolutely mis-
guided.

Perhaps the most obvious explanation of the Aristotelian
sympathies of St. Thomas is the combination of historical

---

p. 37). How, asks Pomponatius, can the soul, whose immortality
would require it to be a *quod est*, be the *quo est* of the composite
man (*ibid.*)? In other words, how are immortality and substantial unity compatible? Driven to this conclusion, we may either
retrace our steps, accept the doctrine of plurality of forms and
follow the Platonic tradition, or we may go on and make of the
soul a pure *quo est* of the composite and admit its mortality.
Pomponatius sees considerable wisdom in the Platonic position:
"Quare sapienter mihi visus est Plato dicere, ponens animam im-
mortalem, quod verius homo est anima utens corpore, quam compositum ex anima et corpore, et verius ejus motor, scilicet corporis,
quam ejus forma, cum anima sit illud quod vere est, et vere existit, et potest induere corpus, et eo spoliari. *Non video enim, quin
et D. Thomas non habeat hoc dicere*" (*ibid.; ed. cit.*, p. 38). But
the criticism of plurality of forms, in which St. Thomas himself
played the leading part, precludes the possibility of such a means
of escape. Hence, forced to accept the implications of substantial
union, we must say: "*Ex quibus modo est syllogizanda conclusio
principalis intenta, scilicet, quod anima humana simpliciter materialis est, et secundum quid immaterialis*" (*Tractatus*, cap. ix;
ed. cit., p. 46).

The experiences of Pomponatius with the problem of the soul,
therefore, are important as illustrating the materialistic conclusions to which, in his eyes, a Thomism that is consistent with its
Aristotelian point of departure must necessarily lead. Furthermore, it is important to note the rôle which Pomponatius assigns
to Platonism in this problem. For him Platonism is a means of
escape from the materialistic implications to be found in the psychology of Aristotle. This sequence of ideas in Pomponatius will
become all the more significant when we shall find that St. Thomas
has outlined all the difficulties which led to the Platonic conception of man, only to discard them. Apart from the clear picture
which Pomponatius thus presents of the place of St. Thomas in
the thought of the early sixteenth century, his account is important for the difficulties which it sees in the adoption of an Aristotelian position, and, in this way, renders the action of St. Thomas
even more perplexing and, historically, even more significant.

circumstances and conflicts that faced his age. While this will not explain the origin of Thomism, it will throw light on its mode of development. The full significance of these historical circumstances, however, does not appear until we confront them with some statements to be found in St. Thomas. In the *Contra Gentiles* he writes: *propositum nostrae intentionis est veritatem, quam fides catholica profitetur, pro nostro modulo manifestare, errores eliminando contrarios. Ut enim verbis Hilarii utar, "ego hoc vel praecipuum vitae meae officium debere me Deo conscius sum, ut eum omnis sermo meus et sensus loquatur."*[19] St. Thomas thus consecrates his life to a theological ideal. Now he finds himself in a set of circumstances which he has described and in which he has laid down a course of action to be followed by a doctor of the Church. In the introduction to a treatise addressed to Pope Urban IV in 1263, St. Thomas remarked that the rise of errors always gave the doctors of the Church an opportunity to restate more clearly and more carefully the doctrines which belonged to their faith, eliminating thereby the possibility of any influence at the hand of these errors: *errores circa fidem exorti, occasionem dederunt sanctis Ecclesiae Doctoribus, ut et quae sunt fidei maiori circumspectione traderent ad eliminandos errores exortos.* This is particularly true of St. Augustine (*egregio Doctorum*), who spoke more carefully concerning the freedom of the will in those books which he wrote after the rise of the Pelagian heresy. It is not surprising, therefore, he goes on to say, if *moderni fidei Doctores,* considering the errors which arose in their day, have spoken more guardedly concerning those doctrines around which heresies have arisen. It is, therefore, the need of the day which determined the formulation of a particular doctrine, and which, according as it saw the rise of new and hitherto unconsidered exigencies, introduced into the doctrines of

---

19. *Contra Gentiles*, I, 2.

faith the required precision. Nor is this all. For, while we are now possessed of a principle according to which we can meet the changing conditions of an age, we are also left with the difficulty of not knowing how to treat the formulations of doctrine that the past has to offer and that the present cannot use. Again in his rôle of theologian, St. Thomas continues: *unde si aliqua in dictis antiquorum Doctorum inveniuntur, quae cum tanta cautela non dicantur, quanta a modernis servatur, non sunt contemnenda, aut abjicienda, sed nec etiam ea extendere oportet, sed exponere reverenter.*[20] It is clear that the expression of the truth is of greater importance to St. Thomas than are the men who have expressed it. The idea uppermost in his mind is to safeguard the truth of faith, to express the same truth that the past expressed, in language, and with the precision which the past would have used had it but known the problems of the present. For St. Thomas, therefore, his separation from St. Augustine meant also a doctrinal allegiance to St. Augustine, or, more accurately, an allegiance to the truth that St. Augustine had found in the Epistles of St. Paul. The immediate object of St. Thomas' criticism lies in the thirteenth century, not in St. Augustine. The difficulties latent in Platonism, which Jewish and Arabian thinkers exploited to the full, but which the thirteenth century, thanks to the searching and often merciless criticism of Aristotle, could see in clear relief, are exactly the point at which the *moderni fidei Doctores* were called upon to restate a number of doctrines vital to the Christian tradition.

---

20. *Contra Errores Graecorum*, Proem.; ed. P. Mandonnet, *Opuscula Omnia* (Paris, 1927), vol. iii, p. 279. Cf. also *op. cit.*, cap. xxxii; ed. cit., vol. iii, p. 328, where, in referring to the author who occasioned this treatise, St. Thomas writes: *utitur etiam et ipse aliquibus modis loquendi, quos in auctoritatibus sanctorum Patrum invenit, qui, sicut superius dictum est, magis sunt reverenter in dictis Patrum exponendi, quam ab aliis usurpandi . . .*

St. Thomas thus invites us to consider the doctrines current in his day in order to explain the starting point of the reconstruction he effected; he invites us also to consider these same doctrines in order to account for his attitude towards St. Augustine. Consequently, if we would understand his philosophical decisions, if we would understand the Thomism of St. Thomas, it is to the historical circumstances in which St. Thomas reached his decisions that we must look.

Of the many problems that the thirteenth century was called upon to consider, that which is concerned with the nature of the soul illustrates remarkably well the many and different factors involved in the formation of attitudes towards Aristotle and in the solution of difficulties raised by his metaphysics. This problem illustrates also the theological repercussions to which a philosophical question can give rise, as well as the deeply Christian motives underlying each tradition. The problem of the soul, indeed, touches upon questions whose solution is of tremendous import in a Christian universe. It is not surprising, therefore, that the psychology of Aristotle, with its rigorous conception of soul and body, should raise innumerable difficulties both for those who rejected his ideas and for those who came to accept the value of his criticism.

In order to see the development of this problem, we must begin at a point where Aristotle met stubborn opposition. Now, it was the express intention of St. Bonaventure never to abandon the doctrinal tradition of St. Augustine. In principle, such an intention extended much farther than might at first sight be apparent, for to the mind of St. Bonaventure it implied also that he could dispense with Aristotle because what was good in Aristotle could be found in St. Augustine. Such a conception of Aristotle settles, *a priori,* the question of St. Bonaventure's attitude towards him. But when such an attitude is developed in a terminology borrowed from Aristotle, the possibility of complicating circumstances becomes very real. If the terminology which he used carried with it a whole metaphysics, to what extent was St. Bonaventure able to free himself from the implications of this metaphysics or to reconcile it with a number of doctrines that it appeared to eliminate? In other words, to what extent could St. Bonaventure accept the ideas of Aristotle, or, rejecting them, avoid the difficulties to which such a rejection committed him? Such is the problem to which we must first turn our attention.

II. ST. BONAVENTURE AND THE PROBLEM OF THE SOUL AS SUBSTANCE.

St. Bonaventure's mental attitude is clearly expressed in the reasons that he gives for adhering to the thought and tradition of St. Augustine. If he feels unwilling to depart from this tradition, it is because of St. Augustine's high position as an interpreter of Scripture. On one occasion he wrote that to say *Augustinum deceptum fuisse . . . valde absurdum est . . . de tanto patre et Doctore maxime authentico inter omnes expositores sacrae Scripturae.*[1] Such an eminence explains also the gifts of wisdom and knowledge which he had received from the Holy Ghost and which,

---

1. *De Scientia Christi,* q. iv, concl.; *Opera,* vol. v, p. 23.—St. Bonaventure will be cited principally according to the Quaracchi edition of his works: *Doctoris Seraphici S. Bonaventurae Opera Omnia,* 10 vols., ad Claras Aquas (Quaracchi), 1882-1902. A convenient table showing the arrangement of the various treatises in this edition may be found in E. Gilson, *La philosophie de saint Bonaventure (Etudes de philosophie médiévale,* iv), Paris, 1924, p. 41-42. Some of the works have been printed in other editions, or have been reprinted, in smaller and more convenient form, from the large edition. Cf. *De Humanae Cognitionis Ratione Anecdota Quaedam . . .,* Quaracchi, 1883, which contains, among selections from other writers, a question on knowledge and a *sermo* on the text of St. Matthew (xxiii, 10) from among the works of St. Bonaventure; *S. D. Sancti Bonaventurae Tria Opuscula ad Theologiam Spectania,* 4th ed., Quaracchi, 1925 (for the *Breviloquium,* the *Itinerarium* and the *De Reductione Artium*); *S. D. Sancti Bonaventurae Decem Opuscula ad Theologiam Mysticam Spectantia,* 3rd ed., Quaracchi, 1926. Finally, we may note two collections of texts that have appeared recently: *D. S. S. Bonaventurae Prolegomena ad sacram Theologiam spectantia ex operibus eius collecta,* ed. Thaddaeus Soiron (Florilegium Patristicum, xxx), Bonn, 1932; *Philosophia S. Bonaventurae textibus ex eius operibus selectis illustrata,* ed. B. Rosenmöller (Opuscula et textus, Series Scholastica, xv), Monasterii, 1933.

therefore, made him the equal of both Plato and Aristotle: *inter philosophos datus sit Platoni sermo sapientiae, Aristoteli vero sermo scientiae. Uterque autem sermo . . . per Spiritum sanctum datus est Augustino, tanquam praecipuo expositori totius Scripturae, satis excellenter, sicut ex scriptis eius apparet.*[2] St. Augustine thus appears as a *praecipuus* interpreter of Scripture, and his doctrines become all the more important when we perceive St. Bonaventure's conception of the relations between Scripture and philosophy. Scripture is the source of true knowledge, and he who would learn must study the text of Scripture in the same way that boys study their alphabet. When we leave the Scriptures, we are open to the danger of error. Even the masters of *Summae,* who, indeed, depend on Scripture, are possible sources of error, and in dealing with them one must be careful *ut semper adhaereat viae magis communi.* If we are forced to descend to philosophers, we must not abandon the waters of Siloe, in which is to be found the greatest perfection, and go to the waters of the philosophers, in which is to be found an eternal deception.[3] The text of Aristotle will be scanned not in the spirit of interpretation, but in the spirit of criticism and with the desire to safeguard the purity of doctrine. Thus, St. Bonaventure refuses to commit himself as to which interpretation of Aristotle is correct: *quod horum*

---

2. Cf. the text of the sermon on Matthew, xxiii, 10, in *De Humanae Cognitionis Ratione . . .,* p. 81. St. Bonaventure then proceeds to show that St. Paul and Moses possessed these gifts of wisdom and knowledge in a higher degree, and that Christ was, in the highest degree, *solus . . . principalis magister et doctor.*—On the unity of Christian wisdom which this last point implies, cf. E. Longpré, *La royauté de Jésus-Christ chez s. Bonaventure et le b. Duns Scot,* 2nd ed., Montreal, 1927; E. Gilson, *La philosophie de saint Bonaventure,* p. 89-118: *La critique de la philosophie naturelle.*

3. Cf. *Collationes in Hexaemeron,* coll, xix, 7, 11, 12; *Opera,* vol. 5, col. 421, 422.

magis verum est, ego nescio; but he is sure of the attitude which he must take towards Aristotle if the latter taught that the universe was absolutely eternal: *hoc unum scio, quod si posuit mundum non incepisse secundum naturam, verum posuit . . . Si autem hoc sensit, quod nullo modo coeperit, manifeste erravit*.[4] St. Bonaventure departs from Scripture very rarely, and then it is only to join the thought of the most eminent interpreter of Scripture.

Consequently, the problem of the soul and its nature has a definite starting point. According to St. Bonaventure, it is in Scripture that we shall find a true explanation of the nature of the soul. Now, in St. Bonaventure's *Breviloquium,* which is a sort of compendium of Christian doctrine, we find an account of the soul according to Scripture: *de anima igitur rationali haec in summa tenenda sunt secundum sacram doctrinam . . .*[5]

According to such a point of departure, we must consider the soul as being a form that exists, has life, is intelligent and enjoys the exercise of freedom. St. Bonaventure attaches a particular significance to each of these attributes. By the soul as an existing form he means a form that exists neither through itself nor as a part of the divine nature, but derives its existence through creation *ex nihilo* by God.   By its possesssion of life, furthermore, St. Bonaventure understands a characteristic that is intrinsic, not adventitious, perpetual not mortal. Then, as an intelligent form, the soul is capable of knowing not only the creature, but also the Creator; it is, in fact, made in the image of God. On this point the influence of St. Anselm is very noticeable.   Finally, the soul is free. This attribute, however, implies only a freedom from external force or compulsion, the presence of the powers of reason and will in the soul; it does not imply freedom

---

4. *In II Sent.,* d. 1, p. 1, a. 1, q. 2, concl.; *Opera,* vol. 2, p. 23.

5. *Breviloquium,* II, 9, 1; ed. minor, p. 82

from the wretchedness and guilt which the loss of original innocence[6] brought with it. The soul's freedom is a freedom of nature, not of condition.[7]

To understand such a nature, we must consider the blessedness and the goodness of God. It is because God is most good that He seeks, in His perfect goodness, to communicate His blessedness to others. Now, God communicates His blessedness to others in a twofold way. To the spiritual substances, which are near Him, God communicates His blessedness directly; to the corporeal substances, which are far from Him, He communicates His blessedness mediately. The soul of man, therefore, holds an important place in the economy of the universe, because, in being, unlike the angels, a spirit joined to a body, it enables material substances to participate in the blessedness of God; or, in the language of the Pseudo-Dionysius, the soul acts as a means of the return of the matter to God.[8] It appears, in this way, that one of the most important reasons for the union of soul and body

---

6. On St. Bonaventure's conception of the state of original justice in man, cf. J.-B. Kors, *La justice primitive et le péché originel d'après s. Thomas (Bibliothèque thomiste, ii)*, Paris, 1930, ch. v. *passim*.

7. *Breviloquium, ibid.*—For St. Anselm, cf. *Monologion*, ‹ap. 13; P.L., vol. 158, col. 160c.

8. *Breviloquium*, II, 9, 2; ed. minor, p. 83.—For the Pseudo-Dionysius, cf. *De Ecclesiastica Hierarchia*, cap. v, no. iv; P. Graeca, vol. 3, col. 504c; *De Coelesti Hierarchia*, cap. iv, no. iii; P.G., vol. 3, col. 192c.

As it is known, the transmission of the divine goodness to matter is ultimately St. Augustine's strongest argument for the union of soul and body. Cf. E. Gilson, *Introduction à l'étude de saint Augustin (Etudes de philosophie médiévale, xi)*, Paris, 1929, p. 59-63. Such an attitude implies that, apart from mutual benefits which the union may produce, the service of the soul to the body is much greater and much more necessary than that of the body to the soul.

lies in the rôle of the soul as a transmitter of the divine blessedness to matter. This point is quite fixed, and will become more prominent as we proceed.

The soul is, therefore, a form capable of receiving beatitude from God. This capability requires the presence of certain other attributes. Through *freedom* the soul is able to merit beatitude. Furthermore, the fact that the soul was made for beatitude implies that it will come into possession of beatitude in such a way as never to lose it. Hence, the fact that the soul was made by God for beatitude implies necessarily that the soul is incorruptible and immortal. The soul, therefore, as capable of beatitude, is immortal: *ut beatificabilis, est immortalis.*[9] Now, precisely because it is incorruptible and immortal, the soul cannot come into existence through generation. On the other hand, as its beatitude depends on a being other than itself, the soul is changeable with reference to its well-being or degree of happiness. Consequently, while the soul has an incorruptible *esse*, it is, nevertheless, *mutabile secundum bene esse.* Thus, immortality and mutability belong to the soul because it is made for beatitude: *Ex his apparet, qualiter finis beatitudinis necessitatem imposuit praedictarum conditionum ipsi animae ad beatitudinem ordinatae.*[10]

As immortal, the soul is joined to the body in such a way that it can be separated from it. However we may conceive this union, clearly it cannot be such as to endanger the immortality of the soul. That is why St. Bonaventure hastens to qualify his conception of the soul as a *forma* when the question of its union with the body arises: the soul is not only a form, it is also, in the language of Aristotle, a *hoc aliquid* or substance: *non tantum forma est (sc. anima) verum*

---

9. *Breviloquium*, II, 9, 2-5; ed. minor, p. 83-84.

10. *Breviloquium*, II, 9, 4; ed. minor, p. 84—Cp. *In II Sent.*, d. 19, a. 1, q. 1, concl.; *Opera*, vol. ii, p. 460.

etiam hoc aliquid.[11] In this way, while the nature or essence of the soul gives to the body its perfection as a human body, it is the substantiality of the soul which is the source at once of its immortality (and, therefore, its separability from the body), and its power to act on the body. This twofold aspect of the relation of soul to body is brought out by two different names: *perfectio* and *motor*. As a form, the soul is joined to the body in the capacity of *perfectio*; as a *hoc aliquid*, the soul is joined to the body as a *motor*.[12]

The body itself is characterized especially by its fitness to be joined to the soul and its subjection to the soul in that union. Thus, the organization of its parts was most perfect, and its submission to the soul was complete when man came from the hand of God. And man was, St. Bonaventure goes on to say, a masterpiece, for his very existence and nature, produced by God as a sort of climax to His creative act, was an eloquent witness to the eminence of the divine power, wisdom and goodness. In the genus of substance, spirit and matter are the most ultimate divisions that exist. And yet God could and did bring together into one nature and one personality two substances so radically different from each other. The composition of man, therefore, because it is the union of soul and body, which belong to the most ultimate divisions of the category of substance, reveals the greatness of God's power. The fitness of the union, once effected, and the perfect adaptation of the body to the nature and purpose of the soul reveal the wisdom of God. Finally, the absence of any guilt or suffering or attending punishment in man,

---

11. *Breviloquium*, II, 9, 5; ed. minor, p. 84.

12. "Quoniam autem ut beatificabilis est immortalis; ideo, cum unitur mortali corpori, potest ab eo separari; ac per hoc non tantum *forma* est verum etiam *hoc aliquid*; et ideo non tantum unitur corpori ut *perfectio*, verum etiam ut motor; et sic perficit per essentiam, quod *movet* pariter per potentiam" (*Breviloquium, ibid.*)

who was essentially good and consequently innocent, reveals the goodness of God.[13]

Such, in brief, is St. Bonaventure's conception of the soul. Its chief characteristics are an earnest desire to safeguard immortality and substantiality, or (what is more nearly correct), to stress the substantiality of the soul in order to insure its immortality. The soul is thus not only a *forma* or *perfectio,* but also a *hoc aliquid.* Now, in the actual exposition of his doctrine, and particularly of the significance of these terms, St. Bonaventure was naturally called upon to consider the metaphysical implications which these terms embodied and the problems they had raised in the course of their history. The *locus* of the most elaborate discussion of the questions is his commentary on the *Sentences* of Peter Lombard.

Of the four definitions of the soul collected by Eduard Lutz from the works of St. Bonaventure,[14] one (which we have already examined) is taken from the *Breviloquium,* while the other three are taken from the commentary on the *Sentences.* The first of these three definitions states that the soul is a *hoc aliquid;*[15] the second, that the soul is the *perfectio* of a body intended by nature to be informed by rational life;[16] the last, that the soul is a *perfectio* with respect to substance and a *motor* with respect to powers.[17] What meaning does the Seraphic Doctor attach to these names that he applies to the soul? Taking them in order, we must consider the significance of *hoc aliquid* and *perfectio;*

---

13. *Breviloquium*, II, 10, 1-5; ed. minor, p. 87-89. Let us note a fundamental principle in the union of soul and body: . . . *corpus unitur animae ut perficienti et moventi et ad beatitudinem sursum tendenti* (*Breviloquium*, II, 10, 4; ed. minor, p. 88).

14. Eduard Lutz, *Die Psychologie Bonaventuras* (*Beiträge*, ed. C. Bauemker, vi, 4-5), Münster, i. W., 1909, p. 9.

15. *In II Sent.*, d. 17, a. 1, q.2, concl., opinio 3; vol. ii, p. 414.

16. *In II Sent.*, d. 2, p. 2, a. 2, q. 3, ad 3; vol. ii, p. 82.

17. *In IV Sent.*, d. 44, p. 1, a. 3, q.2, ad 4; vol. iv, p. 914.

and, as we shall see, it is in the explanation of the soul as a
hoc aliquid [18] that St. Bonaventure will bring forth ideas
and arguments which lend to his whole doctrine its own
distinctive individuality.

Indeed, the analysis of the soul as a *hoc aliquid* or substance will carry us to the very center of St. Bonaventure's
metaphysics. Let us consider the soul in its most fundamental aspect, namely as a *created* substance. Its most
characteristic attributes now become readily apparent, for,
as created, the soul, like all created substances, suffers the
necessary imperfection of being composite. However we may
explain it, there is a radical sense in which it is true to say
that the soul has parts.[19] In distinguishing between God
and His creatures, we must note, first of all, that God *is* what
He is, while the creature *has received* all its attributes, in-
cluding its very existence. From this point of view, receptivity is the most distinctive mark of the soul; and it is
this characteristic which requires that a principle be present
within the essence of the soul itself to serve as the basis of
the soul's substantial existence. Furthermore, the soul, as
substance, must contain within its nature a principle which
will allow it to be the subject of its changes. Hence, it
appears that the finitude and the accompanying mutability
of the soul require the presence of an element which will be

---

18. As it is known, *hoc aliquid* or τόδε τι is Aristotle's technical
expression for concrete individual substance or what he calls the
ultimate subject of predication. Cf. e.g., *Metaphysics*, IV, 8, 1017b
10-25; VIII, 7, 1049a-25-35; *Categories*, III; and the innumerable
references in the Index of Hermann Bonitz, s.v. οὐσία: *Aristotelis
Opera*, vol. v (Berlin, 1870), p. 544-546. For a recent discussion of
this doctrine of substance in Aristotle, cf. Régis Jolivet, *La notion
de substance, essai historique et critique sur le développement des
doctrines d'Aristote à nos jours* (*Bibliothèque des archives de
philosophie*) G. Beauchesne, Paris, 1929, p. 13-34.

19. Cf. *In II Sent.*, d. 8, p. 2, art. unicus, q. 2, concl. 1; vol. i,
p. 168.

at once the subject of existence (since the soul is a substance) and of the changes to which it will be exposed.
Such a principle is matter.

Whatever surprise and disquietude may be caused by
this doctrine of the matter in spiritual substances is alleviated
by St. Bonaventure's distinction between the matter of
spiritual and corporeal substances.[20]   To understand this
distinction, we must note that in the Seraphic Doctor's view,
as distinguished from that of St. Thomas, the term *corporeal*
fills only part of the extension of the term *matter;* and we
must note also that matter applies to beings, not because
they are corporeal, but because they are creatures.   It is
only then that we shall understand the famous doctrine about
the hylemorphic composition of spiritual substances associ-
ated with the name of St. Bonaventure and with the main
Franciscan tradition after him.[21]

More specifically, matter may be considered from two
points of view. We may examine its nature in itself, or we
may consider matter as it actually exists. The first question
is a metaphysical one and seeks to determine what is to be
included *de jure* within the essence of matter; the second
question is concrete and seeks to determine the various states
or conditions in which *de facto* matter finds itself. Now, in
itself and apart from the conditions of its actual existence,
matter is absolutely formless and its essence is a pure and
absolute capacity for the various forms of existence.   Its
very nature, therefore, is just this capacity or possibility to
receive forms: *materia secundum sui essentiam est informis
per possibilitatem omnimodam; et dum sic consideratur, ipsa*

---

20. *In II Sent.*, a. 1, q. 2, concl., opinio 3; vol. ii, p. 414-415.

21. Cf. the Scholion of the Quaracchi Fathers appended to St.
Bonaventure, *In II Sent.*, a. 3, p. 1, a. 1, q. 1 (vol. ii, p. 92-94).
With the exception of John of Rupella, the whole Franciscan
school down to the sixteenth century held the doctrine of spiritual
matter (*ibid.*, p. 95, v). Cf., however, *infra*, p. 68, note 88.

formarum capacitas est sibi pro forma.[22] Matter thus presents the aspect of a kind of unity and infinity: unity, because it is, in itself, absolutely undifferentiated and indeterminate, receiving all its diversity from the diversity of forms; infinite, because its complete lack of forms is equivalent to an endless possibility and capacity to receive forms.[23] Hence, all we may say of matter, *in se considerata,* is that it is a completely indeterminate and undifferentiated capacity to receive whatever forms with which actual existence will endow it.

As it is found in *rerum natura,* however, matter is involved in a set of contingent circumstances which serve as the principles of its diversification. Thus, it always exists in a particular place and at a particular time; it is always subject to rest and motion. Under these conditions, matter is never separated from form: *et hoc modo . . . impossibile est, materiam informem existere prae privationem omnis formae.*[24] It is existence, therefore, which introduces dis-

22. *In Sent II.,* d. 12, a. 1, q. 1; vol. ii, p. 294. On the formlessness of matter, St. Bonaventure invokes the *Confessions* of St. Augustine. Cf. St. Augustine, *Confessions,* xii, 3; 6; ed. J. Gibb and W. Montgomery, Cambridge U. Press, 2nd. ed., 1927, p. 366-367, 368-369.

23. "Illa est unitas magis possibilitatis, quae adeo ampla est ut sustineat receptionem majoris multitudinis diversitatis formarum super adjectarum quam unitas formae alicujus universalis, etiam generis generalissimi; et hoc est propter summam possibilitatem. Unde dicitur una numero, *quia est una sine numero,* quemadmodum ovis carens signo ovium habentium signum dicitur esse signata: per hunc modum intelligi potest materia numero una" (*In II Sent.,* d. 3, p. 1, a. 1, q. 3, Concl.; vol. ii, p. 100). " . . . de se est infinita et ad formas infinitas . . . quae infinitas venit ex summae possibilitatis imperfectione" (*ibid.*).—Cf. also A. Forest, *La structure métaphysique du concret selon s. Thomas d'Aquin* (*Etudes de philosophie médiévale,* xiv), Paris, 1931, p. 116-118.

24. "Respondeo: Ad praedictorum intelligentiam est notandum, quod dupliciter est loqui de materia; aut secundum quod existit in natura, aut secundum quod consideratur ab anima. Si secundum

tinctions in matter; or, what is the same thing, matter as existing is always united to some form. That is why it is possible to distinguish between the matter of spiritual and the matter of corporeal substances. For, while matter in itself is capable of receiving indifferently spiritual or corporeal forms, and is thus metaphysically prior to both determinations, nevertheless, it is never separated from some kind of existence. As a result, once it has received corporeal existence, matter is never despoiled of it, just as it is never despoiled of the spiritual existence it receives in being joined to a spiritual form.[25] That is why St. Bonaventure can say that matter in itself is one, and hold at the same time that the matter of spiritual substances is different from that of corporeal substances, because such a difference is derived, not from matter, but from the diversity consequent upon

---

quod consideratur ab anima, sic potest considerari informis, sive per privationem formae distinctae, sive per privationem etiam omnis formae; et sic docet Augustinus in duodecimo *Confessionum* essentiam materiae intelligere. Nam materia secundum sui essentiam est informis per possibilitatem omnimodam; et dum sic consideratur, ipsa formarum capacitas sive possibilitas est sibi pro forma.—Est iterum loqui de materia secundum quod habet esse in natura; et sic nunquam est praeter locum et tempus, sive praeter quietum et motum; et hoc modo non solummodo non congruit, immo etaim impossibile est, materiam informem existere prae privationem omnis formae" (*In II Sent.*, d. 12, a. 1, q.1; vol. ii, p. 294).

25. "Quod obiicitur de potentia suscipiendi, dicendum quod potentia materiae secundum se consideratae non est magis ad hanc formam quam ad illam, immo indifferenter se habet ad omnem. Nam materia in se considerata nec est spiritualis, nec corporalis; et ideo capacitas consequens essentiam materiae indifferenter se habet ad formam, sive spiritualem, sive corporalem; sed quia materia numquam expoliatur ab omni esse, et quae semel sub esse corporali numquam exuitur et similiter illa quae est sub esse spirituali: hinc est, quod materia consequens esse in spiritualibus et corporalibus est alia et alia (*In II Sent.*, d. 3, p. 1, a. 1, q. 2, ad 3; vol. ii, p. 98).

existence and the forms of existence: *hinc est, quod materia consequens esse in spiritualibus et corporalibus est alia et alia.*[26]

Let us now consider the rôle of matter in the soul. Since the soul is a substance, it exists through itself and since it is created it has received its existence. The soul has, therefore, a received but subsistent existence. It is matter which governs both of these aspects in the soul: matter or possibility at once limits and receives the act of existence which makes the soul a subsistent creature.[27] St. Bonaventure's doctrine on this point is distinctive, for his pre-occupation is twofold: the *subsistence* as well as the *existence* of the soul. What distinguishes the soul as a creature is not that it is the form of the composite (which would be true of any other substantial form), but that it is self-subsistent, i.e., that the subject of its existence is not the body of man to which it is joined, but matter within its own essence. It is this matter which *fixes,* as St. Bonaventure says, the existence of the soul in itself and renders it thereby subsistent. ''Since the rational soul is a *hoc aliquid,* naturally subsists by itself and acts as well as receives actions, we must follow a mean and say that it contains, within itself, the foundation of its own existence, a material principle through which it exists and a formal principle through which it has being. On the other hand, this is not necessary in the case of the brute soul be-

---

26. *Ibid.*

27. "Nulla creatura est actus purus, quia in omni creatura, ut dicit Boethius, differt *quo est* et *quod est;* ergo in omni creatura est actus cum possibili; sed omnis talis habet in se multiformitatem et caret simplicitate" (*In I Sent.,* d. 8, p. 2, art. un., q. 2, quod. 1; vol. i, p. 167).—"Creaturae autem compositae sunt nec vere simplices, quia habent esse mixtum ex actu et potentia, quia habent esse limitatum, et ita in genere et specie per additionem contractum, quia habent esse aliunde datum, quasi habent esse post Deum unum, a quo deficiunt; et ita cadunt in compositionem" (*ibid.,* epilogus; p. 168).

cause it is *founded* in the body. Consequently, since it is a
material principle through which the existence of a creature
is *fixed* in itself, we must admit that the human soul contains
matter.   This matter, however, is above the conditions of
extension, privation and corruption, and is, therefore, called
spiritual matter.''[28]   In a passage such as this it is important to note not only the ideas expressed, but also their
sequence.

---

28. "Et ideo est tertius modus dicendi, tenens medium inter
utrumque, scilicet quod anima rationalis, cum sit hoc aliquid et
per se nata subsistere et agere et pati, movere et moveri, quod
habet intra se *fundamentum suae existentiae* et *principium materiale* a quo habet *existere*, et *formale*, a quo habet *esse*. De
brutali autem non oportet illud dicere cum ipsa fundetur in corpore.   Cum igitur principium, a quo est fixa existentia creaturae
in se, sit principium materiale; concedendum est, animam hu-
manam materiam habere.   Illa autem materia sublevata est supra
esse extensionis, et supra esse privationis et corruptionis, et ideo
dicitur materia spiritualis" (*In II Sent.*, a. 1, q. 2, concl., opinio 3;
vol. ii, p. 414-415).—Cf. "Individuum enim habet esse, habet etiam
existere. Existere dat materia formae, sed essendi actum dat forma
materiae" (*In II Sent.*, d. 3, p. 1, a. 2, q. 3, Resp.; vol. ii, p. 110).
It is to be noted that for St. Bonaventure substantiality and
mutability are inseparable, for, as E. Gilson has observed, it is
because of its mutability that the soul is a substance: cf. *La philosophie de saint Bonaventure*, p. 306.   St. Bonaventure's reason for
this inseparability is clearly based on Aristotle's doctrine that
only substances can receive contraries: μάλιστα δέ ἴδιον τῆς οὐσίας
δοκεῖ εἶναι τὸ ταὐτὸν καὶ ἐν ἀριθμῷ ὂν τῶν ἐναντίων εἶναι δεκτικόν
(*Categories*, iii; ed. Didot, p. 5, 1. 45-47).   Every being that in
changing is capable of receiving contraries is a *hoc aliquid* and a
substance existing in a genus. Such beings are composed of matter and form. Now the soul in changing is capable of receiving
joy and sorrow, and is therefore composed of matter and form:
"Omne illud quod secundum sui mutationem est susceptibile con-
trariorum est hoc aliquid et substantia per se existens in genere,
et omne tale compositum est ex materia et forma; sed anima secundum sui mutationem est susceptiva gaudii et tristitiae: ergo
anima rationalis composita est ex materia et forma" (*In II Sent.*,
d. 17, a. 1, q. 2, fund. 5; vol. ii, p. 414).

Indeed, such a conception of the theory of matter and form is capable of leading us to a new interpretation of unity and change in substance, for the idea of development and perfectibility dominates the doctrine of substance. In fact, the theory of matter and form as interpreted here has as its natural complement the doctrine of the plurality of forms and is connected also with the old Stoic doctrine of seminal reasons. And there is one problem which appears in all these doctrines and acts as a common thread binding them together, the problem of development. This will appear quite clearly if we turn to a rather serious objection which is brought against St. Bonaventure's conception of the soul as a substance composed of matter and form. The objector expresses the fear that the soul is now so complete a substance in itself, that it is incapable of being united to the body. For, to be composed of matter and form as essential parts is really to be a substance and something complete. Nothing, however, that is complete in itself can be joined to something else in order to constitute a third thing. But the soul does join the body in the composition of man in such a way that the new substance man is a real and essential unity. Apparently, therefore, the objector sees a conflict between the substantiality of the soul and its capacity to be the form of man in an essential unity; and as the union of soul and body is a fact, the soul cannot be a *hoc aliquid*. Nor, obviously, is it matter. Hence it must be a pure form— *forma pura*.[29]

It is not always true, St. Bonaventure replies, to say that

---

29. "Item, omne quod habet materiam et formam ut partes constitutivas, est hoc aliquid et est completum; nihil autem, quod est hoc aliquid et completum in se, venit ad constitutionem tertii; sed anima rationalis venit ad constitutionem tertii, ita quod ex anima et corpore fit unum per essentiam; ergo anima non est hoc aliquid; ergo vel materia, vel forma pura; non materia, ergo forma" (*In II Sent.*, d. 17, a. 1, q. 2, obj. 6; vol. ii, p. 413).

a being composed of matter and form cannot enter into further composition to constitute another substance. It is true only under one condition, namely, that matter and form, when joined to one another, exhaust all the possibilities that both have for further development. The matter must satisfy completely and thus terminate the appetite of the form for matter; and the form must satisfy and terminate the appetite for form to be found in matter. When such a condition is realized there is no appetite either in the matter or in the form for further composition, and the inclination and appetite of both is terminated by each other and in union with each other as ultimate complements. Consequently, the fact that soul and body are composed of matter and form does not prevent their union with each other, for in the eyes of St. Bonaventure, the determining factor in this question is not the composite character of the soul or the body, but solely the degree to which matter and form develop all the possibilities for further composition in each other. If an *appetitus* still remains, that indicates that either of the components is only partially developed. Such is the case of soul and body, whose individual composition makes them to be substances but does not develop them completely. The soul, though a composite substance, has the natural inclination and appetite to perfect a corporeal substance, while the body itself, though a composite substance, has an appetite to receive the soul.[30] In a real sense, therefore, a true com-

---

30. "Ad illud quod obiicitur, quod compositum ex materia et forma est ens completum, et ita non venit ad constitutionem tertii; dicendum, quod hoc non est verum generaliter, sed tunc, quando materia terminat omnem appetitum formae, et forma omnem appetitum materiae; tunc non est appetitus ad aliquid extra, et ita nec possibilitas ad compositionem, quae praeexigit in componentibus appetitum et inclinationem. Licet autem anima rationalis compositionem habeat ex materia et forma, appetitum tamen habet ad perficiendam corporalem naturam; sicut corpus organicum ex materia et forma compositum est, et tamen habet ap-

posite substance is one in which there is a perfect proportion between matter and form and in which, consequently, the component elements find in each other their highest development: *Ad hoc quod debite constituatur aliquod compositum, necesse est, materiam et formam proportionari ad invicem.*[31]

And it is on this point that Plato and his followers went astray, for they did not recognize that soul and body were intended by nature to be joined to each other. St. Bonaventure is thinking especially of Macrobius.[32] It is impossible to concede to these Platonists that the body is the prisonhouse of the soul or that souls migrate from body to body, for such doctrines do not recognize that the soul is the true perfection of the body.[33] Nor do they agree with reason or experience, because in reality the soul does not want to be separated from the body, and this fact would be difficult to explain if the soul did not have a natural aptitude and inclination for the body. The body is the companion, not the prison, of the soul.[34] Contrary to the disparaging views of

---

petitum ad suscipiendam animam" (*In II Sent.*, d. 17, a. 1, q. 2, ad 6; vol. ii, p. 415-416).

31. *In II Sent.*, d. 19, a. 2, q. 1, fund. 3; vol. ii, p. 465.

32. An analysis of Macrobius' commentary on the *Somnium Scipionis*, to which St. Bonaventure refers, will be found in T. Whitaker, *Macrobius*, Cambridge Univ. Press, 1923, p. 57-82.

33. *In II Sent.*, d. 18, a. 2, q. 2, concl.; vol. ii, p. 449.

34. "Contra rationem et sensibilem experientiam est, quia videmus, animam, quantumcumque bonam, nolle a corpore separari; secundum quod dicit Apostolus: 'Nolumus expoliari, sed supervestiri' (II *Corinth.*, 5, 4); quod mirum esset, si ad corpus naturalem aptitudinem et inclinationem non haberet sicut ad suum sodalem, non sicut ad carcerem" (*ibid.*).—Cf. *In II Sent.*, d. 43, a. 1, q. 1, fund. 4; vol. iv, p. 883, which is plainly reminiscent of the same Pauline text, and argues in exactly the same way about the natural appetite of the soul for the body; *In II Sent.*, d. 32, a. 3, q. 2, ad 3; vol. ii, p. 773.—For further references, cf. E. Gilson, *La philosophie de s. Bonaventure*, p. 316, note 1.

the Platonists, it is neither accidental nor ignoble for the soul to be joined to the body: it is not accidental, because through such a union the soul becomes the substantial form of man; it is not ignoble, because such a union makes the soul the most noble form in the whole realm of nature and because such a union terminates and completes the appetite of all nature for form: *Hoc enim, quod est animam uniri corpori humano sive vivificare corpus humanum, non dicit actum accidentalem nec dicit actum ignobilem: non accidentalem quia ratione illius est anima forma substantialis; non ignobilem, quia ratione illius est anima nobilissima formarum omnium, et in anima stat appetitus totius naturae.*[35]

St. Bonaventure, therefore, has every intention of defending at once the substantiality of the soul and its real union with the body. Thus, in his eyes there is no incompatibility between the matter-and-form composition of the soul and the unity of man. As a matter of fact, St. Bonaventure develops a doctrine of substantial unity which appears to require, rather than to exclude, the theory of

---

35. *In II Sent.*, d 1, p. 2, a. 3, q. 2, opinio 3; vol. ii, p. 50.

We may note here that this inclination of the soul for the body is the fundamental ground of difference between it and an angel. To reach this conclusion, St. Bonaventure rejects two opinions: 1⁰ The soul and the angel do not differ when considered in their relation to God, because the *deiformitas* which belongs to the angel will belong to the glorified soul as well. In addition, the separated soul will have the same *modus* of knowing as the angel. As a result this basis of difference is only accidental (opinio 1, p. 49-50). 2⁰ Nor is it permissible to say that the angel is of a higher degree and dignity than the soul. St. Bonaventure considers it very doubtful that the angel is so much superior to the soul. For how is an angel higher in dignity than the best conceivable human soul, that of Christ, which does not abandon its humanity (opinio, 3, p. 50)? Cf. *In II Sent.*, d. 1, p. 2, a. 2, q. 2; vol. ii, p. 46, and St. Thomas, *In II Sent.*, d. 16, q. 1, a. 3, ad 4; ed. P. Mandonnet, vol. ii, p. 403.

the plurality of forms;[36] for in a doctrine such as his it is not the unicity of the form, but the degree to which matter and form exhaust the latent capacities of each other, which really determines the unity of the composite. We have already examined this point in part; we shall see its further development in St. Bonaventure's conception of the human body and its organization. This question leads him naturally to consider the problem of seminal reasons and the manner of their presence in matter.[37]

---

36. As historians have remarked, St. Bonaventure does not discuss the theory of plurality of forms *ex professo*, but rather develops a doctrine which implies such a theory. Cf. M. de Wulf, *Le traité* De Unitate Formae *de Gilles de Lessines* (*Les philosophes belges*, 1), Louvain, 1901, p. 44; E. Gilson, *La philosophie de saint Banoventure*, p. 310; G. Théry, *L'augustinisme médiéval et l'unité de la forme substantielle*, in *Acta Hebdomadae Augustinianae-Thomisticae*, (Taurini-Romae, Marietti, 1931, p. 140-200), p. 158-159. As G. Théry notes (p. 158, note 4), that is also the opinion of the Quaracchi editors of St. Bonaventure: *Opera S. Bonaventurae, In II. Sent.*, d. 13, a. 2, q. 2; vol. ii, p. 322-323.

37. St. Bonaventure acknowledges explicitly that the term *rationes seminales* comes from St. Augustine: "et ab ipso (scil. Augustino) potissime habeamus horum nominum usum" (*In II. Sent.*, d. 18, a. 1, q. 2, concl.; vol. ii, p. 436). For an account of the various points defended in the doctrine of seminal reasons in the later part of the thirteenth century, cf. the useful text of Peter Olivi, *Quaestiones in Secundum Librum Sententiarum*, q. 31; ed. B. Jansen, vol. 1 (Quaracchi, 1922), p. 508-570. Avicenna, it may be noted, is one of the influences which determined Olivi's practical rejection of the doctrine of *rationes seminales*: *Quaestiones in Secundum Librum Sententiarum*, q. 72; ed. cit., vol. iii (Quaracchi, 1926), p. 8-9. Neither Olivi nor Duns Scotus after him is convinced by one of St. Bonaventure's favorite arguments, namely, that the presence of *rationes seminales* in matter is necessary to reserve the creative act for God: Cf. Olivi, *Qu. in II Sent.*, q. 31, ad 1; ed. cit., vol. i, p. 551-553; Duns Scotus, *Opus Oxoniense*, II, d. 18, q. unica, no. 667; ed. Quaracchi, 1914, vol. ii, p. 603. If we turn now to St. Thomas, *De Veritate*, XI, 1, we may note how the Aristotelian *via media* between the *latitatio formarum* of Anaxa-

The problem comes to this: How are forms present in matter, and what degree of causality is to be attributed to a created agent in the eduction of these forms from matter? Faced by three different solutions, St. Bonaventure has to steer a very careful course in order to meet two requirements which the solution to this problem demands. Let us suppose that changes take place in nature through the interaction of substances. The existence of such changes indicates that these substances produce something, but not in the sense that they create it; rather, the production is one of form in matter. Now, matter and form, while always found together in nature, are not parts of each other. Hence, the production of forms in matter does not mean that the forms come from matter. Nor may we say that they are produced from nothing, for that would make created substances creators. Clearly, a created substance does produce something through its own causality, but it does not create. We must, therefore, discover an explanation of change which will reserve creative activity for God and, at the same time, attribute some causality to creatures. It is the doctrine of seminal reasons with its conception of matter as in some

---

goras and the *dator formarum* of Avicenna was a contributing cause in the elimination of this doctrine from the Franciscan tradition. John Pecham, however, is too near the scene of conflict as well as too involved in the defence of the Seraphic Doctor's ideas not to criticize St. Thomas for rejecting what he considers to be the tradition of St. Augustine: cf. *Chartularium Universitatis Parisiensis*, I, p. 634 and E. Gilson, *La philosophie de saint Bonaventure*, p. 31 ff.

A comparison between *In II Sent.*, d. 7, p. 2, a. 2, q. 1, concl.; vol. ii, p. 197-199 and *De Veritate*, XI, 1, will show the different conceptions of matter in St. Bonaventure and St. Thomas. E. Gilson, *op. cit.*, p. 285, brings this difference out in a striking sentence: "La matière de saint Thomas est un miroir où peut se propager une lumière; la matière de saint Bonaventure est un sol qui contient des graines, non des plantes, mais dont les plantes peuvent être par conséquent tirées."

sense pregnant with all things to be produced in the course of time which meets these requirements.[38]

The exact significance of this doctrine for St. Bonaventure can be seen by distinguishing it, with him, from the errors of Anaxagoras and Avicenna. For it would seem that both of these thinkers sinned against the efficacy of second causes. In brief, St. Bonaventure accuses Anaxagoras of placing all future changes ready-made in nature, and Avicenna of attributing all the changes in nature to God. The doctrine of Anaxagoras, which presupposes that forms are actually present in matter,[39] is an impossible interpretation of change in nature not only because it posits the co-existence of contraries in matter, but also because the activity of the external agent is reduced to an uncovering of what is already present in matter and not, as it should be, to a causal participation in its production. Coming to the same conclusion so far as second causes are concerned, the doctrine of Avicenna, however, differs from the *latitatio*

38. "Supponamus nunc quod natura aliquid agat, et illud non agit de nihilo, et cum agat in materiam, oportet quod producat formam. Et cum materia non sit pars formae, nec forma fiat pars materiae necesse est aliquo modo formas esse in materia antequam producentur; et substantia materiae est praegnans omnibus: ergo rationes seminales omnium formarum sunt in ipsa" (*In IV Sent.*, d. 43, a. 1, q. 4, concl.; vol. iv, p. 888).—For the metaphysical significance of the problem in the thirteenth century, cf. E. Gilson, *L'esprit de la philosophie médiévale*, Première Série, Paris, 1932, p. 133-152, 268-275.

39. Cf. H. Diels, *Die Fragmente der Vorsokratiker*, 4th ed., Berlin, 1922, vol. i, p. 399 ff., especially fragment 4, p. 401, 1. 10-17. There is a well-known account of Anaxagoras in Lucretius, *De Rerum Natura*, I, 830 ff. Aristotle is naturally the most prominent source of his doctrines for the thirteenth century: Cf. *Metaphysics*, I, 3, 984 a 11; *Physics* III, 4, 203a19; *De Generatione et Corruptione*, I, 1, 314a18.—A brief analysis of Anaxagoras, especially his theory of nature and change, will be found in A. Rivard, *Le problème du devenir et la notion de la matière dans la philosophie grecque* . . ., Paris, 1906, p. 189-199.

formarum of Anaxagoras, for in the doctrine of Avicenna it is the *dator formarum,* that is, the intelligence which presides over the changes that take place in the sublunar world, which produces the changes observable in nature. In this doctrine also, second causes are deprived of their causality, because all they do is prepare the way for the activity of the *dator formarum.*[40] Anaxagoras and Avicenna, therefore, deprive second causes of all causality bearing directly on the production of any effect, and in this way render any conception of creatures as causes meaningless.

It is Aristotle who points the way to the right solution, for he enables us to avoid the absolute extrinsecism of Avicenna and the absolute intrinsecism of Anaxagoras. And it is Aristotle whom the doctors in philosophy and theology follow; only, their interpretations of Aristotle fall into two groups, for, if they agree that the forms to be educed from matter are *potentially* present in matter, they do not agree on the interpretation of this potential presence.

Those who adhere to the first group contend that the potential presence of forms in matter means simply that the matter is capable of receiving these forms. According to this interpretation, the matter is passive but also coöperative in the sense that it will receive certain forms and not others according to different aptitudes under different circumstances. The form itself comes from the agent which possesses, in virtue of its own form and nature, the power of multiplying its form. Thus a candle, though one, is able to light many candles and to have many images in mirrors. In this way, a form so produced is not produced *ex nihilo* (and thus the creative act is reserved for God alone), but from the action of the agent on the matter.[41]

---

40. For Avicenna, cf. *infra,* ch. v.

41. It is St. Thomas to whom St. Bonaventure is here referring. Cf. St. Thomas, *In II Sent.,* d. 18, q. 1, a. 2; ed. Mandonnet, vol. ii, p. 451-453. It is a very significant text of Deuteronomy which

This interpretation of the eduction of forms which is the interpretation St. Thomas adopts, St. Bonaventure will not accept. To see his reasoning on such a fundamental question and to appreciate the ground for his rejection of this interpretation, we must examine the view which he accepts. Forms are indeed in the potency of matter, but this capacity is not that in which (*in qua*) and from which (*a qua*) the forms are produced; it is that out of which (*ex qua*) the form comes. To be sure, this does not mean that the forms are derived from the essence of the matter itself. It means, rather, that there is something in matter, created with the matter itself, out of which the agent acting on the matter produces the form. Nor are we to suppose that this something in matter is a kind of part of the form to be produced. On the contrary, it is something which can and does become the form just as a rosebud becomes a rose: *illud potest esse forma et fit forma, sicut globus rosae fit rosa.* In fact, the agent does not introduce any new essence into the matter, but gives to the essence present in the matter a new mode of existence. Hence the activity of the agent consists precisely in changing an essence really existing in matter from a potential to an actual form. To attribute this causality is not to attribute too much to a created agent.[42] Therefore, in

---

serves as part of the *Sed Contra* to this artitle: *Dei perfecta sunt opera (Deuter.,* xxxii., 4).—That the doctrine of seminal reasons is part of a larger metaphysical attitude to which St. Thomas is opposed may be seen from *De Veritate,* XI, 1, *Respondeo.*

42. This discussion of the eduction of forms is taken from the question that St. Bonaventure devotes to it: *In II Sent.,* d. 7, p. 2, a. 2, q. 1, concl.; vol. ii, p. 197-199.—The text is too long to quote in its entirety; but here is the passage which states the view acceptable to St. Bonaventure: "Alia via est, quod formae sunt in potentia materiae, non solum *in qua* et *a qua* aliquo modo, sed etiam *ex qua.* Et hoc dicunt, non quia ipsa essentia materiae sit, ex qua res producitur, sed quod in ipsa materia aliquid est *concreatum,* ex quo agens, dum agit in ipsam, educit formam; non inquam ex illo tanquam ex aliquo, quod sit tanquam aliqua pars formae producendae

rejecting the opinion which St. Thomas adopts, St. Bonaventure is anxious to limit the causality of creatures in such
a way that for them to be causes does not in any way imply
even the suspicion of their being creators.   In brief, the
doctrine of St. Bonaventure is: *Haec igitur est summa
positionis, quod agens creatum nullam quidditatem, nec
substantialem nec accidentalem omnino producit, sed entem
sub una dispositione facit esse sub alia.*[43]

The progressive development of the active potencies
contained within the seminal reasons begins with the indeter-
minateness of the essence and its latent capacities for future
development.[44] The process of development, which we need
not follow in detail, is one in which, through an internal
finality and a progressive appetition for form, the elements
coalesce to form a mixture, which in turn is able to receive
the form of a complexion.[45] It is at this stage that the soul

---

sed quia illud potest esse forma et fit forma, sicut globus rosae fit
rosa.   Et ista positio ponit, quod in materia sint *veritates* omnium
formarum   producendarum naturaliter; et cum producitur, nulla
quidditas, nulla veritas essentiae inducitur de novo, sed datur ei
nova dispositio, ut quod erat in potentia fiat in actu.   Differunt
enim actus et potentia, non quia dicant diversas quidditates, sed
dispositiones diversas eiusdem; non tamen sunt dispositiones acci-
dentales sed substantiales. Et hoc non est magnum, si est in potentia agentis creati, ut quod est uno modo faciat esse alio modo
(Concl., 2-3; p. 198).   Cp. *In II Sent.,* d. 7, dub. 3; vol. ii, p. 206-207.
—Peter Olivi finds at least twelve difficulties with the doctrine that
the complete essence of the form is present in matter, not to mention three further difficulties with the action of the external agent
on such an essence: *In II Sent.,* q. 31; ed. cit., p. 537-538.

43. *In II Sent.,* d. 7, p. 2, a. 2, q. 1, ad 6; vol. ii, p. 189—The animal souls also are developed from seminal reasons; cf. *In II Sent.,*
d. 15, a. 1, q. 1; vol. ll, p. 374.

44. *In II Sent.,* d. 18, a. 1, q. 3, Concl., opinio 2; vol. ii., p. 441.

45. *In II Sent.,* d. 15, a. 1, q. 2, concl.; vol. ii, p. 378.   A complexion is the complete interpenetration of the four elements, and
is necessary for the activity of animal life.—According to the accepted astronomical ideas, the conciliation of the four elements

enters the body. The stages through which the body passes
until the soul enters into it must be considered as so many
partial steps leading to the organization that belongs to the
human body and requiring, therefore, an order and a development enabling the body to take its proper place in the
economy of the human composite.[46] The intermediate forms
or dispositions leading to such an end do not yield their
place to the succeeding forms but are, each of them, perfected
by the succeeding form and indeed make that form possible.
That is why it is possible to say that in the philosophy of
St. Bonaventure the doctrine of the plurality of forms, far
from excluding the union of soul and body, requires and
indeed makes possible such a union.[47] For, clearly, if the
dispositions are the *sine quibus non* of their successors, they
must be present to effect the entrance of the more perfect
form; so that the coming of the soul into the body cannot
suppress what it needs for its entrance, just as the body it-

---

took place under the influence of the celestial bodies. Cf. *In II
Sent.*, d. 17, a. 2, opinio 3; vol. ii, p. 422-423.

46. " . . . est . . . vere . . . organizatio quae competit corpori
humano, quae quidem est a virtute formativa, cum seminibus delata
. . . Nec quaecumque qualitas mixtionis est illa quae facit ad
veritatem corporis humani, sed illa quae habet virtutem specifica-
tam, hominis completivam et directivam" *(In II Sent.*, d. 8, p. 1,
a. 2, q. 1, ad 2; vol. ii, p. 215). Cp. *In II Sent.*, d. 17, a. 2, q. 1,
concl. 2; col. ii, p. 419. On the difference between the soul and an
angel in the use of the body, cf. *In II Sent.*, d. 8, p. 1, a. 3, q. 2,
ad 2; vol. ii, p. 222.

47. " . . . sed is est ordo, quod forma elementaris unitur animae
mediante forma mixtionis, et forma mixtionis disponit ad formam
complexionis" *(In II Sent.*, d. 17, a. 2, q. 2, ad 6; vol. ii, p. 423). Cf.
E. Gilson, *La philosophie de saint Bonaventure*, p. 312. The foregoing text is to be interpreted according to the following principle
governing the realms of nature and grace alike: *"Observatio justitiae disponit ad eam (scil. sapientiam) habendam, sicut appetitus
materiae inclinat ad formam et facit eam habilem ut conjungatur
formae mediantibus dispositionibus; non quod illae dispositiones
perimentur, immo magis complentur sive in corpore humano, sive*

self cannot be complete until it has been endowed with the most perfect form in the whole realm of nature, the human soul, for which it was made and to the reception of which it points all its energies.[48]   And that is why the appetite of soul and body for each other, which is St. Bonaventure's explanation of the reason for their union, affects the very essence of both and is not to be considered as a sort of external tie between them.   In their developments, it is toward each other that they are constantly tending, and their union satisfies and completes the most essential aspect of their being.

St. Bonaventure finds another opportunity to insist on the real unity of man when he considers the problem of the origin of the soul. Two errors can be discarded immediately.

---

in aliis.   Observatio igitur justitiae introducit sapientiam" (*In Hexaemeron*, Coll. ii, 2; vol. v, p. 336).

48. "Corpus enim humanum nobilissima complexionatum; ideo non completur nec natum est compleri nisi nobilissima forma sive natura" *(In II Sent.*, d. 1, p. 2, a. 3, q. 2, opinio 3; vol. ii, p. 50).

We may note here that St. Bonaventure requires the presence of three spirits to make possible the union between a spiritual and a material substance. As he admits *(In I Sent.*, d. 10, a. 2, q. 3, concl.; vol. i, p. 204), he derives his definition of *spiritus* from the *De Differentia Spiritus et Animae* of Costa-ben-Luca: "Spiritus est quoddam corpus subtile, quod in humano corpore oritur ex corde et fertur in venis pulsus ad vivificandum corpus; operatur quoque vitam et anhelitum atque pulsum. Et similiter oritur ex cerebro et nervis et operatur sensum atque motum" (cap. i; ed. C. S. Barach, Innsbruck, 1878, p. 121). These are known respectively as the *spiritus vitalis* and the *spiritus animalis* (op. cit., cap. ii; ed cit., p. 130). As Costa-ben-Luca does not admit three spirits, and as Alfredus Anglicus distinctly fights against the addition of a third, the *spiritus naturalis*, this tradition cannot be St. Bonaventure's source. (For Alfredus Anglicus, cf. *De Motu Cordis*, ix, 9; ed. C. Baeumker, *Bieträge*, xxiii, 1-2, Münster, 1923, p. 42). Baeumker points out *(ibid.*, note 1) that the doctrine is from Galen.

For some historical indications on the doctrine of spirits, cf. E. Lutz, *Die Psychologie Bonaventuras*, p. 35-37.

Since the soul is spiritual, it is not traduced with the body;[49] and since it is a substance in its own right and is in no way subservient to the perpetuation of the species, it is impossible to agree with any Averroistic attempt to inculcate a doctrine which was equivalent to holding one soul for the entire human race.[50] After the elimination of these errors, the problem becomes this: At what moment was each soul created? Concerning the soul of Adam, St. Bonaventure thinks it possible that it was created before the body, but he thinks it more reasonable that Adam's soul was joined to his body immediately after its creation.[51] As to the souls of human beings after Adam, St. Bonaventure is more positive. None of them exists before its body, because then the soul would not be joined to the body as its true perfection; and since, as Aristotle says, the proper form naturally is brought into existence in its proper matter, to accept such a theory as the foregoing is to deny that in each individual case the soul is the true perfection of the body.[52] The Manichaean doctrine will be rejected also, for it contradicts faith, philosophy and experience: faith, because any doctrine of sin in a prior existence contradicts the statement of St. Paul;[53] philosophy, because on the assumption it makes, man

---

49. "Et ideo est tertius modus dicendi catholicus et verus, quod animae non seminantur, sed formatis corporibus a Deo creantur et creando infunduntur et infundendo producuntur" (*In II Sent.*, d. 18, a. 2, q. 3, opinio 3; vol. ii, p. 453).—For St. Augustine's doubts on this point and his solution, cf. the references of the Quaracchi editors, *ibid.*, n. 2.

50. This is St. Bonaventure's reduction of Averroes' doctrine that the active and possible intellects are separate. That is why he insists on the qualification "intellectualis": cf. *In II Sent.*, d. 18, a. 2, q. 1, error 2; vol. ii, p. 446.—Cf. E. Gilson, *La philosophie de saint Bonaventure*, p. 307-309.

51. *In II Sent.*, d. 17, a. 1, q. 3, concl.; vol. ii, p. 417.

52. St. Bonaventure is aiming at Macrobius, Cf. *supra*, notes 32-33, and *De Anima*, II, 2, 414a 25-27, for the reference to Aristotle.

53. *Romans*, IX, 11.

would not be a real unity, nor would soul and body be made
for the express purpose of establishing that unity; experience, because, as we have already seen, the soul does not
desire to be separated from the body. There is an additional
point on which the teaching of the Manichaeans conflicts
with experience, namely, the acquisition of knowledge. We
are not aware of knowing any more than we learn in this
life, and the theory of reminiscence runs directly counter
to the facts of experience.[54]   Consequently, only one conclusion is possible, namely, that each soul is created in its
own individual body and not before it. On this point, says
the Seraphic Doctor, there is no room for *opinari probabiliter;*
we must *credere fideliter.* What is more, when we meet a
doctrine which has some claim to authority and which appears
to speak of a priority of soul over body, this priority must
be understood as being one of nature and not of time.[55]

In this way, the doctrine of St. Bonaventure on the substantiality of the soul and the unity of man presents the
aspect of a complete and consistent whole. In the problem
of the soul, whatever may be the terminology he uses, St.
Bonaventure has little, if any, room in his system for an
Aristotelian conception of the soul as the form of the body.
To accuse him, therefore, of making an ineffectual synthesis
between the tradition of St. Augustine and the new Aristotelianism is to misconceive the direction of his thought

---

54. *In II Sent.*, d. 18, a. 2, q. 2, concl.; vol. ii, p. 449.—On the true
unity of man, cf. *In III Sent.*, d. 5, a. 2, q. 4, ad 5; vol. iii, p. 139,
and especially, *In III Sent.*, d. 22, a. 1, q. 1, ad 4; vol. iii, p. 453.

55. *In II Sent.*, d. 18, a. 2, q. 2, concl.; vol. ii, p. 449-450. This is
the principle which will govern the definitions of the soul to be
found in Gregory Nazienzen, John of Damascus and St. Augustine.
As St. Augustine is quoted from the *De Spiritu et Anima*, it would
appear that St. Bonaventure did not share the opinion that this
work is apocryphal. Cf. St. Thomas, *Quaest. Disp. de Anima*, a.
xii, ad 1 (and not ad 2, as Ueberweg-Geyer, *Grundriss.* 11th ed.,
p. 261, has).

and to judge it according to the metaphysical standards of Aristotle.[56] Properly speaking, there is no problem of reconciling St. Augustine and Aristotle confronting St. Bonaventure. He will not only test Aristotle by a theological formation whose corner-stone is St. Augustine; he will even use the language of Aristotle to convey doctrines that are not Aristotelian. In any Aristotelian sense, the doctrine of the soul as form of the body has almost no place in the thought of the Seraphic Doctor; and that is why he does not see problems where an Aristotelian would. Thus, if in the eyes of an Aristotelian the doctrine of plurality of forms destroys the unity of the composite substance, for St. Bonaventure it is the successive and preparatory presence of these forms which leads to the perfect unity of the individual. This idea of the preparatory function of forms is so dominant in his mind that he cannot understand how a form is joined to matter without the mediation and disposition of intervening forms: *Unde insanum est dicere, quod ultima forma addatur materiae primae sine aliquo, quod sit dispositio vel in potentia ad illam, vel nulla forma interiecta.*[57] Such a conception of form will remain a distinctive feature of Franciscan thought even in the face of the criticism to which St. Thomas subjected the doctrine of plurality of forms. We may see this point illustrated by some statements to be found in St. Bonaventure's immediate disciples.

Matthew of Aquasparta, whose *Quaestiones de Incarnatione* were held in Rome between 1281 and 1287, sees no difficulty in the doctrine of plurality of forms. In fact, he writes that *secundum sententiam Magistrorum Parisiensium* an individual could have many *esse* or acts of beings and still remain one being. Many substantial forms perfect the

---

56. Cf. E. Lutz, *Die Psychologie Bonaventuras*, p. 8-9, and the criticism of E. Gilson, *La philosophie de saint Bonaventure*, p. 323-324.

57. *In Hexaemeron*, Coll. iv, no. 10; vol. v, p. 351.

same individual according to different degrees of being and
locate him in different genera. Thus, one and the same man
is in the genus of substance through the form of substance;
in the genus of corporeal substance through the form of
body; in the genus of mixture through the form of mixture;
in the genus of complexion through the form of complexion;
in the genus of living substances through the vegetable form;
in the genus of animals through the sensible form; in the
species man through the intellectual form. The intellectual
form is the form which completes man in an absolute sense,
while the other forms, far from fixing or perfecting the being
of the individual in any final sense, give it only a partial
perfection and a disposition to receive finally its complete
being through the intellectual form. In this way, the intermediate forms can be considered from two points of view.
In their relations to matter they must be considered as
giving it *being* at a particular degree; in their relations to
the succeeding forms, they are, as it were, material dispositions and are indeed all material with respect to the last
form.[58]   All these forms remain in the individual as the

---

58. "Rursus, quilibet homo, quamvis unus homo sit, tamen in
uno et eodem homine sunt plura esse, quia plures formae substantiales perficientes secundum diversos gradus essendi, et per
quas reponitur in diversis generibus gradatim ordinatis, secundum
communem sententiam Magistrorum Parisiensium. Unde unus et
idem homo per formam substantiae reponitur et collocatur in
genere substantiae; et per formam corporis in genere substantiae
corporeae; et per formam mixtionis in genere corporis mixti; et
per formam complexionis in genere complexionati; et per formam
vegetabilem in genere vivi; et per formam sensibilem in genere
animalis; et per formam intellectivam sive rationalem in specie
hominis, ita tamen, quod ista est forma specifica et ultimo com-
pletiva, aliae autem non dant esse completum simpliciter, sed in
tali gradu, nec dant esse fixum, sed ordinant et disponunt ad istam
ultimam. Et ideo, etsi per comparationem ad materiam sint formae dantes esset in tali gradu, tamen respectu formae ulterioris
materiales sunt dispositiones et tenent se ex parte materiae, et

disposing principles through which the later forms enter.[59] The presence of these forms does not oppose the unity of the individual because such a unity is derived, not from the substantial form, but from the completing individual form.[60] And that is why, Matthew concludes, the doctrine of the unity of the substantial form is untenable and therefore rightly condemned by the masters at Paris.[61]

William de la Mare, the *Corrector Fratris Thomae,* comes to the same conclusions. The plurality of substantial forms does not affect the unity of the composite because the forms

---

ideo aeque sunt materiales respectu ultimae" (Matthew of Aquasparta, *Quaestiones Disputatae Selectae,* II, *Quaestiones de Christo,* qu. ix, *Respondeo;* ed. Quaracchi, 1914, p. 167.

59. "Tu obiicis: in formis, quae sibi invicem succedunt, una adveniente, altera cedit. Dico quod verum est in formis contrariis et quae simul se non compatiuntur, sicut in eadem materia succedunt sibi formae elementares, quae simul esse non possunt; in aliis autem formis veritatem non habet; nam, ut saepe dictum est, in eodem homine primo praecedit forma vegetabilis, quia primo vivit vita plantae et illa disponit ad sensitivam, et, ea adveniente, manet; et sensitiva praecedit intellectivam, quia prius est animal quam homo, et utrumque disponit ad intellectivam, cum qua simul et aliae manent" (*Quaestiones de Christo,* qu. ix, ad 1; ed. cit., p. 171).

60. "Ad cuius intelligentiam notandum, quod esse duplex est, vel dupliciter dicitur: substantiale essentiale et individuale sive personale et hypostaticum. Esse substantiale vel essentiale est a forma substantiali communi; esse autem individuale, personale vel hypostaticum est a forma propria vel per materiam appropriatam. Hoc dico in creaturis. . . In eodem igitur impossibile est esse plura esse personalia, quia una est tantum proprietas personalis; sed in eodem possunt esse plura esse substantialia sive formalia, quia idem individuum sive suppositum potest reponi et collocari in diversis sive pluribus generibus. (*Quaestiones de Christo,* qu. ix, *Respondeo;* ed. cit., p. 170).—Cp. *ibid.,* ad 8; ed. cit., p. 173.

61. *Quaestiones de Christo,* qu. ix, *Respondeo;* ed. cit., p. 168. Matthew has in mind here the controversies which occupied the third quarter of the thirteenth century and which resulted in the large scale condemnation of 1277: cf. *Chartularium Universitatis Parisiensis,* vol. i, p. 543 ff.

which precede the ultimate form are incomplete and in potency
to the complete being which will be introduced by that form.[62]
These forms, therefore, which come after the first, are not
accidental because they are essential complements of the
hitherto incomplete individual.[63] In what sense, then, does
the intellectual form, which is the last to enter the human
composite, give existence to the composite? To answer this
question, we must distinguish two possible meanings which
it may have. Such a question may mean: is or is not the
intellectual form the one and only source of the existence
of the compound? If the question is to be interpreted in

---

62. "Ad secundum dicendum quod quaelibet istarum formarum
dat aliquod esse; sed sicut prima forma est in potentia ad secundam completivam ipsius, ita esse quod dat prima forma est in-
completum et in potentia ad esse completum. Pluralitas ergo formarum non est contra unitatem compositi essentialem nisi sint
tales quae non se habent secundum esse completum et incom-
pletum ita quod non possint convenire ad aliquam unitatem
essentialem" (*Correctorium Corruptorii "Quare"*, art. xxxi in
primam partem; ed. P. Glorieux (*Bibliotheque thomiste*, ix), Le
Sauchoir, Kain 1927, p. 133).—What is more, for William de la
Mare the unity of the substantial form is condemned by faith,
philosophy and Scripture: "Haec positio de unitate formae substantialis reprobatur a magistris, primo, quia ex ipsa plura
sequuntur contraria fidei catholicae; secundo, quia contradicit
philosophiae, tertio, quia repugnat Sacrae Scripturae" (*ibid.*, ed.
P. Glorieux, p. 129).

63. "Ad tertium cum dicitur quod haec: homo est animal,
est praedicatio per accidens, dicendum quod non oportet; formae
enim ordinatae quae praedicantur ad invicem sunt dupliciter;
quaedam enim sunt accidentia illi supposito immediate, quae
praedicantur de se invicem praedicatione accidentali, sicut cum
dicitur superficiatum est coloratum, quia nec superficies est de
essentia subiecti nec color; item nec reponitur in specie completa per colorem qui accidit ei; aliae autem formae sunt quae
sunt de essentialibus suppositi, ratione cuius de se invicem
praedicantur in concretione, ubi nunquam est praedicatio acci-
dentialis" (*Correctorium Corruptorii "Quare"*, art. xxxi in primam
partem; ed. P. Glorieux, p. 133).

this way, then the intellectual form is not the principle whereby the compound exists, because it is not the source of that existence which the compound has through the preceding forms. Rather, the existence which the intellectual form gives is the complement and the perfection of all the preceding forms and of the existence which they give. If the existence in question, however, is said to be absolute as opposed to accidental existence, then it is true to say that the intellectual form is *simpliciter* the source of the existence of the composite. For just as the preceding forms are in potency to this form as to an essential complement, so the existence of these forms is in potency to the existence of the intellectual form.[64]   Consequently, the soul as a substantial form is to be understood as perfecting the existence of the composite, and not as being the principle of that existence. His conclusion, therefore, is this: *ad argumentum tamen dicimus quod esse animae et esse compositi est esse duarum*

---

64. "Ad sextum, scilicet quod aliter intellectiva non daret esse simpliciter, dicendum quod si per ly esse simpliciter intelligat totum esse quod est in composito, verum est quod non dat illud esse totum quod datur per formas praecedentes, sed esse quod dat est completivum et perfectivum omnium formarum praecedentium, et esse istarum formarum. Si autem intelligat esse simpliciter, secundum quod dividitur ex opposito contra esse quod dat accidens, secundum quem modum dicit Philosophus I⁰ de Generatione, quod substantia generatur dicitur generatio simpliciter, sic dico quod forma intellectiva dat esse simpliciter; quia sicut formae praecedentes erant in potentia ad illam tamquam ad essentiale complementum, sic etiam esse formarum praecedentium ad esse eius; et ideo in adventu formae completivae est generatio vera, vel generationis essentiale complementum, quamvis non sit generatio vera, in adventu formae accidentalis" (*Correctorium Corruptorii "Quare"*, art. xxxi in primam partem; ed. P. Glorieux, p. 134-135). The reference to Aristotle is *De Generatione et Corruptione, I*, 3; ed. Didot, vol. ii, p. 439. —Cf. *Correctorium Corruptorii "Quare"*, art. v in I Sent.; ed. P. Glorieux, p. 423.

rerum et non unius rei; *et hoc non est inconveniens quod
duarum rerum sint duo esse.*[65]

Such a doctrine, to which John Pecham,[66] Roger
Marston [67] and John Peter Olivi [68] adhered faithfully, is

---

65. *Correctorium Corruptorii "Quare"*, art. iv in I Sent.; ed.
P. Glorieux, p. 421.

66. If the soul is composed of matter and form, how can
man be a unity? To this question Pecham gives identically the
same answer as St. Bonaventure: although the soul is composed
of matter and form, it was made to be joined to the body, and
therefore its own composition is only a step, as it were, in the
perfection of the soul. Cf. John Pecham, *Quaestiones Tractantes
de Anima*, q. xxv; ed. H. Spettmann (*Beiträge*, xix, 5-6), Münster
i, W., 1918, p. 183-184, 186-188, especially the reply to objections 1-3, p. 187.

Pecham's firm allegiance to St. Augustine and to the development of his thought in Alexander of Hales and St. Bonaventure
had as its natural counterpart an uncomprising opposition to the
Aristotelian ideas which had invaded the *solidior doctrina* of the
Augustinians. Cf. *Chartularium Universitatis Parisiensis*, vol. i,
p. 634-635. On the personal relations between Pecham and St.
Thomas during this period, cf. the important but controverted
paper of A. Callebaut, *Jean Pecham, O.F.M. et l'augustinisme,
Aperçus historiques* (1263-1285), in *Archivum Franciscanum
Historicum*, xviii (1925), p. 441-472.

67. Roger Marston, *Quaestiones Disputatae, De Emanatione
Aeterna*, q. 1, ad r; ed. Quaracchi, 1932, p. 20; q. ii, ad 9; ed.
cit., p. 36.—On the question whether or not Marston was a pupil
of St. Bonaventure, cf. the introduction of the Quaracchi editors, *op. cit.*, p. xiii-xvi.

68. " . . . idcirco simpliciter teneo in corpore humano
praeter animam esse alias formas realiter differentes ab ipsa et
etiam credo omnes gradus formales qui in eo sunt concurrere
ad unam perfectam formam constituendam, quarum principa-
lior et omnium quodam modo forma et radix est illa quae ultimo
advenit" (*Quaestiones in II Sent.*, qu. L. Respondeo; ed. B.
Jansen, vol. ii, Quaracchi, 1924, p. 35).—The opening paragraph
of the *Respondeo* (*ibid.*, p. 29) contains a summary of the
Thomistic doctrine on the unity of the substantial form, a doctrine to which Peter Olivi's first reaction is that "opinio autem
haec non potest habere in se veritatem" (*ibid*).

capable of bringing to light two different metaphysical traditions underlying a common philosophical language. The *Quodlibeta* of Godfrey of Fontaines furnish an interesting commentary on this difference, and the testimony of Godfrey is all the more significant for the distinction of philosophical traditions because his unwillingness to choose definitely between the partisans of unity and the partisans of plurality of forms led him to a thorough analysis of the problem and, what is more important, to an appreciation of the different metaphysical presuppositions that a uniform terminology concealed.

In the long development of the question in the second Quodlibet,[69] Godfrey adopts a decidedly critical attitude towards pluralism. Distinguishing three different types of the doctrine of plurality of forms,[70] he considers the first to be a confusion of logic and physics, or, in other words, the attribution to reality of distinctions produced by the mind.[71] The second type Godfrey considers to be a mis-

---

69. *Les quatres premiers Quodlibets de Godefroid de Fontaines,* ed. M. de Wulf and A. Pelzer (*Les philosophes belges,* ii), Louvain, 1904, Quodl. II, q. vii (p. 95-133): *Utrum homo habeat esse ab una forma substantiali vel a pluribus.*

70. *Quodl.* II, q. vii; ed. M. de Wulf-A. Pelzer, p. 96-97.

71. In spite of his hesitations, therefore, it would appear that Godfrey of Fontaines was inclined to look upon the doctrine of plurality of forms as an example of Platonic realism. Such texts as the following make this abundantly clear: "Et ideo logicus qui est artifex rationalis dicit genus praedicari de speciebus univoce propter unitatem rationis et conceptus, secundum quod genus dicitur aliquod unum solum secundum rationem; physicus vero qui est artifex realis dicit genus praedicari aliquo modo aequivoce sive non simpliciter univoce, eo quod uni conceptui et rationi secundum intellectum non respondet una forma et natura in re extra, et secundum hoc latent aequivocationes in genere" (*Quodl.* II, q. vii; ed. cit., p. 103). From this principle Godfrey proceeds to reduce pluralism to a plurality of predicable relations *cum fundamento in re concepta*: "Et sic non valet fundamentum dictae positionis. Quamvis autem ab una et

interpretation of Averroes on the permanence of elements in a mixture.[72] To the third type of pluralists in the doctrine of substantial forms he objects that they destroy the unity of man. It belongs to the nature of a form to give existence, and if that form is a substantial form, however incomplete, then it is the source of existence in an absolute sense: *hoc est de ratione formae quod det aliquod esse in actu et de ratione formae substantialis cuiuscumque quantumcumque incompletae quod det esse simpliciter.*[73]

In spite of these and many other objections, Godfrey

---

eadem re sumatur ordo praedicabilium quae distinguuntur secundum genus et differentiam et speciem, item secundum genus generalissimum et subalternum (haec autem multitudinem quandam important), tamen ordo huiusmodi cui non respondet multitudo realis ex parte formae cui imponuntur non est vanus, quia ordo praedicamentalis non dicit ordinem aliquorum plurium realium differentium, sed secundum rationem quae fundantur in una re concepta sub diversis rationibus ex comparatione ad aliqua diversa in aliquo etiam communicantia. Et ideo cum talis pluralitas habeat fundamentum in re non est cassa; provenit enim huiusmodi diversitas rationum non ex pluribus formis existentibus in eodem sed ex parte eiusdem secundum eandem formam ad diversa. Quamvis etiam eadem sit forma qua asinus est asinus et qua est animal, unumquodque autem intelligatur intellecta sua forma, non oportet tamen quod intellecto animali intelligatur asinus nisi in universali, quia anima non imponitur ad significandum determinate asinum et eius formam sed indeterminate; unde dicit aliquid quod indeterminate se habet ad asinum et multa alia; et contractum ad asinum non dicit aliam formam in asino ab illa qua asinus est asinus" (*Quodl.* II, q. vii; ed. cit., p. 108-109).

72. *Quodl.* II, q. vii; ed. M. de Wulf-A. Pelzer, p. 109-111.—Cp., however, St. Thomas, *Quaestio Disp. de Anima*, q. ix, ad 10, and A. Forest, *La structure métaphysique du concret selon saint Thomas d'Aquin*, p. 197-199. The point of the Thomistic criticism in the *De Anima* will be seen by referring to a text of the Arabian commentator quoted by the editors of Godfrey of Fontaines, *ibid.*, p. 110, note 1.

73. *Quodl.* II, q. vii; ed. M. de Wulf - A. Pelzer, p. 114.

does not absolutely discard the doctrine of plurality of forms, nor does he adhere definitely to the doctrine of the unity of the substantial form. His difficulty is the same in both instances: "Consequently, although both positions are difficult—I mean, to posit only one form in man and to avoid all the objections brought against this doctrine, or to posit many forms and to avoid the contrary objections—nevertheless, the objections urged against the doctrine of plurality of forms contain the greater difficulties. In fact, it would appear that the strongest difficulties urged against those who posit one form are effective also against those who posit many forms, for all such objections are based on an extremely serious difficulty which arises as follows: The rational soul is considered to be an immaterial substance, independent of matter, being a *hoc aliquid* and a self-subsistent creature; it is considered also to be so simple that it is neither divisible nor capable of extension either essentially or accidentally. Nevertheless, in spite of such characteristics, the soul is held to be capable of joining prime matter in existence in such a way that it is the source of the first and substantial existence of the composite as well as of the corporeal and extended matter. And this is very difficult to understand no matter which of the above interpretations we accept.'"[74] After thus noting that *magna difficultas remanet utrobique,* Godfrey concludes that the arguments for the unity of the substantial form in beings other than man appear to have equal weight when applied to man, and that there is only one form in man.[75] Here, therefore, with its nuances and reservations, is the conclusion that he reaches: *Ideo per modum saltem probabilis opinionis, et ut mihi videtur, eis quae fide certa teneri oportet non repugnantis, potest teneri quod in homine non sit nisi una forma, aliam tamen positionem non reprobando*

---

74. *Quodl.* II, q. vii; ed. M. de Wulf - A. Pelzer, p. 123-24.
75. *Quodl.* II, q. vii; ed. M. de Wulf - A. Pelzer, p. 124.

*nec impossibilem vel erroneam reputando. Et quid visum
est mihi quod rationes reprobantes pluralitatem formarum
in aliis ab homine habent efficaciam aequalem etiam in homine, ideo, quia nolo asserere tanquam necessarium et cuius
contrarium sit impossibile et erroneum, quod in homine sit
tantum una forma, sed solum hoc dicendo per modum probabilis opinionis,—ideo etiam volo asserere in aliis ab homine
non posse esse nisi unam formam, paratus tenere determinate
in homine esse plures formas, si appareant aliae rationes
efficaciores, vel si ex determinatione Ecclesiae determinetur
aliquid circa corpus Christi esse tenendum quod nondum est
determinatum, vel aliud ratione cuius oporteat ponere in homine plures formas.*[76]

While Godfrey of Fontaines thus gives only a conditional
assent to the doctrine of the unicity of the substantial form,
and considers the alternative solution possible, he does not
show any hesitation in separating the two distinct metaphysical conceptions underlying the conclusions facing him. Re-
turning to the question in the recently published tenth
Quodlibet, he still refuses to adhere to either solution: *non
asseram in homine plures formas esse nec etiam contrarium;*[77]

---

76. *Quodl.* II, q. vii; ed. M. de Wulf - A. Pelzer, p. 125-6.

77. *Quodl.* X, q. x; ed. J. Hoffmans (*Les philosophes belges*,
IV, 3), Louvain, 1931, p. 347.—He would follow the interpretation of Henry of Ghent who held (according to the testimony
of Godfrey) "quod in homine sit duplex forma, una scilicet
educta de potentia materiae, alia vero ab extrinseco, scilicet a
Deo creatore" (*Quodl.* X, q. x; ed. cit., p. 344)—an opinion, be
it noted, in which *philosophi plurimi consenserunt et etiam
videntur sanctorum dicta, prout ad litteram sunt conscripta, con-
cordare* (*ibid.*)—, were it not for the following difficulty: "in
hac positione ut sic generaliter intelligitur solum est difficultas ex hoc quod ratio propter quam in aliis negatur pluralitas
formarum videtur hoc etiam in proposito persuadere, maxime
cum supponatur quod anima intellectiva sit forma substantialis
dans esse substantiale et primum materiae illam informando"
(*ibid.*). Such an argument naturally caused considerable per-

but he also points out the different philosophical background
underlying each tradition. The occasion of this observation
was the following question: *utrum homo sit vere et realiter
compositus ex eo quod in ipso est materia et forma.*[78]

Some answered the question negatively, holding that man
was not really a composite substance. A real composition requires a real multiplicity of component principles, and matter and form do not produce a multiplicity. A real multiplicity, in fact, will exist only when each of the component
principles has its own being, its own actuality and its own
existence. Now in man, matter does not possess its own being or its own existence, for otherwise man would not be a
real unity. Consequently, since there is only one principle
of existence in man, there is no real composition in him.[79]

---

plexity: "Et ideo semper fuit perplexitas circa hominem de hoc
articulo et apud philosophos et apud theologos catholicos propter
ignorantiam naturae rationalis animae et modi quo unibilis sit
materiae" (*ibid.*). This is the atmosphere which explains the
personal hesitations of Godfrey of Fontaines: "Propter quod ego
etiam super hoc nec scio nec audeo aliquid diffinire, licet mihi
visum fuerit alias et adhuc videatur circa istum articulum quod
probabiliter possit sustineri quod non sit nisi una forma substantialis in homine, scilicet anima rationalis omnes praecedentes virtute continens" (*ibid.*).

78. *Quodl.* X, q. ix; ed. J. Hoffmans, p. 336-342.

79. "Circa primum quaerebatur primo unum pertinens ad
materiam eius, scilicet utrum homo sit vere et realiter compositus ex eo quod in ipso est materia et forma. Et arguitur quod
non. Quia per id quod cum alio non facit aliquam pluralitatem
vel multitudinem non potest aliquid esse vere et realiter compositum, quia compositio realis requirit aliquam realem pluralitatem vel multitudinem. Sed materia cum forma non constituit
aliquam pluralitatem vel multitudinem, quia aliqua non possunt
esse plura vel multa nisi quodlibet illorum habeat propriam entitatem et actualitatem et proprium esse. Sed materia non habet
propriam entitatem vel proprium esse, alioquin illud in quo est
materia et forma non esset unum simpliciter sed multa. Quare.
Et cetera" (*Quodl.* X, q. ix; ed. J. Hoffmans, p. 336).

Those who defended the real composition of man used the same argument, namely, that whenever two things have their own being and their own actuality, each distinct from the actuality of the other, then they can produce a real multiplicity in the composite to which they belong. Now matter has its own actuality and its own existence, for otherwise, if matter be merely a pure potency, then it would be simply a relation. And this is false.[80]

Whatever solution be given to this problem, it is important to note the two conceptions of matter upon which the alternatives rest; and indeed the first consideration of Godfrey is to point out this difference and to determine which of these conceptions of matter is compatible with the unity of man. If, he writes, it is possible for many substantial forms to exist in any one composite substance, then matter can be called a subject existing in potency, not in the sense that it excludes all actuality, but in the sense that it possesses a very small and imperfect actuality in the genus of substance. For if it does not violate the unity of the composite substance to say that there is an incomplete form in it which, in the development of the composite, assumes the rôle, as it were, of matter upon the entrance of the complete form which is the source of complete and perfect existence, then it can be said also, by way of resolution to the ultimate subject or matter, that matter itself is a being possessed of a certain small actuality in the genus of substance, destined to be perfected by a greater and more per-

---

80. "Contrarium arguebatur ostendendo oppositum virtute eiusdem medii. Quia illud quod habet esse proprium et propriam actualitatem distinctam ab esse et actualitate alterius facit cum illo compositionem realem. Sed materia habet propriam actualitatem et proprium esse, alioquin si materia non esset nisi ens in pura potentia sive quaedam potentia tantum, cum potentia non sit nisi relatio, materia non esset nisi relatio. Hoc autem est falsum. Ergo. Et cetera" (*Quodl.* X, q. ix; ed. J. Hoffmans, p. 336).

fect actuality.[81] Now, observes Godfrey, such an explanation may be possible, but it cannot claim the authority of Aristotle, because the idea of matter which it has is not Aristotelian, but comes from the *antiqui* who held that matter is something actually existing: *unde secundum eos qui hoc ponunt, non potest argui quod talis materia sit qualem posuit Philosophus, sed qualem posuerunt antiqui: quod materia erat aliquod ens in actu.*[82]

Matter, therefore, according to the *antiqui,* was a kind of infinitesimal substance, possessed of a small but positive existence, to which the introduction of substantial forms contributed a further disposition and a more perfect development. In such a tradition there is no question of considering the substantial form as that which at once bounds and limits the existence of the composite and of the matter of the composite; rather the distinctive function of the substantial form is to develop and to complete an already existing substance. In thus pointing out the idea of matter which this tradition upholds, as well as the complementary idea of form, Godfrey is anxious to point out also that it has nothing to do with the Aristotelian interpretation of matter; so that when we turn to Aristotle's conception of matter and form, we invest our ideas with a new metaphysical background. And

---

81. "Responsio. Dicendum quod si in uno ente quocumque substantiali composito possunt inesse plures actus substantiales, videtur quod materia possit dici subiectum ens in potentia, non quidem omnimodam actualitatem excludens sed includens actualitatem minimam et imperfectissimam in genere substantiae. Si enim non repugnat unitati compositi substantialis quod in illo sit forma incompleta cedens quasi in ratione materiae et forma completa dans esse perfectum et completum, ita poterit dici resolvendo usque ad illud quod materia dicitur, quod ipsa nihil aliud est quam ens secundum actualitatem minimam in genere substantiae nata perfici per quamcumque aliam actualitatem maiorem et perfectiorem" (*Quodl.* X, q. ix; ed. J. Hoffmans, p. 336).

82. *Quodl.* X, q. ix; ed. J. Hoffmans, p. 336-337.

the problem which in the eyes of Godfrey of Fontaines may require the transition to Aristotle is the unity of man. How, indeed, can man be one and yet have many substantial forms or principles of a *per se* existence? It is according as we answer that question that we shall agree with the *antiqui* or with Aristotle.

The Aristotelian alternative, according to the analysis of Godfrey, requires that matter in the genus of substance be only a purely potential being and include no actuality within itself. To be one or a unity in the genus of substance, a being must possess one source of its substantiality; so that as a substantial component matter must be the pure subject of that substantial existence. For an Aristotelian, therefore, there is a definite and necessary connection between the unity of substance and the pure potentiality of matter, and, as a corollary, between the unity of substance and the unicity of the substantial form: *Si autem nihil potest dici unum simpliciter ubi sunt plures actualitates, oportet dicere quod materia in genere substantiae sit ens in pura potentia nulla actualitatem includens.*[83] Consequently, in speaking of man as a composite substance and as possessing parts, we must note that there is a special sense in which this composition is to be understood, and does not imply the presence in man of many actual entities: *Et tale compositum non debet dici compositum ex pluribus entibus simpliciter et absque distinctione; sed, ut dicit Philosophus octavo Metaphysicae, debet distingui huiusmodi plura, dicendo quod plurium ex quibus constituta est substantia materialis unum est potentia simpliciter, ut materia; aliud vero, ut actus. Et haec est ratio quare ex istis constituitur unum.*[84] Such is the Aristotelian alternative.

---

83. *Quodl.* X, q. ix; ed. J. Hoffmans, p. 337.

84. *Quodl.* X, q. ix; ed. J. Hoffmans, p. 338.—Cf. Aristotle, *Metaphysics*, VII (VIII), 6; ed. Didot, p. 562-563 and St. Thomas, *In Metaph. Aristotelis Commentaria*, Lib. VIII, lect. v; ed. M.-R.

Between Godfrey of Fontaines, therefore, and the acceptance of the doctrine of plurality of forms lies the problem of the unity of man as a substance. Godfrey was frankly perplexed; he did not know whether the presence of many actual entities in a substance was compatible with the unity of that substance. Now it would appear that where Godfrey of Fontaines hesitated Duns Scotus assented. For the Subtle Doctor there is no more incompatibility between unity and plurality of forms than there is between unity and composition: *dico quod sicut non repugnat per se uni quod sit compositum, ita non repugnat ei quod sit ex aliquibus actualibus entitatibus realiter distinctis.*[85] Now, since a substance that is subject to change must necessarily be composite, it follows that such a substance is composed *ex aliquo et aliquo, sicut ex materia et forma.*[86] For Duns Scotus this means that matter is not something purely potential, but an actually existing being: *cum enim sit (scil. materia) principium et causa entis, oportet necessario quod sit aliquod ens;* it is a *realitas distincta a forma* and a *quid positivum.* And if it is called *ens in potentia,* the reason is that the less actuality a being has, the more potentiality it has; and since matter is capable of receiving all subsantial and accidental forms, it is in potency with reference to these forms. The potentiality of matter is thus a potentiality of indetermination; it is the potentiality of an actual being which is capable of further distinction and development.[87]

Cathala, 2nd ed., Taurini, 1926, no. 1755-1767, especially no. 1767.

85. *Opus Oxoniense,* II, d. 12, q. 1; ed. M. F. Garcia, Quaracchi, vol. ii, 1914, no. 556, p. 505.

86. *Opus Oxoniense,* II, d. 12, q. 1; ed. M. F. Garcia, vol. ii, no. 554, p. 504.

87. *Opus Oxoniense,* II, d. 12, q. 1; ed. M. F. Garcia, vol. ii, no. 554, p. 504.—Later on, Suarez followed Scotus in holding that matter had *suam propriam entitatem*: cf. J. F. McCormick, *Suarez on Matter and Form,* in *Proceedings of the Tenth An-*

Such a decision is neither isolated nor novel in the Franciscan tradition. As E. Longpré has insisted, the rôle of Duns Scotus in this as in other doctrines was to defend and develop the ideas that had become distinctively Franciscan under the guidance of St. Bonaventure.[88] Before Duns Scotus, Peter Olivi had defended the doctrine of the actuality of matter and considered it to be of Augustinian origin: *moti autem sunt ad hoc ex ratione et ex dictis Augustini.*[89] Matthew of Aquasparta held the opinion to which Olivi is here referring, for, on the principle that matter and form have distinct essences, he concludes that every essence is a being and has its own existence and that, *de omnipotentia Dei,* it could exist without a form.[90]

---

nual Convention of the Jesuit Educational Association, Chicago, Loyola U. Press, 1931, p. 172-183.

88. E. Longpré, *La philosophie du b. Duns Scot*, Paris, 1924. —Nevertheless, we must note that this unity in the Franciscan tradition did not prevent the gradual infiltration of some ideas reflecting the influence of St. Thomas. Thus, Duns Scotus abandons the doctrine of seminal reasons which Pecham had numbered among the cardinal principles of the Augustinian heritage received by Alexander of Hales and St. Bonaventure. Cf. *supra*, note 37; E. Gilson, *L'ésprit de la philosophie médiévale*, Première série, p. 269-270, note 11; E. Longpré, *op. cit.*, p. 74. It appears also that Duns Scotus followed St. Thomas in rejecting the hylemorphic composition of spiritual substances: cf. E. Longpré, *op. cit.*, p. 265.

89. After mentioning the Aristotelian conception of matter as pure potentiality, Olivi continues: "Alii autem dixerunt et, ut credo, verius et rationabilius quod materia secundum suam essentiam dicit aliquem actum seu actualitatem, distinctam tamen sufficienter ab actu qui est idem quod forma; hoc autem dicunt, sumendo nomine actus quodcumque positivum reale et quamcumque realem entitatem. Moti autem sunt ad hoc ex ratione et ex dictis Augustini" (*Quaestiones in II Sent.*, q. 16; ed. B. Jansen, vol. i, Quaracchi, 1922, p. 305-306).

90. Basing his teaching on Augustinian texts, Matthew argues first that matter "habet essentiam distinctam ab essentia formae, ac per hoc habet suam ideam in Deo"; from which it follows

Such, in outline, is the conception of matter which the immediate disciples of St. Bonaventure defended.[91]   If we ask now what is distinctive in this interpretation of matter and its capacity for existence without form, it is that Aristotle cannot be considered its author. As a matter of fact, Olivi denied such a parentage. The soil in which pluralism *could* grow—and Godfrey of Fontaines has noted this point—is furnished by the *antiqui,* but the actual doctrine, as it will appear, is an importation. Who were the *antiqui?* Briefly they were the representatives of mediaeval thought prior to the arrival of Aristotle late in the twelfth century. Peter Lombard summarized well the prevailing ideas. The question is this: how are we to understand the informity of matter?

In principio creavit Deus caelum et terram (*Gen.* I, 1). *Caelum* refers to the angels; *terram* refers to the confused and chaotic mass of matter which was to be developed into the four elements. According to St. Augustine, this original chaos was called *terra* because of all the elements earth is the least ornate.[92] But, however we may call it, its most characteristic and indeed essential aspect is formlessness. Does this mean that the original matter of creation had no form? Clearly not, because it is impossible for a corporeal substance which has no form whatever to exist. On the contrary, it was called formless because it was confused and the elements were not distinguished, and because it was not yet adorned

---

that "quoniam omnis natura et essentia habet esse sibi correspondens, hoc ipso quod non nihil est, ens est, et si ens est, esse habet".—Cf. the text as a whole, edited by E. Longpré, *La philosophie du b. Duns Scot,* p. 72-73, from among the unpublished *Quodlibeta* of Matthew of Aquasparta.

91. St. Bonaventure himself, according to his best interpreters, held that matter can be separated from form and exist without it: cf. E. Longpré, *La philosophie du b. Duns Scot,* p. 70.

92. Peter Lombard, **Sent.,** II, d. 12, c. 3; ed. Quaracchi, 1916, vol. i, p. 359-360.—For St. Augustine, cf *De Gen. contra Manichaeos,* vii, 12; P.L., vol. 34, col. 179.

with the beautiful and visible and distinctive form or appearance it now possesses. The original matter was thus created *in forma confusionis*. All corporeal substances were created at the same time in a sort of confused unity; it was the work of the six days which arranged and ordered them.[93]

It does not even occur to Peter Lombard, therefore, to connect form and existence. For him, form is a disposition introduced into the basic reality, matter; and the indetermination of matter itself refers to the capacity for further development. The doctrine of matter which Peter Lombard thus reveals is representative of the age. As M. De Wulf and G. Théry have pointed out, and as the cosmologies of the school of Chartres well illustrate, the preoccupations of the age were not especially metaphysical.[94] The question of the unity or plurality of substantial forms cannot be found here. It is true that these thinkers are advocates of a doctrine of matter which can be pressed into the service of pluralism once the problem of forms arises. But, if pluralism it is, the conception of matter and its development is so native to the cosmo-

---

93. "Ad illud igitur quod primo positum est, breviter respondentes dicimus, illam primam materiam non ideo, dictam fore informem, quod nullam omnino formam habuerit, quia non aliquid corporeum tale existere potest, quod nullam habeat formam; sed ideo non absurde informem appelari posse dicimus, quia in confusione et permixtione informem subsistens, nondum pulchram apertamque et distinctam receperat formam, qualem modo cernimus. Facta est ergo illa materia in forma confusionis ante formam dispositionis: in forma confusionis prius omnia corporalia materialiter simul et semel sunt creata, postmodum in forma dispositionis sex diebus sunt ordinata" (Peter Lombard, *Sent.* II, a. 12, c. 5; ed. Quaracchi, vol. i, p. 361).—The ideas and even the expressions of this text can be found in Hugh of St. Victor, *De Sacramentis*, Lib. I, P. i, c. 3, 4; P.L., vol. 176, col. 189c.

94. M. De Wulf, *Le traité* De Unitate Formae *de Gilles de Lessines*, p. 26-28; G. Théry, *L'augustinisme médiéval et l'unité de la forme substantielle*, in *Acta Hebdomadae Augustinianae-Thomisticae*, Taurini-Romae, 1931, p. 141-144.

logical speculations of the twelfth century that it is more the expression of a definite Christian tradition than a philosophical position defended in the face of controversy.

On the other hand, if we compare these commentaries on the work of the six days with the ideas advanced by Dominicus Gundissalinus on the same subject, the differences are striking. In the thirteenth century, Thomas of York referred to him as *Gundissalinus imitator, immo compilator Algazel et Avicennae . . .;*[95] to which we may add the name of Ibn Gebirol, for the works of the archdeacon of Segovia embody not only the ideas of Ibn Gebirol and Avicenna, but also their texts.[96] In the *De Processione Mundi,* which is concerned with the existence of God and the creation of the universe, Avicenna is the guide that Gundissalinus follows in the first problem, while Ibn Gebirol is his guide and master in the question of the nature and constitution of creation. It is in this second problem that we are here interested.

Since every created being contains within itself some diversity, God created simple but diverse principles, matter and form, which are purely possible and require that they be united for actual existence.[97] The universe was made out of these two principles in the following way: The first form joined to matter was the form of substantiality, but along with it came the form of unity, because everything that is, is because it is one. These two forms were joined to matter prior to all others because it is the substance which

95. Thomas of York, *Sapientiale,* II, 28; quoted by E. Longpré, *Fr. Thomas d'York, O.F.M.,* in *Archivum Franciscanum Historicum,* **XIX** (1926), p. 900.

96. The *De Processione Mundi* is particularly significant in this respect. Cf. G. Bülow, *Des Dominicus Gundissalinus Schrift "Von dem Hervorgange der Welt" (De Processione Mundi) (Beiträge* **XXIV**, 3), Munster i. W., 1925. As G. Théry has pointed out (*art. cit.,* p. 149, with note 1), the *De Unitate* also is dependent textually on the *Fons Vitae* of Ibn Gebirol.

97. *De Processione Mundi;* ed. G. Bülow, p. 21, 24, 27-28.

they constitute that is the subject of all future determinations and therefore *mediates* between matter and the determinations to come.[98]   Two forms now follow which divide the whole realm of substance, the form of corporality, *corporalitas,* and the form of spirituality, each of which can be either substantial or accidental: the form of corporality can be constitutive of the existence of a corporeal substance, and then it would be called *corporeity,* or it could be simply a quality or accident of the corporeal substance already constituted; the form of spirituality could be substantial, as is the form of rationality in man, or accidental, as is knowledge.[99]   In brief: *Sic igitur processit totius mundi constitutio de nihil esse ad possibiliter esse, de possibiliter esse ad actu esse et de actu esse ad corporeum et incorporeum esse; et hoc totum simul, non in tempore . . . Et sic de nihilo ad simplicia, de simplicibus ad composita, de compositis ad generata facta est progressio.*[100]

Apart, therefore, from the work of Avicenna and Ibn Gebirol which he translated, Gundissalinus also introduced to the middle ages the most significant of their ideas.[101] With reference to Ibn Gebirol in particular, it is clear that Gundissalinus is indebted to the *Fons Vitae* [102]

---

98. *De Processione Mundi;* ed. G. Bülow, p. 41-42, 43.

99. *De Processione Mundi;* ed. G. Bülow, p. 42-43.

100. *De Processione Mundi;* ed. G. Bülow, p. 54.

101. On the influence of Avicenna on Gundissalinus in the problem of knowledge, cf. E. Gilson, *Les sources gréco-arabes de l'augustinisme avicenisant (Archives d'hist. doctr. et litt. du moyen age,* iv, 1929), p. 79-92; on the same influence of Avicenna on the proof of the existence of God in Gundissalinus, cf. *De Processione Mundi;* ed. G. Bülow, p. 4-5, 7, 8, 16, with the references of the editor to the *Metaphysica* of Avicenna.

102. For purposes of reference, we may note the following points in the *Fons Vitae* of Ibn Gebirol: Matter and form are the two irreducible constituant roots *(radix)* of the whole physical universe *(Fons Vitae,* I, 5; ed. C. Baeumker *(Beiträge,* I.

for the doctrines of universal matter[103] and plurality of forms.

2-4), Münster i. W., 1892-1895, p. 7). Matter is absolutely undifferentiated, and all the diversity that we observe in corporeal substances is caused by form *(Fons Vitae*, I, 12; *ed. cit.*, p. 15). Matter is thus the base or ground of all existence, while form is the source of all diversity *(Fons Vitae*, I, 17; *ed. cit.* p. 22; cf. *ibid.*, I, 10; p. 13-14; V, 30; p. 312-313). After the third book which is devoted to proving the existence of simple substances the fourth book proceeds to show that these substances also are composed of matter and form. None of them indeed is form without matter, because then nothing would act as the subject or support of existence: quomodo est possibile ut formae *sustineantur sine sustinente (Fons Vitae*, IV, 1; *ed. cit.*, p. 212-213)? Cp. *ibid.*, IV, 4; p. 217. The human soul, being a simple substance, is subject to the law governing such substances *(Fons Vitae*, II, 1 and III, 28; *ed. cit.*, p. 25 and 145). Now, why is it necessary for all substances, spiritual and corporeal, to be composed of matter and form? The reason is that everything below the pure unity of the One is limited and derived *(Fons Vitae*, V, 23; *ed. cit.*, p. 300). Since, in fact, in a derived existence it is necessary to have a subject of existence, matter is present in all derived substances as that which receives the form and supports its existence. The conception, therefore, of matter as the *fundamentum existentiae* which St. Bonaventure defended (cf. *In II Sent.*, a. 1, q. 2, concl., opinio 3; vol. ii, p. 414-415) appears to have Ibn Gebirol as its source.—For the definition of form as unity coming from the One, cf. *Fons Vitae*, II, 20; *ed. cit.*, p. 60-61, and for the progressive subsistence of one form in a higher as well as for the same conception of matter, cf. *Fons Vitae*, II, 2; *ed. cit.*, p. 26-27.

A summary of the *Fons Vitae*, with translated extracts, will be found in S. Munk, *Mélanges de philosophie juive et arabe*, Paris, 1859 (reprinted, 1927), p. 173ff. On Ibn Gebirol as a whole, cf. I. Husik, *A History of Medieval Jewish Philosophy*, New York, 1916 (reprinted, 1930), p. 59-79. What Husik (*op. cit.*, p. 61) says of Duns Scotus must now be attributed to Vital du Four, the author of the *De Rerum Principio*. For Duns Scotus, cf. *supra*, note 88.

103. Some reservation must be made for the *De Immortalitate Animae* of Gundissalinus. If Gundissalinus is the author of all the treatises attributed to him, and if, as G. Bülow supposes

From the beginning of his philosophical career St. Thomas attributed both of these doctrines to Ibn Gebirol and considered him to be their author.[104] On the other hand, the disciples of St. Bonaventure, confronted by the criticism of St. Thomas, invoked the testimony of St. Augustine on the existence of spiritual matter. William de la Mare writes unhesitatingly: *quod autem sit ponere materiam spiritualem patet per Augustinum.*[105] Now it is possible to find indications of the doctrine of spiritual matter in St. Augustine,

---

(*Des Dominicus Gundissalinus Schrift "Von dem Hervorgange der Welt"*, p. xxvi), this treatise is the last that Gundissalinus wrote, then we must suppose that after accepting the doctrine of universal matter from the *Fons Vitae* which he and John of Spain had translated into Latin, Gundissalinus finally rejected this doctrine and refused to admit the presence of matter in the soul: *et de primo modo manifestum est, quoniam ipsa (scil. anima) est pura forma et substantia immateriata et incomposita in se huiusmodi compositione quae est ex materia et forma* (*De Immortalitate Animae*: ed. G. Bülow, *Des Dominicus Gundissalinus Schrift "Von der Unsterblichkeit der Selle"*, (*Beiträge*, II, 3, Munster i. W., 1897, p. 28). Cp. *ibid.* p. 103, 133.

104. "Quidam enim dicunt quod in omni substantia creata est materia, et quod omnium est materia una; et hujus positionis auctor videtur Avicebron, qui fecit librum *Fontis Vitae*, quem multi sequuntur (*In II Sent.*, d. 3, q. 1, a. 1, Resp.). . . ." . . . nisi forte dicatur, secundum positionem libri *Fontis Vitae*, esse unam primam formam, et sic in materia primo distinctas" (*In II Sent.* d 12, q. 1, a. 4, *Resp.*) As we shall see, St. Thomas does not consider such an explanation very plausible.

105. *Correctorium Corruptorii "Quare"*, art. x in primam partem; ed. P. Glorieux, p. 50. Here is the text that he cites: "Non itaque temporali, sed causali ordine prius facta est informis formabilisque materies, et spiritualis et corporalis, de qua fiet quod faciendum esset, cum et ipsa, priusquam instituta est, non fuisset; nec instituta est nisi ab illo utique summo Deo et vero, ex quo omnia sunt" (*De Genesi ad Litt.*, V, 5, 13; P.L., vol. 34, col. 326). Cf. E. Gilson, *Introduction à l'étude de saint Augustin* (*Etudes de philosophie médiévale*, ix), Paris, 1929, p. 254.

held, however, somewhat hesitatingly.[106]   Furthermore, it
has been shown that Neoplatonism was the common source
from which St. Augustine and Ibn Gebirol could derive this
doctrine.[107]   Only, here, as in the doctrine of plurality of
forms, what St. Augustine and the earlier middle ages had
held without being aware of the underlying metaphysics was
crystallized into the systematic form in which it can be found
in Gundissalinus, St. Bonaventure and his disciples under
the influence of the *Fons Vitae*.

St. Bonaventure himself is clearly not involved directly
with this movement.   Concerned as he was to maintain intact
the fundamental doctrines of Christianity, he entered the
field of controversy only when he feared for the safety of
Christian ideas or of speculations coming from the high
authority of St. Augustine.   In the problem of the soul, he
has one principal consideration, namely, to safeguard its
immortality.   This he does by making the soul a complete
substance and thus insuring its independence of the body.
In such an attitude there is obviously no question of inserting
an Aristotelian definition of the soul.   On this point, at
least, St. Bonaventure is an Aristotelian only in language.
He does indeed insist on the unity of man, but the question
which presents itself is whether the explanation of the union
between soul and body which he adopts is compatible with
that unity.

Now, in associating pluralism with the *Fons Vitae* and
its Platonic speculations, St. Thomas undertook to show the
underlying metaphysical method which characterized the

---

106. On the question of matter and its forms in St. Augustine cf. E. Gilson, *Introduction à l'étude de saint Augustin* p.
253-265. Cp. G. Théry, *L'augustinisme médiévale et l'unité de
la forme substantielle*, *loc. cit.*, p. 145, 148-149, 199, note.

107. Cf. P. Correns, *Die dem Boethius fälschlich zugeschrie-
bene Abhandlung des Dominicus Gundisalvi De Unitate* (*Beiträge*, I, 1), Münster, 1891, p. 42-48.

Platonic tradition. For the Angelic Doctor, however, such a method had been refuted at its source by the work of Aristotle. For St. Thomas, therefore, the immediate problem of the age, raised by the presence of a completely Platonic metaphysics, was to take into account the long and minute examination to which Aristotle had subjected the teachings of his master. For the first time, the mediaeval world had come to see the full significance of the Platonic metaphysics. *Augustinus autem Platonem secutus quantum fides catholica patiebatur.*[108] But how far was an age, better informed on the significance of Plato as well as on the cardinal fault of his thought, to follow in his footsteps or in those of his disciples?

These historical circumstances mark the starting point of the Thomistic reconstruction. But St. Thomas had been a student of the learned Albert, and in seeking the origins of his thought it is natural to turn to the works of his teacher. What effect did the Aristotelian conception of change, substance, unity, have on the outlook of St. Albert? What will be his attitude towards such doctrines as universal matter, plurality of forms, the completeness of the soul as a substance? His answer to these questions will enable us to measure more accurately what his own age considered to be the *novitas* of the Angelic Doctor.

---

108. *Quaest. Disp. de Spiritualibus Creaturis,* art. **X**, ad 8. E. Gilson has insisted repeatedly on the importance of this text for interpreting the relations between St. Thomas and St. Augustine: cf. *Pourquoi saint Thomas a critiqué saint Augustin* (*Archives d'hist. doctr. et litt. du moyen âge,* I, 1926-1927), p. 119, 125.

III. ST. ALBERT THE GREAT AND THE PROBLEM OF THE SOUL AS FORM AND SUBSTANCE.

The philosophical activity of St. Albert the Great has not always been interpreted in the same way. While all are generally agreed that he was, in the words of Ueberweg-Geyer, "der erste hochragende Bannerträger des Aristotelismus im dreizehnten Jahrhundert",[1] all are not agreed on the nature of his Aristotelianism and more particularly, on his relations to St. Thomas Aquinas. While some are of the

---

[1]. B. Geyer, *Grundriss*, 11th ed., p. 409. P. Mandonnet speaks constantly of a common work undertaken by St. Albert and St. Thomas *(Siger de Brabant*, I, ch. 2 *passim)*. Such a conception is unquestionably true when it refers to the introduction of Aristotle to the Latin west, and the polemic of St. Albert against David of Dinant is clear witness on this point (cf. *supra*, ch. i, note 14). But the reality of such a continuity between St. Albert and St. Thomas has been questioned seriously when it is intended to express a common tradition in philosophical ideas. Cf. M. De Wulf, *Le traité* De Unitate Formae *de Gilles de Lessines*, p. 45 with note 3; C. Baeumker, *Petrus von Hibernia der Jugendlehrer des Thomas von Aquino und seine Disputation vor König Manfred* (Sitzungsberichte der Bayerischen Akad. der Wissenschaften, Phil.-phil. und hist. Klasse, 1920, 8. Abhandlung), München, 1920, p. 35-36; E. Gilson, *Pourquoi saint Thomas a critiqué saint Augustin* (Archives d'hist. doctr. et litt. du moyen âge i, 1926), p. 121; A. Forest, *La structure métaphysique du concret selon saint Thomas d'Aquin*, p. 199-203 (with some qualifications in favor of a continuity between St. Albert and St. Thomas).

For St. Albert I am using the edition of his works by C. A. Borgnet: *B. Alberti Magni Ratisbonensis Episcopi, Ordinis Praedicatorum, Opera Omnia . . .*, Parisiis, Apud Ludovicum Vivès, 38 vols., 1890-1899.

I must here express my indebtedness to Professor E. Gilson for the use of valuable notes on St. Albert. Several bibliographical indications are due to his kindness.

opinion that St. Albert and his famous pupil shared in the
common task of reviving Aristotle and that the work of the
master laid the foundations upon which was to be built the
magnificent structure of his disciple, others appear to question this continuity of thought between St. Albert and St.
Thomas, and thus to lay greater stress on what has been
called the originality of the Angelical Doctor. Hence arises
the problem of determining the Aristotelianism of St. Albert,
for in this way we may hope to discover not only the influences at work in the first significant effort to familiarize
the Latin West with the doctrines of the Stagirite, but also
to determine the nature and the extent of the legacy received
by St. Thomas from his faithful teacher and friend. The
problem of the soul is particularly adapted to such a purpose, for in studying this problem we shall be able to observe
the forces at work in the formation of St. Albert's thought,
his constant effort to be true to the old as well as to the new,
and those ideas which made it possible for him to be a faithful observer of tradition at the very moment when he was
embracing the philosophical doctrines of the new Aristotle.

In the second part of the *Summa de Creatur*is,[2] which
deals with man (*de homine*), the first problem which St.
Albert meets is concerned with the substance and the nature
of the soul.[3] He observes that there are two ways of studying the soul. The first proceeds to study the substance and
nature of the soul directly because this will lead to the
knowledge of the accidents of the soul's various parts. Such
a method is *a priori*. The second proceeds from a study of

---

2. This work dates from about 1245, and will thus give us St.
Albert's ideas before he came into contact with his pupil. On the
chronology, cf. Ueberweg-Geyer, *Grundriss*, 11th ed., Berlin, 1928,
p. 408.

3. *Sum. de Creat.*, P. II, tract. 1, q. 1; vol. 35, p. 1. The first
article of this *tractatus* (p. 2) asks the question whether the substance of the soul is to be treated before its parts, or whether it
is to be the body, or the composite of soul and body.

the accidents to that of the parts and finally to that of the soul. This way is *a posteriori,* because in it the *principia* of knowledge are the accidents that form the basis of further knowledge. On the other hand, these accidents are not really known except in relation to their cause. This cause is clearly the substance and the nature in which they inhere, namely, the soul. Thus the *a priori* method is the one with which we ought to begin, though both are found to be necessary.[4] This necessity arises because to study the soul in a purely dialectical way, and thus to disregard all its properties, is to transcend the condition of existing things and to render our knowledge vain and useless.[5] Dialectic, therefore, must be tempered by experience. Hence, we have two points to consider. There is a logical definition of the soul as well as an empirical one. The logical definition is useless without the empirical, while the empirical is groundless without the logical. That is why in the study of the soul they complete one another and are both necessary in order to insure at once the applicability of reasoning to individual facts and the grounding of these facts in their causes.

With this distinction in mind we are ready for the first

---

4. "Et respondendum est quoad primum, quod duplex est via in cognitionem animae, quarum una est, quod per cognitionem substantiae ipsius et naturae cognoscuntur causae accidentium, quae sunt passiones partium animae: omnis enim passio causatur a principiis substantiae: et haec via prior est. Alia via est a passionibus sive accidentibus propriis, quae inferunt sibi passiones procedentes in cognitionem partium animae, quibus illa accidentia inferunt passiones, sicut color visui, et sonus auditui, et sic de aliis. Et haec via posterior est: eo quod in ea principia cognitionis sunt accidentia, quae supponuntur cognita: non autem sunt cognita nisi ex causis suis: causa autem accidentium est substantia et natura subjecti illius, cui accidunt accidentia illa. Et ita patet, quod prima via praecedit secundam: utraque tamen est necessaria" *(ibid.,* ad 1; p. 2-3).

5. "Unde si aliqua diffinitio datur de substantia et natura subjecti in universali, ex qua non cognoscitur determinatum

question.   Following St. Albert's order, this question is:
Utrum sit anima?[6]   Seven contentions are here ranged in
defense of the negative solution. Quoting the Book of Wisdom, the first objector shows that the soul is smoke rising
from the heart; breath escaping from the nostrils, apparently
to release the pressure on the heart; natural heat becoming
articulate, and thus serving as a rational principle on the
occasion of whose extinction the body wastes away and gives
forth the corporeal spirit which it had received from the
air. It appears, therefore, that the soul is either nothing or,
at any rate, not different from the body.[7]   The second
objector is of the same mentality, while the third undertakes
to prove his contention *per rationem.* If there is a soul, it
is either a substance or an accident. It is not an accident
because it is impossible for an accident to constitute a substance, while body and soul do constitute the substance of
man. Likewise, it is not a substance because a substance is
either matter or form or the composite of these two.[8]   The

---

esse partium sub illis aut istis passionibus naturalibus, illa erit dia-
lectica, id est, transcendens esse rei quod habet in natura; et vana,
quia non concludit passiones de subjecto si ponatur medium in
demonstratione" *(ibid.).* The same note is struck many years later
in the *Summa Theologiae*, P. II, tract. 12, q. 69, mem. 2, a. 3; vol.
33, p. 18.

6. *Ibid.*, a. 2; vol. 35, p. 6-7.

7. *Ibid.*, obj. 1; p. 6. The scriptural reference is *Sapientia*, II,
2-3, while that of the second objector is *Genesis*, II, 7. A little
farther down the fourth objector uses *Deuteron.*, XII, 23, to the
same effect, that "ergo videtur eadem ratione, quod in nulla ani-
matorum sit aliquid, vel erit corpus." The fifth, sixth and seventh
objections are drawn from Aristotle, Augustine and Gregory of Nyssa
(i.e., Nemesius, whose *De Natura Hominis* was very influential,
though Gregory of Nyssa was held to be the author. Cf. *infra*, note
13).

8. This division is drawn from Aristotle's *De Anima*, II, 1,
412b 6-9: "λέγομεν δὴ γένος ἕν τι τῶν ὄντων τὴν οὐσίαν, ταύτης δὲ
τὸ μὲν ὡς ὕλην, ὁ καθ' αὐτὸ μὲν οὐκ ἔστι τόδε τι, ἕτερον δὲ μορφὴν
καὶ εἶδος, καθ' ἥν ἤδη λέγεται τόδε τι, καὶ τρίτον τὸ ἐκ τούτων."

soul is not matter, because matter (i.e., that of the soul), plus matter (i.e., that of the body), will not produce unity. It is not a composite, because a composite exists as such and cannot enter into further composition,[9] whereas it is required of the soul that it be joined to a body. Apparently, then, we must say that the soul, if it exists, is a form. It does not exist, our objector continues, because, as the *De Trinitate* of Boethius shows,[10] no form can be the subject of accidents. The soul, however, can be the subject of vice, virtue and knowledge. Therefore, it is not a form. And since, by elimination, it is neither a substance nor an accident, the soul either does not exist or is identical with the body.[11]

On the opposite side St. Albert advances many arguments. His preoccupation in these arguments is to identify the name *anima* with the principle in certain bodies which

---

9. This is a fundamentally Aristotelian point which will be urged effectively by St. Thomas against the doctrine of the soul as composed of matter and form.

10. " . . . formae vero subjectae esse non possunt . . .

Forma vero, quae est sine materia, non poterit esse subjectum, neque enim esset forma, sed imago" *(De Trinitate*, cap. II; Patrologia Latina, vol. 64, col. 1250 C-D).

11. "Item, per rationem videtur idem: quia si anima est, aut est substantia, aut accidens. Constat, quod non est accidens: nam ex accidente non fit substantia, ex anima autem et corpore fit substantia: ergo non est accidens. Similiter non videtur esse substantia: substantia enim est materia, et forma, et compositum; sed anima non est materia, quia ex materia et materia non fit unum: cum igitur sit corpus materia, ex corpore et anima non fieret unum. Similiter ipsa non est compositum: quia compositi in quantum hujusmodi est, non est compositio: sed anima componitur corpori: ergo ipsa non est compositum. Ergo relinquitur, quod sit forma, si est. *Sed contra*: Dicit Boethius in libro de *Trinitate*, quod nulla forma potest esse subjectum alterius accidentis. Anima autem est subjectum accidentium, scilicet vitii, et virtutis, et scientiarum. Ergo non est forma. Cum igitur nec sit substantia, nec accidens, vel nihil erit, vel erit corpus" *(Sum. de Creat. loc. cit.*, obj. 3; vol. 35, p. 6-7).

accounts for the manner of their constitution. Thus, he proves from Avicenna that the difference between a body, such as a stone, and another body, such as a flower or an animal, is not that they are bodies, but that the flower and the animal have a principle in their essence, over and above their corporeal nature, from which their activities of growth and reproduction emanate. This is the soul.[12] If we examine the movements of this principle in bodies, we shall discover what kind of agent it is.[13] St. Albert therefore concludes that if we understand this point we are granting his position, because the dispute does not concern the name but what is

---

12. "Item, per Avicennam: Nos videmus corpora quae non nutriuntur, nec augmentantur, nec generant: et videmus alia quae nutriuntur, et augmentantur et generant sibi similia: sed non habent hoc ex sua corporeitate: restat igitur ut sit in essentia eorum principium hujusmodi praeter corporeitatem, et principium illud a quo emanant istae affectiones, dicitur anima" *(ibid., Sed contra,* 2; p. 7-8).—Avicenna took this from Aristotle: "τῶν δὲ φυσικῶν *(scil.* σωμάτων) τὰ μὲν ἔχει ζωήν, τὰ δὲ ουκ ἔχει· ζωὴν δὲ λέγομεν τὴν δι' αὐτοῦ τροφήν τε καὶ αὔξησιν καὶ φθίσιν. ὥστε πᾶν σῶμα φυσικὸν μετέχον ζωῆς οὐσία ἄν εἴη, οὐσία δὲ οὕτως ὡς συνθέτη" *(De Anima,* II, 1, 412b 13-16).

13. "'Ex natura motuum cognoscitur natura motorum; sed in plantis et hominibus inveniuntur quidam motus, qui non inveniuntur in aliquo alio corpore, sicut attractio nutrimenti et nutrimentum secundum rationem debitam magnitudinis est hujusmodi: ergo ista opera specialem habebunt motorem qui non erit in aliis corporibus: et istum vocamus *animam:* ergo illud quod vocamus animam, est: non enim disputamus de nomine, sed an hoc sit quod hoc nomine significare consuevimus" *(Sum. de Creat., loc. cit., Sed Contra,* 7; p. 8).

This argument is somewhat expanded in *Summa Theologiae,* P. II, tract. 12, q. 68; vol 33, p. 2-7. Here the argument proceeds from act to power and then to substance.—In this connection St. Albert makes considerable use of Nemesius, *De Natura Hominis.* On the translations of Nemesius in the Middle Ages, namely, that of Alfanus in the eleventh century, and that of Burgundio in the twelfth, cf. the references in Leopold Gaul, *Alberts des Grossen Verhältnis zu Plato, Beiträge* . . . Band XII, Heft 1, Münster i.

customarily called by that name. The *Summa Theologiae* [14]
points to the same conclusion. In it he quotes Aristotle very
frequently and, along with him, Nemesius (whom St. Albert
quotes as "Gregory"), anxious apparently to insure the
immortality of the soul by showing it to be an incorporeal
substance.[15]

Having given an affirmative answer to the first question,
we are ready for the second: *Utrum anima sit substantia?*[16]

W., 1913, p. 76, note 1. As to which of these translations St. Albert used, Gaul says, "Die Frage, welche von beiden Uebersetzungen
Albert vorgelegen hat, ist durch einem Vergleich leicht zu entschei-
den," and he proceeds to tabulate his texts from St. Albert that
refer to Nemesius, with the translations of Alfanus and Burgundio
on either side. He concludes that the translation used by St.
Albert was that of Burgundio. "Der Vergleich ergibt, das nur die
Uebersetzung des Burgundio in Betracht kommen kann, wenn eine
der beiden Uebersetzungen dem Albert als Vorlage gedient hat"
(ibid.). (On Burgundio's activities, in which translation was only
a part, cf. C. H. Haskins, *Studies in Mediaeval Science*, Harvard
University Press, Cambridge, 1924, p. 206-208).—Geyer expresses
well and concisely Nemesius' attitude towards Aristotle's definition
of the soul when he observes that "er shient darin eine Gefahr für die
Substantialität der Seele, wie er auch Aristoteles und Dikäarch die
Leugnung einer substanziellen Seele zuschreibt" *(Grundriss*, 11th
ed., p. 120)). Indeed, the whole proceeding of Nemesius was based
on the assumption that if the soul is a form of the body, it must
be a form dependent on the body, unsubstantial, and therefore not
immortal. Hence, his "Gefahr."

14. *Loc. cit.*

15. "Quod anima rationalis sit, et non sit corpus, sed incorporea
substantia, probat Gregorius Nyssenus (i.e., Nemesius; cf. note 13)
in libro quem fecit de *homine*, supponens quod et verum est, et ab
Aristotele in II de *Anima* probatum, scilicet quod actus praevii sunt
potentiis, et objecta actibus secundum rationem. Ex quo de necessitate sequitur, quod cujus est actus, ejus de necessitate est potentia: et cujus est potentia, ejus est substantia de qua fluit illa
naturalis potentia" *(ibid.).*

16. *Summa de Creaturis*, P. II, tract. 1, q. 2: *De diffinitionibus
Sanctorum de eo quid sit anima* (p. 9-20); q. 3: *De diffinitionibus
Philosophorum de eo quid sit anima* (p. 20-30); q. 4: *De diffinitioni-*

The method followed here is historical, and we meet, in order, the definitions of the soul to be found in the *saints* and then in the philosophers. The first definition is taken from the psuedo-Augustinian *De Spiritu et Anima,* which, however, St. Albert attributes to Augustine: "Dicit ergo Augustinus in libro *De spiritu et Anima,* quod anima est substantia rationis particeps, regendo corpori accomodata":[17] the soul is a substance; it partakes of reason; it was made to rule the body. The second definition is from Remigius of Auxerre:

---

bus animae secundum Aristotelem (p. 31-62). The *Summa Theologiae* is somewhat different: P. II, tract. 12, q. 69: *Quid sit anima?* Mem. 1: *De septem definitionibus Sanctorum de eo quid sit anima* (vol. 33, p. 7-11); 2: *De tribus definitionibus Philosophorum de eo quid sit anima*: a. 1: *De prima definitione animae, quae est Avicennae* (p. 11-13); a. 2: *De secunda definitione animae secundum Philosophos quae est Aristotelis* (p. 13-18); a. 3: *De tertia definitione animae quam idem ponit Aristoteles* (p. 18-19).

17. *Sum de Creat.,* P. II, tract. 1, q. 2, a. 1. p. 10. It is also found in *Sum. Theol.,* P. II, tract. 12, q. 69, mem. 1; vol. 33, p. 7. Thus, St. Bonaventure (cf. *supra,* p. 52) and St. Albert both attribute the *De Spiritu et Anima* to Augustine. Apparently, the statement of St. Thomas did not trouble them *(ibid.).* It is generally attributed to Alcher of Clairvaux, a Cistercian of the middle of the twelfth century (cf. Leopold Gaul, *op. cit.,* p. 85, note 4). As Gaul observes, St. Albert knows of the opinion which does not attribute this work to Augustine, because he mentions this fact in *Isagoge in Libros de Anima,* a. 2; vol. 5, p. 508. However, though he agrees that there is a distinction between the soul and its faculties as against Augustine, because this opinion "Solemnior et verior videtur esse," in c. 4, he proceeds to say, "Item Augustinus in libro *De Spiritu et Anima* dicit quod . . ." as though the question of authenticity did not trouble him at all.—The definition is really taken ultimately from Augustine, *De Quantitate Animae,* XIII, 22; Patrologia Latina, vol. 32, col. 1048, from where it was incorporated in the compilation, *De Spiritu et Anima* (P.L., vol. 40, col. 781), and in that form given to the Middle Ages. Cf. E. Gilson, *Introduction à l'étude de saint Augustin (Etudes de philosophie médiévale,* XI), Paris, 1929, p. 55, note 1.

"anima est substantia incorporea regens corpus",[18] and adds little to the first from which it is apparently taken. St. John of Damascus says: the soul is a living, incorporeal substance, immortal, rational, etc., "organico utens corpore, . . . "[19] St. Bernard says: "anima est res incorporea, rationis capax, vivificando corpori accomodata".[20] The *Summa Theologiae* adds the following: I. "Alexander nequam in libro de *Motu Cordis*, sic: 'Anima est substantia incorporea, illuminationum quae sunt a primo ultima relatione perceptiva' ".[21] II.

---

18. It is Augustinian, also; cf. preceding note.—On Remigius of Auxerre, cf. Geyer, *op. cit.*, p. 179, especially for his Platonic realism.

19. *De Fide Orthodoxa*, II, 12; Patrologia Graeca, vol. 94, col. 924B.

20. This definition is not taken from St. Bernard, but from the *Epistola ad Fratres de Monte Dei*, printed in Migne among the works of St. Bernard and ascribed there to Guigo, *quinti Prioris Majoris Carthusiae*: P. L., vol. 184, col. 307-364. For the definition, cf. *Epistola ad Fratres de Morte Dei*, ii, c. 2, 4; P.L., vol. 184, col. 340B. This work was ascribed to William of Saint-Thierry by Mabillon (cf. P.L., vol. 184, col. 297-300)), and quite recently A. Wilmart has defended this attribution: cf. *Les écrits spirituels des deux Guiges*, in Revue d'ascétique et de mystique, V. (1924), p. 59-79, 127-158. For William of Saint-Thierry and the *Epistola*, cf. p. 152-158. Bernard Geyer, *op. cit.*, p. 257-258, appears to say, somewhat inexplicably, that Wilmart rejects this attribution to William of Saint-Thierry.

21. *De Motu Cordis*, Prologus, 1. 7-9, ed. C. Baeumker, *Beiträge . .* Band XXIII, Heft 1-2, Münster i. W., 1923, p. 2. This work, written by Alfredus Anglicus and dedicated to Alexander Neckham, was generally cited in the thirteenth century either without an author or as the work of *sapiens quidam* (e.g., as St. Albert does himself: "Anima prout est spiritus, sic diffinitur a *quodam sapiente* in libro de *motu cordis* . . ."; *Isagoge in Libros de Anima*, cap. 1, vol. 5, p. 506), or it was ascribed to Alexander Neckham and even to Augustine *(De Motu Cordis, ibid.*, note 4). It is necessary to see the full quotation which St. Albert uses. The beginning is, "*In se enim considerata* . . ."; St. Albert's text follows, and then the *De Motu Cordis* continues: ". . . ut Aristoteles in Metaphisica capitulo quod K inscribitur; a qua diffinitione *nec Ariopagita* in Ierarchia sua dissentit. *Relata vero* anima perfectio est corporis phisici or-

"Seneca sic: 'Anima est spiritus intellectualis ad beatitudinem in se et in corpore ordinatus'".[22]   III. "Cassiodorus sic: 'Anima est substantia spiritualis a deo creata, proprii sui corporis vivificatrix'".[23]   IV. "Item Augustinus sic: 'Anima est spiritus intellectualis, rationalis, semper vivens, semper in motu, bonae malaeque voluntatis capax'".[24]

In the rest of the article St. Albert adduces arguments to prove the substantiality of the soul which these definitions embody. From Costa-ben-Luca he argues that whatever can receive opposites, while continuing to remain one in number,

---

ganici" *(loc. cit.,* p. 2-3). In the same note, Baeumker remarks of this definition: "Die Definition, welche die neuplatonische Emanationslehre voraussetzt, steht natürlich nicht in echten Aristoteles, sondern stammt ohne Frage aus einer arabischen Quelle." For our present purposes, let us note that Alfredus Anglicus implies quite clearly a two-fold definition of the soul.

22. This definition apparently does not appear in Seneca. Cf. A. Schneider, *Die Psychologie Alberts des Grossen, Beiträge,* Band IV, Heft 5-6, Munster i. W., 1903-1906, p. 369, note 3. That this definition is in agreement with Seneca's thought can be readily seen from *Epist.* xcii, 1-2; ed. R. M. Gummere (Loeb Classics), vol. 2, London, 1920, p. 446.

23. M. Aurelii Cassiodori *De Anima,* cap. ii: "Anima autem hominis, ut veracium doctorum assentit auctoritas, est a Deo creata, spiritualis propriaque substantia, sui corporis vivificatrix, rationalis quidem et immortalis, sed in bonum malumque convertibilis" (Patrologia Latina, vol. 70, col. 1283A; cf. *Expositio in Psalterium. Psal.* L, vers. 13; col. 367 B-C).

24. This is found in the *De Spiritu et Anima,* and comes from Alcuin, *Liber de Animae Ratione ad Eulaliam Virginem,* cap. x; Patrologia Latina, vol. 101, col. 643D-644A. Alcuin continues: " . . .; secundum benignitatem Creatoris libero arbitrio nobilitatus, sua voluntate vitiatus; Dei gratia liberatus; ad regendum carnis motus creatus, invisibilis, incorporalis, sine pondere, sine colore, circumscriptus, in singulas suae carnis membris totus; in quo est imago Conditoris spiritualiter primitiva creatione impressa" *(ibid.).* The influence of St. Augustine is unmistakable. Cf. Geyer, *Grundriss,* 11th ed., p. 161, for the use made by Alcher of Clairvaux of Alcuin's phychology.

is a substance. The soul receives virtues and vices though
it is immutably one in number in its essence. The soul must,
therefore, be a substance.[25] Further, whatever moves a substance from place to place must itself be a substance. Again,
therefore, the soul is a substance.[26] The third proof is taken
from the translator John of Spain (Toletanus), who has
several other names,[27] and argues that, since whatever is, is

25. "Constabulinus in libro de *Differentia Spiritus et Animae*:
Quicquid recipit opposita, cum unum sit numero immutabile in
sua essentia, substantia est: sed anima rationalis recipit virtutes
et vitia, cum sit una numero: ergo recipit opposita: igitur est
substantia" *(Sum. de Creat.*, P. II, tract. 1, q. 2, a. 1, ad *sed in
Contrarium;* p. 11-12). The definition is taken from cap. 3, ed.
C. S. Barach, Innsbruck, 1876, p. 131. It is curious to remark of
Costa-ben-Luca that though he gives the definitions of Plato and
Aristotle on the soul, cap. 3, he does not bother to compare them,
but proceeds at the close of the chapter to say, "Et quia jam exposuimus utrasque definitiones, Platonis scilicet et Aristotelis, et
patefecimus interpretationes uniuscuiusque partis earum, nunc lo-
quamur de virtutibus animae, et dicamus . . ." etc. (p. 137); and
apparently that is the end of the matter.—On the translation of
this treatise by Johannes Hispalensis, cf. Leopold Gaul, *op cit.*, p.
87, note 1.

26. This is also from Costa-ben-Luca (p. 131): "Item dicamus:
quicquid movet substantiam, est substantia; sed anima movet corpus,
corpus autem substantia est, anima ergo substantia est." St. Albert
writes: "Item, Quicquid movet substantiam secundum loca diversa,
est substantia; anima est talis: ergo, etc. Prima harum rationum
probat, quod anima rationalis est substantia. Secunda, quod est et
sensibilis" *(Sum. de Creat., loc. cit.).* Thus, he does not accept
this argument without criticism, even though a little further on
Costa-ben-Luca argues for the immateriality of the soul.—It may
be significant to observe here that both of these arguments drawn
by St. Albert from Costa-ben-Luca are used by that author to eluci-
date the *Platonic* definition of the soul: "Nunc autem exponemus
has duas definitiones et incipiamus a prima, *quae est Platonis*, et
ostendamus, quod anima sit substantia . . ." *(loc, cit.).*

27. Toletanus, Collectanus, Avendehut, Avendeath. Cf. L. Gaul,
loc. cit., who refers to A. Schneider, *Die Psychologie Alberts des
Grossen, Beiträge*, . . . Band IV, Heft 5, Münster i, W., 1903, p. 13,
note 2; cf. also Geyer, *Grundriss*, 11th ed., p.343.

either a substance or an accident, when the presence of something constitutes, just as its absence destroys, the species of substance, that something must be not an accident but a substance. Such, in fact, is the soul in the plant, the animal and man. The soul is, therefore, a substance.[28]   Finally, St. Albert draws an argument from Avicenna for the substantiality of the soul. It is impossible for the proper subject of the soul to be what it is except through the soul itself, which is its constitutive cause; and as the soul, therefore, gives perfection and specific existence to the body, it is a substance.[29]

In the *Summa Theologiae* several difficulties are raised in connection with the definition of the *saints* quoted by St. Albert in defense of the soul as a spiritual substance. Of these we shall examine his reply to the second, in order to determine more exactly his position on the meaning of substantiality, before we proceed to his discussion of the philosophers' definitions. The objector to the second definition, which was drawn, as we have seen, from the pseudo-Augustinian *De Spiritu et Anima,* says that to define the soul as a spiritual substance able to rule the body is to give a defini-

---

28. "Item, Collectanus: Quicquid est, aut est accidens aut substantia: nihil autem quod adveniens constituit speciem substantiae et recedens destruit eandem, est accidens: quaelibet species animae adveniens constituit speciem plantae, animalis, et hominis, et recedens destruit eandem: ergo quaelibet species animae est substantia" *(Sum. de Creat., loc.cit.).*

29. "Item, Avicenna: Proprium subjectum animae impossibile est esse id quod est nisi per animam, et ipsa est causa unde est: si ergo anima dat actum et rationem specificam corpori in genere quod est substantia, ergo est substantia." To interpret this text clearly, we must compare it with the original text of Avicenna, *Liber VI Naturalium,* P.1, cap.3 (Venetiis, 1508) f. 3va, which is quoted and discussed by E. Gilson, *Les sources gréco-arabes de l'augustinisme avicennisant (Archives d'histoire doctrinale et littéraire du moyen âge, IV,* 1929) p. 42, with the explanatory texts in note 1.

tion which will be applicable to an angel as well, whenever
the angel assumes a body; because under such circumstances
an angel would be a spiritual substance capable of ruling the
body.[30]   To this objection St. Albert replies that in that
definition St. Augustine (i.e., pseudo-Augustine) was giving
the general nature of the soul and its proper function towards
the body. Now the objection does not hold, because an angel
and the human soul are called incorporeal substances equivocally. The reason is that though the angel is not, the soul
is, naturally able to join the body. If an angel assumes a
body, this does not mean that the body will be ruled with
a view to its natural operations of life; rather, it means that
the angel will perform what is fitting from the standpoint
of appearance, but not, therefore, what is natural to the body
itself. As a result, though both an angel and a human soul
are spiritual substances, there is this distinction between
them, namely, that the soul has a natural affinity for the
body.[31]

---

30. *Sum. de Creat.*, P.II, tract.12, q.69, mem.1; p.8.

31. "Secunda definitio quae est Augustini accipitur a generali
natura animae et proprio actu quem habet in corpus. Ad (the text
mistakenly has *ab*) objectum contra, dicendum quod aequivoce
dicitur Angelus substantia incorporea et anima. Angelus enim
substantia incorporea est non unibilis corpori: anima autem substantia incorporea unibilis corpori. Similiter Angelus quando
assumit corpus, non regit corpus ad operationes vitae, sed ad con-
gruentias operationum, quas ministerio suo operatur circa eos
quibus apparet, ut dicit Augustinus. Cum autem anima regendo
corpori accomodata dicitur, intelligitur quantum ad operationes
vitae naturalis" *(ibid.; p.9)*. The reply to the fifth objector en-
forces the same conclusion: "Et licet Angelus sit substantia a
Deo creata, tamen non est carnis unibilis: et ideo aliter est spiritualis quam anima: *nec est creata substantia Angelus ad imaginem
creantis sicut anima.* Unde licet in multis sit imago anima, in hoc
tamen *etiam* est imago, quod sicut Deus vivificat omnia, ita anima
vivificat omnia sua, et unumquodque membrum ad suum proprium
actum vitae" *(ibid.);* cf. also q.4, a.1, Solutio; p.34. The following
is very clear: "Item nota, quod licet angelus cum assumit corpus

Hence, this is the point that St. Albert's discussion has reached thus far. By appealing to Avicenna and to the *saints,* he defends the substantiality of the soul through denying that it is an accident of the body, which is exactly the procedure of Avicenna,[32] and then through saying that it is a substance using a body,[33] thus defending its superiority over the body.[34] Briefly, the conclusion which can be drawn from the *saints* assisted by Avicenna is that since the soul is not an accident, it is a substance.

Under the title *De diffinitionibus Philosophorum de eo quid sit anima,* St. Albert considers first the definition of Plato that *"anima est substantia incorporea movens*

---

uniatur ei ut motor, non tamen sicut rector: unde etiam cum vult deponit illud. Spiritus vero humanus habet se ad corpus cui junctus est, ut motor naturalis, et quadam necessitate naturalis inclinationis alligatus. Et propter hoc se habet ad corpus ut rex et rector, quadam necessitate amoris et gubernationis ipsius regimini alligatus; et ob hoc praedicta diffinitio soli animae convenit, et non Angelo" *(Isagoge in Libros de Anima, cap.v, vol.* 5, p. 507).—For a comparison with St. Bonaventure, cf. supra, p. 42, note.

32. This is the point that Avicenna is fighting for when he states the problem: cf. E. Gilson, *loc.cit.,* p.39-42.

33. Cf. note 19. The Platonism of this definition (no doubt via Nemesius) is quite evident. This means really that our determination of St. Albert's position thus far permits us to place him generally in a *Platonic-Augustinian* tradition.

34. To the question, "Utrum anima sit incorporea?" he replies by taking five arguments from Costa-ben-Luca, which he says were used also by Toletanus, but who added another from Avicenna. The soul is incorporeal, because its qualities are invisible: this is Costa-ben-Luca's first argument, while the other four are based on a *reductio ad absurdum,* granting the corporeity of the soul. The argument from Avicenna proves the soul incorporeal by showing that it is impossible for intelligible species to reside in the soul either as in a body or as in a power existing through the body *(Sum. de Creat.,* P. II, tract. 1, q. 2, a. 2, *Sed Contra;* p. 14-15).

corpus"; [35] and the article which follows this new question
is quite naturally entitled, *"Quomodo anima movet corpus?"*
What exactly is this motion which Plato attributes to the
soul? When the soul moves the body, is it itself moved or
unmoved? The first argument proves that Plato held that
the soul was itself moved in moving the body; while the next
four arguments show that this conclusion has to follow as
a necessary consequence partly on the ground that the soul
has to have motion in order to communicate it, and partly
because, as a matter of experience, we see that the soul does
change, as in sorrow, joy and hope, or in the reception of
sensations and intelligible species.[36] But these theses—

---

35. *Sum. de Creat.*, P. II, tract 1, q. 3; p. 20.

36. *Ibid.* p. 21: "Et Plato videtur probare, quod non primo
modo (*scil.* while the soul remained *immobilis*): supponit enim,
sicut dicit Philosophus in I de *Anima*, hoc quod omnes supponebant,
scilicet nihil movere, et quod ipsum non moveatur. Cum igitur
anima moveat, et ipsa movebitur." This is the text of Aristotle:
"ἐπὶ ταὐτὸ δὲ φέρονται καὶ ὅσοι λέγουσι τὴν ψυχὴν τὸ αὐτὸ κινοῦν.
ἐοίκασε γὰρ οὗτοι πάντες ὑπειληφέναι τὴν κίνησιν οἰκειοτάτην εἶναι
τῇ ψυχῇ, καὶ τὰ μὲν ἄλλα πάντα κινεῖσθαι διὰ τὴν ψυχὴν, ταύτην
δὲ ὑφ' ἑαυτῆς, διὰ τὸ μηθὲν ὁρᾶν κινοῦν ὁ μὴ καὶ αὐτὸ κινεῖται."
(*De Anima*, I, 2, 404a20-25). The meaning is quite clear. According to Aristotle, Plato held that the soul was a self moving
being because he held that everything was moved by the soul,
conceiving of motion as most properly belonging to the soul.
Aristotle gives as the reason for this that "they saw nothing move
which was not itself moved." If we remember the tenth book of
Plato's *Laws*, we must observe that Plato's position rests on the
consideration that all motion cannot be transitive, and that as all
motion in material things is transitive, soul or mind is prior to
matter in that it has both immanent and transitive motion. Cf.
Laws, Bk. X, p. 895c (ed. E. B. England, Manchester, 1921, vol. 2,
p. 157-158): "'ΑΘ. [ηναῖος ξένος]. ἐὰν ἰδῶμεν που ταύτην γενομένην ἐν
τῷ γηίνῳ ἤ ἐνύδρῳ ἤ πυροειδεῖ, κεχωρισμένῳ ἤ καὶ συμμιγεῖ, τί ποτε
φήσομεν ἐν τοιούτῳ πάθος εἶναι; —ΚΛ. [εινίας κρὴς]. μῶν ἄρα μὲ
ἐρωτας εἰ ζῆν αὐτὸ προσεροῦμεν, ὅταν αὐτὸ αὐτὸ κινῇ; —'ΑΘ. Ναί.
—ΚΛ. Ζῆν· πῶς γὰρ οὔ; —'ΑΘ. τί δε; ὁπόταν ψυχὴν ἔν τισιν
ὁρῶμεν μῶν ἄλλο ἤ ταὐτὸν τούτω; ζῆν ὁμολογητέον;—ΚΛ. οὐκ ἄλλο."

that the soul moves itself and that sensation is a motion in it—St. Albert rejects. In his defense he invokes the names of Aristotle, Avicenna, Averroes, Costa-ben-Luca, Alfarabi, John of Spain, "et multi alii naturales".[37] The soul moves the body and remains itself unmoved, except *per accidens,* when the body is moved. Indeed, according to St. Augustine, the soul is in the body as God is in the world. That is, just as God is in the world and moves all things without being moved essentially or accidentally, so does the soul move the body, remaining itself unmoved, but not accidentally, because its power of motion falls short of that of God.[38]

Having rejected the idea that the soul is essentially moved in moving the body, St. Albert turns to Aristotle's criticism of Plato.[39] To say that the soul becomes angry or

---

It is easy to see how this could be used by Plato (*Phaedrus,* p. 245c) as an argument for the immortality of the soul. Macrobius, against whom we have seen St. Bonaventure arguing (cf. *supra,* p. 41) knew this argument from the *Laws* and quotes it in *Comm. in Somn. Scip.,* II, 15.—These references will be found in England's note on *Laws* 894b10, vol. 2, p. 468-469.

37. Sum de Creat, P. II, tract 7, *Solutio,* p. 28.

38. " . . . movet autem corpus ipsa existens immobilis per se, per accidens autem mota motu corporis; quia, sicut dicit Philosophus, moventibus nobis moventur ea quae in nobis sunt. Et tamen dicit Augustinus, quod anima est in corpore sicut Deus est in mundo: quia sicut Deus in mundo existens caetera movet ita quod non movetur per se vel per accidens, ita anima movet corpus immobilis manens per se, mota tamen per accidens: quia sicut in omnibus deficit a Deo, ita virtus ejus motiva deficit a virtute divina motiva" (*ibid.*) For Augustine, cf. *De Gen. ad Litt.,* VIII, 26, 48; P.L., vol. 34, col. 391-392. The reference to Aristotle is *De Anima,* I, 4, 408a30-33: "κατὰ συμβεβηκὸς δὲ κινεῖσθαι, καθάπερ εἴπομεν, ἔστι καὶ κινεῖν ἑαυτήν, οἷον κινεῖσθαι μὲν ἐν ᾧ ἐστί, τοῦτο δὲ κινεῖσθαι ὑπὸ τῆς ψυχῆς."

39. We might here notice the reply to the second objection (p. 28). St. Albert as against Plato, denies local motion to the soul, invoking the authority of St. Augustine (*op. cit.,* VIII, 72, 50; col. 392) that "per locum non movetur quod per loci spatia non disten-

is afraid, is the same as saying that the soul weaves or builds. It would be better to say, Aristotle observes, that *man* does these things because of the soul. This is not to be taken as meaning that motion is in the soul, but that at times motion comes as far as the soul, at times proceeds from it. The first is illustrated by sensation, while for the latter Aristotle uses memory. Age would be an example of the change or motion of the soul, but Aristotle remarks that if you give an old man the eye of a young man he would see as a young man. And if the soul is not moved, much less will it move itself.[40] Thus far, then, the soul is found to be unmoved in its relation to the body. This last point has been gained chiefly through the criticism of Aristotle. Now the question which becomes interesting at this stage of St. Albert's development is to know how he would interpret Aristotle's definition of the soul. This is the subject of *quaestio iv*: *De diffinitionibus animae secundum Arsitotelem.*[41]

---

ditur". Hence, Albert concludes: "Quicquid autem per loci spatia distenditur, corpus est: ac per hoc consequens est, quod anima per locum moveri non putetur, si corpus esse non creditur" (*ibid.*).— To another objector St. Albert replies that motion is the *proprietas* that flows from motor to moved; but it does not follow that the motion must be in the motor as in the subject, but rather that the motion comes from the motor as from an efficient cause (*ibid.*).

40. *De Anima*, I, 4, 408b13-31. Cf. especially, "βέλτιον γὰρ ἴσως μὴ λέγειν τὴν ψυχὴν ἐλεεῖν ἢ μανθάνειν ἢ διανοεῖσθαι, ἀλλὰ τὸν ἄνθρωπον τῇ ψυχῇ. τοῦτο δὲ μὴ ὡς ἐν ἐκείνῃ τῆς κινήσεως οὔσης, . . . (b. 13-15) . . . . . .ὅτι μὲν οὖν οὐχ οἷόν τε κινεῖσθαι τὴν ψυχήν, φανερὸν ἐκ τούτων· εἰ δ' ὅλως μὴ κινεῖται, δῆλον ὡς οὐδ' ὑφ' ἑαυτῆς" (b. 30-31).

41. P. 31: "Ponamus igitur diffinitionem animae, quae ponitur in II de *Anima* in principio, ubi sic dicit Philosophus: 'Anima est primus actus corporis physici, potentia vitam habentis. Hujusmodi autem est quodcumque organicum.'" The reference is *De Anima*, II, 1, 412a19-22. Of this definition St. Albert asks five questions: (a) Quomodo anima sit *actus?* (b) Quomodo *primus?* (c) Quomodo *corporis physici?* (d) Quomodo *patentia vitam habentis?* (e) Quomodo hujusmodi est quocumque organicum, et utrum haec sint de diffinitione?

Is the soul the *actus* of the body? Now Avicenna calls the soul the *perfectio* of the body.[42] Apparently, then, according to the first objector, *perfectio* and *actus* ought to mean the same thing. But if the soul is a perfection, the objector continues, it is in a subject perfected and has existence only in that subject; which would mean that the soul is a purely material form. The objector, therefore, does not like the word *perfectio* because, thus explained, it is not applicable to a rational soul.

Here is the solution of St. Albert. We have seen that the substantial difference between an angel and the soul is that the soul is inclined towards the body as its *actus*, while the angel is not. Now we may consider the soul from two points of view. We may consider it in itself, and then it would not be defined with reference to the body, but according as it has existence in itself. Or, we may define it by considering it in relation to the body, and not according to the existence which it has in itself, and this would give us a definition of the soul in relation to the body. Accordingly, we have two definitions of the soul, one of the soul in itself, the other, in relation to the body. The reason for this, says St. Albert, is that some souls can be considered to exist without bodies. That is why, he continues, and here follows a reflection worth noting, Avicenna could say that the name *soul* is not a name indicating the essence of the thing to which it is referred. For this reason the definition of Aristotle does not look to the *esse* or nature of the thing defined, except in so far as it is the source of certain affections or activities. In other words, the definition of Aristotle does

---

42. "Dicit Avicenna in VI de *Naturalibus*, quod anima est perfectio propria corporis physici, etc. Ergo videtur, quod perfectio et actus sunt idem" (1*a* obj.; p. 32). In the reply to this objection he grants that they are the same, and this he takes from Averroes; though he does say, "et si aliquam habent differentiam, illa infra ostendetur" (ad. 1*am.*; p. 34).

not consider the essence of the soul, but certain activities
which are accidental to its nature, though necessary indications of the essence in itself. Avicenna goes on to give an
example which St. Albert takes over from him. If we say
that what moves has a mover, we do not, therefore, know
in this way what the essence of the mover is in itself.
Avicenna means to say, observes St. Albert, acting as interpreter, that just as the mover has a twofold definition, that
is, with respect to that *proprietas,* which makes it a mover,
and, secondly, with respect to its own essence, in the same
way the soul has a twofold definition: it may be considered
in so far as it is a soul, that is, the *actus* of the body and its
motor, or, again, in so far as it is a substance contained,
according to its nature, in the category of substance.[43]

---

43. *"Solutio,* Dicendum, quod supra determinatum est de Angelis, quod substantialis differentia animae et angeli est in hoc
quod anima inclinatur ad corpus ut actus, Angelus autem non.
Et ideo substantiale dicimus animae esse, quod sit actus corporis.

Si autem attenditur id quod est anima, tunc potest considerari
duobus modis, scilicet secundum esse quod habet in se, et sic non
diffinitur in comparatione ad corpus: vel secundum comparationem
ad corpus, et sic definitur. *Et hoc pro tanto dicitur ei accidere,
quia quaedam species animae potest considerari et esse sine corpore.* (That is, because a certain kind of soul is separable from
the body, therefore, St. Albert's argument runs, it is *external*—
indeed, it is accidental, as we shall see—to the soul to be defined
in relation to the body). Et ideo dicit Avicenna in VI. de *Naturalibus,* quod hoc nomen, *anima,* non est nomen hujus rei ex
ejus essentia, nec ex praedicamento in quo continetur: et cum anima diffinitur, sicut diffinita est ab Aristotele, non affirmatur esse
ejus, nisi secundum quod est principium emanandi a se affectiones,
quae non sunt unius modi et sunt voluntariae: *et sic affirmatur
esse ejus ex hoc quod habet aliquid accidens*: Quod tamen accidens valet ad certificandum ejus essentiam et ad cognoscendum
quid sit. Et dat Avicenna simile dicens: 'Fortassis enim jam
dicimus, quod id quod movetur, motorem habet: Tamen non
scimus propter id essentiam hujus motoris quid sit'. Ea intendit
Avicenna, quod sicut motor dupliciter diffinitur, scilicet penes pro-
prietatem hanc quae est movens, vel penes suam essentiam: ita

Thus, Avicenna is St. Albert's master in the definition
of the soul. According to this interpretation, we must distinguish two aspects of the soul. In itself it is a substance.
But it also has certain powers which enable it to act as the
motor of the body. In this way, by means of Avicenna, St.
Albert is enabled to interpret Aristotle's definition in such
a way that it gives a valid but, for all that, not essential
definition of the soul. We can make this point a little more
precise by looking at the sixth objection and its answer.
Referring to the text of the *De Anima,* which we have already
seen,[44] the objector wants to know why Aristotle, if he calls
the soul a *forma,* does not define the soul as the *forma prima*
rather than as the *actus primus* of the body.   St. Albert
replies that there are two reasons why the soul is better
called an *actus* than a *forma.* The first is that the *forma,*
according to natural philosophy, refers to that which has
its existence in this determinate matter and cannot exist
without it; but a *perfectio* can exist according to its substantiality without the being it perfects, as a sailor can exist
without a ship: *sicut nauta sine navi.* Since, therefore, a
particular kind of soul can exist separately, the soul is better
called a *perfectio* or *actus* than a *forma.* The second reason
is that, unlike *forma,* which refers to what is remotest from
its complement, namely, the potency of matter, *perfectio*
refers to, and implies a comparison with, a being that is
perfect not only in its matter, but also in all aspects necessary
to the perfection of that being.   That is, whereas *matter*
would be the subject of form, *body* is the subject of the soul
as *actus* or *perfectio.*[45]

---

anima dupliciter potest diffiniri, scilicet secundum quod est anima,
id est, actus corporis et motor, et secundum quod est substantia
quaedam contenta secundum seipsam in praedicamento substantiae"
(ibid., Solutio; p. 34). For Avicenna, cf. *infra,* note 87.

44. Cf. *Supra,* note 8.

45. "Ad aliud dicendum, quod etiam duplex est ratio quare
melius dicitur actus vel perfectio quam forma. Quarum una est,

The *Summa Theologiae* restates the foregoing doctrine. The definition of Aristotle which we have been discussing defines the soul according as it is the form, species and substance of an animated body in which the soul carries on the functions of life proper to the whole and to the parts of the body; but this definition of Aristotle does not reveal what the soul is in itself. That is why, says St. Albert (and here we must observe closely the Avicennian form in which Aristotle is found), Aristotle proceeds to state that the soul is not separable with respect to those parts according to which it is the *actus* of a body, and outside of which it does not perform any functions of life; because if it were separate according to those parts with respect to which it is the *actus* of the body, then it would have no vital functions at all, and would not thus be a soul. The text ends with "ampliusque manifestum est hoc si sit corporis actus anima sicut natura (*sic;* read: *nauta*) navis".[46]   And here Avicenna enters:

quia forma proprie secundum naturalem philosophiam est illa quae habet esse in hac materia, et non est sine ea. Perfectio autem quaedam bene est sine perfecto secundum suam substantiam, sicut nauta sine navi. Cum igitur anima secundum aliquam sui speciem separatur, convenit magis ei secundum omnem sui partem dici perfectionem quam formam. Secunda est, quia forma dicit comparationem ad id quod remotissimum est a complemento, hoc est, ad potentatem materiae. Perfectio autem dicit comparationem ad perfectionem rei, sicut dicit Philosophus: Perfectum est illud cui nihil deest. Et Avicenna, quod perfectio dicit comparationem ad rem perfectam, ex qua emanat accidens quod perfectio est respectu speciei; et cum sic anima comparatur ad corpus, melius dicitur perfectio quam forma" *(Sum. de Creat.*, P. II, tract. 1, q. 4, a. 1, ad 6; p. 35).

46. *Sum. Theol.*, P. II, tract. 12, q. 69, mem. 1, *Solutio;* vol. 33, p. 15. Aristotle's text *(De Anima*, II, 1, 413a8-9) is as follows: "ἔτι δὲ ἄδηλον εἰ οὕτως ἐντελέχεια τοῦ σώματος ἡ ψυχή ὥσπερ πλωτήρ πλοίου."

The text that St. Albert is using, then, has no negative *manifestum* where the Greek has ἄδηλον; also, the editors must have read *natura* for *nauta*, mistakenly. Clearly, the text should

quod tractans Avicenna in VI de Naturalibus, dicit, says
St. Albert,[47] that the sailor has *two* definitions. In the one

read: "ampliusque immanifestum est hoc si sit corporis actus
anima sicut nauta navis." However, the text without the negative
is exactly the interpretation of Aristotle which St. Albert, following Avicenna, is making, and his whole discussion so far has been
to show that the definition, and therefore the nature, of the soul
as related to the body is not at all that of the soul in itself. That
is why it is possible to say that St. Albert developed an interpretation of Aristotle in which the influence of Avicenna was decisive.

47. Here is the full text of the *Summa Theologiae* (P. II, tract.
12, q. 69, mem. , a.2; vol. 33, p. 15-16): "*Solutio.* Dicendum quod
definitio Aristotelis inducta dicit quod anima secundum quod
anima est forma et species et substantia animati corporis, in quo
secundum totum et secundum partes operatur operationes vitae,
et non est data de anima secundum quod est in seipsa: propter quod
etiam Philosophus dicit ibidem, ubi ponit istam definitionem, quod
secundum partes secundum quas est actus corporis alicujus, extra
quas non exercet opera vitae, non est separabilis: quia si separare-
tur a corpore, et esset in se, secundum illas partes secundum quas
actus est corporis, nullas haberet operationes vitae *et sic non esset
anima.* Substantiale est enim animae operationes vitae facere.
Unde Philosophus ibidem dicit sic: Quod quidem igitur non sit
separabilis anima a corpore: aut si separabilis, pars quaedam
ipsius apta nata est separari, non immanifestum est. Quarundam
enim partium actus est, secundum quas scilicet non contingit eam
separari. At vero secundum quasdam nihil prohibet eam separari,
propter id quod nullius sunt corporalis partis actus. Ampliusque
manifestum *(sic;* read: *immanifestum,* and cf. note 46) est hoc si
sit corporis actus anima sicut natura *(sic;* read: *nauta,* and cf.
note 46) navis. Quod tractans Avicenna in VI, de *Naturalibus,*
dicit, quod sicut nauta duplicem habet definitionem: unam secundum quam consideratur in seipso, secundum quam dicitur artifex
arte regens navim: aliam secundum quam (p. 16) operationes nauticas operatur instrumentis navis, a temone scilicet, malo, velo, re-
mis: ita anima duplicem debet habere definitionem: unam secundum quod operatur opera vitae in corpore et in organis ejus. Et
secundum hoc definitur ab Aristotele secundum quod est endele-
cheia sive perfectio corporis physici organici, potentia vitam ha-

definition he is considered in himself according as he is the ruler of the ship, but not operating. In the second definition, he is considered as performing the *operationes nauticas* by

---

bentis. Et intelligitur de completa potentia, quae perfecte habet in se omnia, et in nullo deficit, quim(?)ex his quae in se habet, operatur opera vitae. Illa enim est perfecta potentia sicut scientia, quae tunc completa est, quando in nullo deficit eorum quae exiguntur ad considerare secundum actum illius scientiae.

Alia definitio est, quae datur de anima secundum se, et secundum quod separabilis est a corpore, maxime secundum partem quae nullius corporis est actus, hoc est intellictivam, secundum quam partem opera vitae operatur in seipsa. Secundum quod dicit Isaac in libro de *Definitionibus*, quod anima rationalis, substantia est in umbra intelligentiae creata. Et hoc est quod dicit Dionysius dicens, quod supremum rationis attingit infimum intelligentiae. Intelligere enim et scire, opera quaedam vitae sunt, sed secundum potentiam, quae nullius corporis est actus. Potentia enim quae alicujus corporis est actus, nihil recipit, et circa nihil operatur, nisi circa hoc quod est de harmonia illius corporis cujus actus est: sicut patet in visu, qui est actus oculi, qui nihil recipit et circa nihil operatur, nisi circa hoc quod est de harmonia perspicui aquei sive diaphani, ex quo componitur oculus: et hoc est lux et color. Et sic est de aure ad sonum et ad crepitum aeris in quo fundatur tympanum auris et auditus."

Isaak Israeli, who is considered to be the earliest Jewish Philosopher of the Middle Ages, lived in Egypt between 845 and 940. Most of his work, written in Arabic, was medical, but we have two philosophical treaties, the *Liber de Definitionibus* and the *Liber de Elementis*, though only in Jewish and Latin translations. Cf. B. Geyer, *Grundriss*, 11th ed., Berlin, 1928, p. 333-334. He is a Neoplatonist, as J. Guttmann shows in *Die Philosophischen Lehren des Isaak ben Salomon Israeli, Beiträge . . .*, Band X, Heft 4 (1911), p. 17-18, 42, note 3 (where Albert's reference is to be found). For St. Albert's estimate of Isaak, cf. *ibid.*, p. 18-19, especially St. Albert's statement, "In idem autem videtur penitus consentire Judaeus Philosophus, qui vocatur Rabbi Moyses, *et Judaeus, qui ante ipsum fuit in Philosophia Magnus*, qui vocatur Isaak" *(Metaphysicorum* XI, tract. 2, c. 10; vol. 6, p. 627).

Notice that St. Albert uses the Neoplatonic position to define the soul in itself.

means of the ship's instruments—topsail, mast, sail, oars.[48] Let us apply this to the soul which also has two definitions. According to one of these, the soul carries on the functions of life in the body and in the organs of the soul. As we have seen, this is the aspect of the soul which Aristotle's definition, by way of Avicenna, reveals. Avicenna's influence on this point is exclusive.

Let us for the moment omit St. Albert's interpretation of the other parts of Aristotle's definition and proceed to the other definition, namely, of the soul in itself and according as it is separable from the body, especially according to that part of itself whch is not the perfection of a body. This is the intellective part of the soul, and it is in this part that the soul carries on its own functions of life.

At this point, St. Albert introduces the Neoplatonic conception of the Jew, Isaak, in which, to carry out another figure, the soul illumines the body in the same way that the sun illumines the physical world.[49] This simile

---

48. More precisely: "Nauta enim movet navim per speciem intellectivam quae est scientia gubernandi: et cum nullam operationem habet nauta in navi, quae non expleatur motu et instrumento corporeo, sicut a temone, vel clavo, vel velo, aut gubernaculo, vel remo: et separatur tamen totus gubernator a navi" *(Liber II de Anima,* tract. 1, cap. IV; vol. 5. p. 199). The sailor or pilot is really distinct from the ship, but he has the knowledge to run the ship; while in putting his knowledge into practice he is exercising *some* of his powers on the ship's instruments, and cannot exercise *these powers except through these instruments.* If we apply this to the soul we shall readily see what St. Albert is intending to enforce. As we have hurriedly noted already, and as it will become abundantly clear presently, this meticulous elaboration in St. Albert proceeds from Avicenna.

49. Cf. J. Guttman, *op. cit.,* p. 38-40. On the soul as standing on the horizon of two worlds, time and eternity, cf. *ibid.,* p. 42, note 3. Isaak, as Guttmann tells us (p. 17), made of the soul a *complete* substance and fought the *Mutakallimin* who made it depend on the body. In other words, the alternative was between the soul as accident and as *complete* substance for Isaak as for Avicenna.—

is quite significant. As St. Albert looks at the soul in itself, he sees that it has certain powers and operations that
are not completed through the body but directly through
the soul. For St. Albert this means that the intellectual
soul is completely separable from the body; and the reason
for such a conclusion is the following: A "part" of the soul
is a power deriving or flowing from the soul. If such is
the case, it is impossible to think that a soul really joined
to a body could have a power whose action was completed
outside of some bodily organ. On the other hand, it is perfectly possible to have powers flowing from what is essentially (*essentialiter*) distinct or separated from the body
into the body, because a higher power can produce the ef-
fects of a lower one, but not *vice versa*. Thus, the prime
mover, who is the most separate substance of all in existence,
is the source of the power moving the *primum mobile*; and
this power does not effect its operation without a body, because only a body can move locally. St. Albert, therefore,
sees no difficulty in having the soul essentially separate from
the body. In fact, he observes that we shall define the soul
as essentially dependent on the body if we are ready to admit
that all the powers which flow from the essence of the soul
operate through the body. But as the power of the soul is
the property of its essence, the soul is included in its definition. Whence, if the intellect is a separate power, the whole
intellectual soul is essentially separate. That is why the
soul is in the body as a pilot is in a ship.[50]

For the *Mutakallimin*, cf. E. Gilson, *Pourquoi s. Thomas a critiqué
s. Augustin*. (Archives . . ., I, 1926-1927), p. 8 ff.

It may be significant here to notice a similar conception of the
Jewish estimate of man in Nemesius, *De Natura Hominis*, c. 1;
Patrologia Graeca, vol. 40, col. 513B-C.

50. "At vero quamdam animam et secundum quasdam partes
nihil prohibet separari, propter hoc quod illae nullius corporis sunt
actus, in quo vitae exerceant actiones, sicut in organo, sicut manifestum erit in sequentibus tam agenti quam possibili, et in parte

St. Albert, therefore, following his Avicennian interpretation of Aristotle, feels called upon to defend him against the criticism of Nemesius. Nemesius objected to the Aristotelian definition because he thought that, logically carried out, it would make of the soul a purely material form. In fact, in the eyes of Nemesius, we shall say either that the

---

in praemissis habitum est. Amplius autem manifestum est non solum de ipsa parte intellectiva, quod separatur, sed de ipsa anima tota intellectiva, quod separetur est manifestum: cujus causa necessaria est, quia cum partes animae sint naturales potestates ejus, ab ipsa fluentes, impossible est quod ab essentia conjuncta cum corpore fluat potestas separata. Sed e converso possibile est quod ab eo *quo essentialiter est separatum,* fluant potentiae operantes in corpore; quia omnis potestas superior potest quicquid potest virtus inferior et non convertitur: cujus probatio est, quod a primo simplici qui maxime substantia separata est inter essentias omnes, fluit virtus motiva primi mobilis, quae nullo modo explet operationem suam sine corpore, eo quod nihil est localiter mobile nisi corpus . . . Patet igitur quod ab eo cujus essentia separata est, fluunt potentiae operantes in corpore. Sed ab eo quod essentialiter subditur corpori, et est virtus in corpore existens, nulla fluit potentia quae sit separata: quia potentia naturalis et operatio sequitur essentiam: et ideo ipsa potentia mixta corpori, magis erit mixta quam ipsa essentia a qua fluit. Adhuc autem naturalis potentia est proprietas essentiae. Est autem subjectum principium passionis, et cadit in diffinitione ejus. Qualiter igitur posset esse, quod essentia conjuncta corpori, causaret potentiam naturalem separatam? Ex his igitur patet, quod si intellectus est potentia separata, tunc oportet quod natura et essentia intellectivae animae sit separata: et cum hoc habebit plurimas potentias corpori conjunctas. Amplius autem manifestatur hoc si dicatur anima intellectiva sive rationalis movere corpus et esse actus ejus, sicut nauta est actus et motor navis . . . (cf. note 48) . . . Et similiter si anima sic movet corpus totum intellectu gubernante aut imperante, ipsa separatur tota essentialiter a corpore, licet habeat multas vires et operationes sensus et vegetationis, quae non explentur sine instrumentis corporeis" *(Liber II, De Anima,* tract. 1, cap. 4; vol. 5, p. 198-199).

Thus we have to observe that St. Albert kept the Avicennian doctrine intact.

soul is a substance, an individual being, ruling the body and itself essentially separate from it—which is the position of Plato; or, we must say that the soul is the entelechy of the body and has no being outside of the body which is its subject—which is the position that Nemesius attributes to Aristotle. Such is the dilemma before which Nemesius places his readers: we must either agree with Plato and say that the soul is a substance, or we must agree with Aristotle and hold that the soul is a material form. Such is also the dilemma that Albert accepts. Only, his interpretation, benefiting by Avicenna's analysis, is able to avoid the difficulties of the dilemma by distinguishing between the definition of the soul in itself and the definition of the soul in relation to the body. He can criticize Nemesius, therefore, quite in keeping with his position, even though we shall have to question the logic of such a position.[51] He will say, then, that Nemesius' (he says, Gregory's) reduction of Aristotle would be valid if Aristotle's definition applied to the essence of the soul: *si anima in se considerata esset endelechia secundum essentiam.* We have seen that such is not the case. Is the soul the entelechy of the body? It is, but only through the *animationem quam facit corpori per opera vitae.* This does not affect the soul in itself, and therefore Aristotle's definition becomes acceptable because it is external—shall we say, accidental?— to the essence of the soul. But in defining the soul in itself we move upon an entirely different level and within an entirely different tradition, for it is to Plato that we turn. We can conclude, therefore, that the soul *in se considerata* ...

---

51. The arguments will be found in *Sum. Theol.*, P. II, tract 12, q. 69, obj. 1-3; vol. 33, p. 13-14. In the reply to the fourth objection St. Albert again uses the simile of the sailor and the ship (p. 16); while in the reply to the seventh we see Plato fully clothed in the Arabian doctrine of the *"dator formarum,"* that is, the active intellect of Avicenna. Cf. E. Gilson, *Pourquoi s. Thomas a critiqué s. Augustin (Archives . . . I, 1926-1927),* p. 38-45.

est spiritus incorporeus, semper vivens, ut dicit Plato.[52]
Consequently, if St. Albert can criticize Nemesius, if he can
succeed where so many others have failed, this, in his own
famous paradox, is the reason why: *Ad aliud dicendum quod
animam considerando secundum se, consentiemus Platoni:
considerando autem eam secundum formam animationis quam
dat corpori, consentiemus Aristoteli.*[53]

Behind this paradox, which indeed we must bear in mind
when we compare St. Albert with his famous pupil, lies a
very earnest desire at once to safeguard the substantiality of
the soul and at the same time to account for the union between the soul and the body. It is here that Avicenna, himself bred in the Neoplatonic tradition, comes to St. Albert's
assistance and makes possible the assimiliation of Aristotle
within a tradition that remains fundamentally Platonic.

After examining the meaning of *actus,* St. Albert turns
his attention to the significance of *primus* in Aristotle's definition.[54]   Again he begins with Avicenna.[55]   The *actus
primus* gives *esse, species* and *ratio* to that of which it is the
actus.   That is, it perfects a being in its specific character,
which in this case results in placing man in his species. The
actus secundus follows upon the first and covers any operation which proceeds from the individual so constituted by
the presence of the soul. Thus, he can now think and feel.[56]

---

52. *Sum. Theol., loc. cit.,* ad 1.

53. *Ibid.,* ad 2.

54. *Sum. de Creat.,* P. II, tract. 1, q. 4, a. 2; vol. 35, p. 38:
Quomodo anima sit actus primus? Solutio; p. 39.

55. "Et ideo dicit Avicenna in VI de *Naturalibus*: . . ." *(ibid.).*

56. "*Solutio.* Dicendum cum Philosopho, quod anima est actus
primus, ut supra dictum est, qui dat esse et speciem et rationem
ei cujus est actus: actus vero secundus non est principium operationum, sed ipsa operatio: . . . Et ideo dicit Avicenna in VI de
Naturalibus: Perfectio prima est, propter quam species fit species
in effectu. Perfectio autem secunda est aliquid ex his quae consequuntur speciem rei, aut ex actionibus ejus, aut ex passionibus:

In the same way, if we seek to determine what St. Albert means by *potentia* in interpreting Aristotle, we meet the usual opening remark, *"Dicendum secundum Avicennam. ."*[57] It is difficult to get a clear meaning of this word in St. Albert. He treats the problem in Article iv before proceeding to a comparison between *potentia* and *organicum* in Article v. [58] The vegetable soul, he says, is a form of soul only in plants, while in an animal it is only a *potentia* or, presumably, power. In like manner, the sensible soul is in man as a power. Now, if you consider *soul* as a class or genus, then *soul* refers to the nature of the soul with respect to its primary operations which are those of the vegetable soul; and from this point of view, the vegetable soul will appear in all the species of soul, being, as St. Albert holds, the lowest implication of the term.[59]

We may apply this analysis to Aristotle's phrase *potentia vitam habentis*. It means, he says, not what Nemesius thought,

---

sicut incidere est ensis, et sicut cognoscere et cogitare et sentire est motus hominis: quia homo species constituta per animam. Primum enim est, quo posito non est necesse sequens ponere. Secundum autem non ponitur sine primo" *(ibid.)*.

57. *Sum. de Creat.*, P. II, tract. 1, q. 4, a. 5, *Solutio;* p. 53.

58. *Ibid., Solutio;* p. 48.

59. *"Solutio.* Dicimus et supponimus hic quod anima vegetabilis prout est species animae, non est nisi in plantis, sed prout est potentia est in animalibus. Etiam sensibilis prout est species animae, non est nisi in brutis: prout autem est potentia, est in hominibus. Similiter rationalis prout est species animae, est in hominibus. Si vero accipiatur secundum suum genus, tunc illud genus ponet naturam animae secundum primas potestates animae, quae postea determinantur per consequentes differentias: et illae sunt potestates vegetabiles; et sic dicta anima vegetabilis secundum genus erit in qualibet suarum specierum. Dico, igitur, quod anima vegetabilis non est actus corporis hominis, nec etiam sensibilis. Similiter non est actus corporis bruti, sed illius; id est, hominis est actus rationalis tantum, et illius, id est, bruti sensibilis, tunc et plantae vegetabilis tantum" *(Ibid.)*. Cf. also the answer to the fourth objection, p. 48-49.

but the relation of matter to the *actus* of the soul which is to live. The phrase, then, indicates the difference which characterizes some physical bodies, such as plants, animals, etc., as opposed to stones and the like. Now this life comes from the soul, and hence we can say that *"vita est animae sicut potentiae activae"*, and that life is *"corporis sicut passivae (scil. potentiae).*"[60] In other words, the phrase, *potentia vitam habentis* refers to the general relationship existing between soul and body, and shows at once whence the act of life comes and that it is the distinguishing mark of some bodies. On the other hand, the term *organicum* as applied to body is explained by St. Albert, again following Avicenna,[61] as meaning the same as *instrumentale*, and as referring, in particular, to the powers of the soul which operate in the body; whereas the phrase *potentia vitam habentis* refers to the soul itself as the source of life.[62]   Hence, St. Albert again

---

60. "Ad primum ergo dicendum . . . Et quod Aristoteles dicit, *Potentia vitam habentis*, ly *potentia* non dicit nisi respectum materia ad actum animae qui est vivere. Ille enim respectus potentiae est, et non actus: numquam enim Aristoteles intendit hoc quod Gregorius (i.e., Nemesius) ei imponit, scilicet quod sit anima actus corporis existentis in potentia ad animam, immo illius non est actus . . . *Potentia* enim *vitam habent* ponitur in diffinitione ad differentiam quorundam physicorum corporum, quae non habent potestatem vivendi sicut mineralia et lapides" *(ibid.).*

"Ad aliud dicendum, quod vita est animae sicut potentiae activae, et corporis sicut passivae' (ad 4; *ibid.).*

61. Cf. *Supra*, note 57.

62. "*Solutio*. Dicendum secundum Avicennam, quod anima est perfectio prima corporis naturalis instrumentalis habentis opera vitae. Et secundum hanc diffinitionem organicum est pars diffinitionis, et instrumentale et organicum accipitur pro eodem.

"Et secundum hoc dicendum ad rationem Constabulini, quod licet corpus organicum accipiatur pro eodem, et secundum hoc supponetur per potentia vitam habentis, tamen ly *potentia vitam habens* alium respectum materiae ad formam sive corporis ad animam dicit: ly *organicum* enim dicit respectum ad potentias animae, quae

concludes that the soul is the *actus corporis organici,* and that this is a part of its definition.

But certain objectors will not grant such a conclusion. They do not think that the body is necessary to the definition of the soul, and, in fact, they throw grave doubt on the possibility of union between soul and body, given such a definition of the soul as St. Albert has outlined. Thus, it is objected that everything organic is a body, perfect in the distinction and composition of its parts and in the shape of its organs. Such a body is therefore actually existing *in toto.* But no actually existing being is so united to another that a real unity results from their union. Hence, from such a body and such a soul no unity will result.[63] And again it is objected that every *motor,* especially with reference to local motion, is not only an actus of the body, but also *actu ens* in itself. This is the case with sensible and rational souls; and therefore between such souls and their respective bodies there is no real unity.[64] Finally, an objector observes that a substance has existence in itself and does not depend on an accident because it is clearly separable from the accident. Since

---

operantur in organis: sed ly *potentia vitam habens* dicit respectum ad ipsam animam: quia vita est actus animae secundum se . . . ." *(Solutio* and ad 1; *loc cit.).*

"Ad aliud dicendum, quod rationalis anima duo dicit, scilicet quod est anima, et quod est rationalis: si accipiatur ut anima, tunc est actus corporis, et habet a se potentias effluentes, quarum quaedam affixae sunt organis, et quaedam non: et ab illa homo est homo: et concedo bene, quod a sensibili vel vegetabili non est homo, cum in homine non sint nisi sicut potentiae, et non sicut actus corporis. Si autem accipitur quod rationis est solum, tunc nullius corporis est actus, id est, nullius partis corporis: quia illae suae potentiae non sunt affixae organis, licet accipiant per apprehensionem a potentia affixa organo, ut est phantasia, vel memoria, vel aestimatio" *(In I. Sententiarum,* d. 8, F, a. 26, *ad quaest.* 2; vol. 25, p. 260-261).

63. Obj. 3; Sum. Theol, *loc cit.,* p. 49.
64. Obj. 4; *ibid.*

the soul is separated from the body and remains in itself, it is a perfect substance in itself. But no such being can be united essentially to another, and it would appear as though the soul cannot be the *actus* of the body.[65] In other words, the substantiality of the soul appears to preclude the possibility of union with the body.

To the first of these three objections St. Albert replies that the body has actual existence only through the soul. When the soul is not present, then the body is not an organic body, except equivocally, as a dead man can be called a man.[66] To the second objector he replies that not every mover is an *actu ens* as well as an *actus,* because an animal soul is clearly not *actu ens,* even though it is the *actus* of an animal body. But if you apply this principle to the human soul, then, he says, the question has been answered already, because, following Avicenna, St. Albert can attach two definitions to the soul, one as substance, the other as *actus*; and it is only according to the second aspect in itself that the soul can be united to the body: if it were just a substance, it would not be able to join the body for the constitution of another substance.[67] The reply to the third objector only helps to en-

---

65. Obj. 5; p. 50.

66. "Ad aliud dicendum, quod corpus organicum non est actu nisi per animam. Cum autem non habeat animam, non est corpus organicum, nisi aequivoce, ut homo mortuus dicitur homo" (ad 3; p. 53).

67. "Ad aliud dicendum, quod haec propositio est falsa si universaliter ponatur: Omnis motor secundum locum processivum non solum est actus, sed actu ens per seipsum: sensibilis enim anima est motor processive secundum locum in brutis, et tamen non est actu ens per seipsam, sed est actus corporis solum. Si vero non universaliter, sed de anima rationali tantum proponitur, tunc supra soluta est argumentio, ubi distinctum est, quod anima rationalis non tantum est substantia per se ens, nec tantum actus, sed substantia et actus: sed si esset substantia per se tantum, non esset unibilis alteri per constitutionem unius per substantiam" (ad 4; *ibid)*.

force what St. Albert has already said. We must not conceive of the body as an actually existing substance which can
be separated from the soul as a subject can be separated from
its accident. It is the soul which gives it its actual existence.
The soul, indeed, depends on the body in the sense that it is
capable of being united to it and will be united to it in the
resurrection. Since, therefore, soul and body depend upon
each other in the way explained, one substance results from
their union.[68]

It is perhaps unnecessary to follow St. Albert's discussion
any farther or to observe how he interprets the other definitions. His Platonic, or, more accurately, Avicennian,
position is clear. What difficulties such a position raises we
shall see presently. We must now turn to consider the substance of the soul. The soul is a complete substance. Every
substance, according to the classic remark of Boethius, is
composite, only God excepted. The soul, then, is composite.
For St. Bonaventure, considerations of receptivity and change
had resulted in the doctrine of the matter-and-form composition of all created substances. Does St. Albert accept this
solution? He does not.

I agree, he says ,that there is a composition of essential
principles in the soul which are *quod est* and *esse*; but I do

---

68. "Ad aliud dicendum, quod corpus bene separatur ab anima
ut materia, sed non ut actu manens ut subjectum separatur ab accidente. Similiter anima rationalis dependentiam habet ad corpus,
eo quod est unibilis ei et unitur ei in resurrectione novissima. Et
ideo cum sic utrumque dependeat ad alterum ex eis fit unum per
substantiam" (ad 5; *ibid.*).

In fact, à propos of this definition of Avicenna, he can say
in the *Summa Theologiae*: Dicendum, quod definitio Avicennae
bona est, et eundem sensum habet cum definitione quam ponit
Aristoteles . . ." (P. II, tr. 12, q. 69, mem. 2, a. 1; vol. 33, p. 12).
We may remark that the only reason for this affinity between
Avicenna and Aristotle is the fact that St. Albert has always interpreted Arsitotle as though he were Avicenna.

not agree that the soul is composed of matter and form, even though *quidam* seem to say this. His reason for rejecting this doctrine is that matter, according to Aristotle—*secundum Philosophum*—is concerned exclusively with the capacity for change present in a substance or with the capacity which a substance may have for local motion. Such a capacity, however, exists only in bodies, and matter will thus be confined to the physical world.[69] That is why St. Albert will say that the soul, though a substance, is not a *hoc aliquid*. It is neither philosophers nor *saints* who call the soul a *hoc aliquid;* it is the *masters—magistri*—who use such a name. St. Albert is not partial to such ideas: *et puto, quod sit dictum falsum.* His reason is that Aristotle applies the term *hoc aliquid* only to the compound of matter and form,[70] and this would exclude the soul. To be sure, he continues, the soul is composite, but not as a *hoc aliquid*, because according to its very nature it depends on the body, though it can exist without the body, and because also the soul's perfection is not absolutely complete without the body.[71]

---

69. *"Solutio.* Consentio in hanc partem, quod anima sit composita ex principiis essentialibus quae sunt quod est et esse, sed non ex materia et forma: licet hoc quidam dicere videantur: et hoc ideo quia secundum philosophum materia determinatur per potentiam ad motum variantem aliquid in substantia, vel ad motum localem: et cum potentia hujusmodi non sit nisi in corporibus, non erit materia nisi in corporibus" (*In I Sententiarum*, d. 8, F. a. 25, *Solutio;* vol. 25, p. 257). As this work dates very early, St. Albert's opposition to the doctrine of spiritual matter which the Franciscans held is very decided from the beginning.

70. He refers to *De Anima* II, 1, 412a5ff. Cfr. note 71.

71. "Ad aliud dicendum, quod anima sit hoc aliquid, hoc est dictum a Magistris, sed non a Philosophis, nec a Sanctis: et puto, quod sit dictum falsum: quoniam in principio libri II de *Anima* habetur, quod materia non est hoc aliquid, nec etiam forma, et quod anima non est hoc aliquid: sed hoc bene concedo, quod anima est substantia composita: sed ipsa non est composita ut hoc ali-

St. Albert's conception of composition raises two problems, namely, the nature of matter and the precise significance of the *quod est* and *quo est* in the soul as substance.

Matter, as absolutely simple, is incapable of definition,
because a definition refers to the parts of the thing defined.
It might then be argued that our statements about matter are
only descriptions. St. Albert will not agree. A description,
he says, refers to the substantial constituents, to the distinction of these constituents by means of their proper accidents,
or to their grouping within one individual. But all of these
attributes belong to a composite thing, and not to a simple
one.[72] If such is the case, our knowledge of matter must be
negative, that is, it refers to what lies beyond the forms.
Hence, we know matter in relation to some form, and it is
only in this way that we can define it—*secundum quod ratio*

---

quid: quia secundum naturam dependentiam habet ad corpus, licet
posset esse sine illo. Sed bene concedo, quod perfectio sua non est
omnio completa sine illo" (*In II Sent.*, d. 17, C, a. 2, ad 2; vol. 27,
p. 299). His objection to *hoc aliquid* is made clear by the following definition: "*hoc aliquid enim est forma contracta per materiam*"
(*Sum. de Creat.*, P. I, tract. 1, q. 2, a. 2, ad diffin. 3, ad 1; vol. 34,
p. 325).—There is no doubt that in St. Albert we are definitely
confronted with the necessity of relating, somehow or other, the
soul to the body in a real unity; and a passage such as this helps
to show that St. Albert was conscious of that necessity.

72. "Quod omnino simplex est, nullo modo est diffinibile; quia
omnis diffinitio dicit partes diffiniti. Materia autem simplex est
omnino. Ergo nullo modo est diffinibilis.

"Si forte dicatur, quod descriptiones sunt. *Contra* hoc iterum
est: quia descriptio vel est ex parte substantialium, sicut ex dif-
ferentiis aggregatis, praeter genus, vel ex substantiali et accidentali, sicut si proprium conjungitur cum genere vel differentia: vel
ex accidentibus aggregatis, sicut Crispus musicus Cleonis filius est
descriptio Socratis. Et unaquaeque istarum descriptionum est de
composito tantum, et non de simplici. Ergo descriptio non potest
esse materiae cum sit simplex" (*Sum. de Creat.*, P. I, tract. 1, q. 2,
a. 2, ad *Contra ultimam*, 2; p. 323).

accipit eam (scil. materiam) ordinatam vel conjunctam.[73]
Matter is thus not a thing, but the privation of a thing, a
pure subject with the order and the aptitude for form.[74]
As existing in time, it always offers the aspect of quantity,
and is always united to a substantial form.[75] These indications are sufficient to show that St. Albert's conception of
matter differs considerably from that of St. Bonaventure, for,
whereas St. Bonaventure had determined his conception of
matter by considering it the receptive principle of existence

---

73. *"Solutio.* Ad ultimum respondemus primo, quod (sicut
dicit Boethius) substantia et entitas materiae in se considerata non
est intelligibilis proprio intellectu, sed intelligitur secundum privationem, scilicet, quod hoc est materia, quod praeter formas acci-
dentales et substantiales invenitur in ente: et ideo si debet intelligi, oportet quod hoc sit per ordinationem ad formam, vel per
conjunctionem ad formam: et sic quodammodo diffinibilis est, et
habet quamdam compositionem rationis, secundum quod ratio accipit eam ordinatam vel conjunctam (*ibid.*).

74. " . . . et ideo non dicit (*scil.* materia) ens simpliciter:
quia non est absolute res a qua scilicet secunda est inchoatio rei
quae est forma, et est secundum veritatem ordo ad formam, *qui
ordo medium est inter ens et non ens.*

"Ad id quod contra objicitur, dicimus quod materia seipsa est
principium desiderii: desiderium enim illius nihil aliud est nisi
privatio formae cum potentia habendi illam, quae potentia est ipsa
materia: ipsa enim entitas materiae est subjectum subjicibile formae: quae subjicibilitas est potentia et desiderium sive appetitus,
et non differt ab ipsa nisi secundum rationem dictam.

"Et si quaeratur, Utrum illa ratio aliquid ponat? Dicendum,
quod secundum rem quae simpliciter res sit, nihil posuit super
subjectum: et hoc contingit ideo, quia non est ratio rei sed privationis rei: et privatio nihil relinquit nisi subjectum cum ordine et
aptitudine ad formam" (*op. cit.*, q. 2, a. 4, *Solutio and ad* 1; vol.
34, p. 329-330).

75. "Ad aliud dicendum, quod materia prima numquam tempore est sine quantitate" (ad 3; *ibid.*).—"Ad aliud dicendum, quod
materia numquam tempore est sine forma substantiali, et tamen
sola est subjectum idem numero manens sub formis diversis" (ad
quaest. 1; p. 330-331).

in creatures, St. Albert limits matter to the realm of physical changes.

Having thus denied the presence of matter in spiritual substances,[76] St. Albert proceeds to his conception of how substances are composed. When a substance is composed of matter and form, neither member is predicated of the compound, and a universal predicate will refer not to the form of the matter in the compound but to the form or nature of the whole. That is, according to this interpretation of a somewhat difficult text, when I predicate *gold* of this individual thing, the name refers not to the form alone but to the form and matter together. Now this form of composition does not exist in some beings. Theirs is the composition of *quo est* and *quod est,* and of these the first is the *forma totius* or nature, the second, the *totum* or whole individual thing which has this nature. However, as there is no matter present in the substances now under consideration, the *forma totius* will be equivalent to the *forma materiae* completely, which was not true before, and the *quod est* will have the position that matter formerly had, namely, that of subject.[77]

---

76. *Ibid.,* a. 5, *Solutio;* p. 333-334. Granting a universal matter, he says, *quidam* have distinguished three classes of substances according as the form received exhausted the potentiality of the matter: I. If this is complete, then you have the first class of substances, entirely spiritual, subject only to spiritual "accidents" such as knowledge, illumination, etc.   II. There are next those substances which, through the presence of quantity, are subject to local motion but not to contrariety; and this, I take it, is the case of the heavenly bodies. III. Finally, there are those bodies which are subject both to local motion and to new forms. This scale is determined by the form and the power to realize the potencies of the matter (cf. p. 333).

77. "Si quid aliter vellet dicere, dicet quod non omnium substantiarum est materia una, quemadmodum dicit auctoritas Aristotelis: et secundum hoc substantia dupliciter componitur: in quibusdam enim substantiis est compositio ex materia et forma, sicut in generabilibus et corruptibilibus, quorum neutrum praedicatur de

St. Albert illustrates. If I say *hoc coelum* I refer to the matter, that is, to the individuating characteristics; but if I say *coelum,* I refer to the nature or form. Likewise, if I say *hunc angelum* or *hanc animam,* I refer to the *suppositum* or individual subject; but if I say *angelum* or *animam,* I refer to the nature of this individual subject.[78]

---

substantia composita: compositum enim neque materia est, neque forma: unde in talibus universale quod praedicatur de composito, non accipitur a forma materiae, sed a forma totius conjuncti. In quibusdam autem non est talis compositio, sed ex quo est et quod est, quemadmodum dicit Boethius: et *quo est* est forma totius, quod est autem dicit ipsum totum cujus est forma: et haec compositio est in incorruptibilibus et in ingenerabilibus, in quibus forma totius non differt a forma materiae: quia non habet materiam: ergo ipsum totum quod supponitur per quod est, non habet distinctionem a materia propter eandem causam. Et hoc praecipue verum est in spiritualibus substantiis, in quibus non est accipere compositionem nisi suppositi et naturae cujus est suppositum illud" (*ibid.;* p. 333-334).

78. "Si autem quaeritur, qualiter debeat significare? Dicendum quemadmodum dicit Aristoteles in primo de *Coelo et Mundo,* quod cum dico *hoc coelum,* dico materiam: sed cum dico *coelum,* dico formam. Similiter cum dico *hunc Angelum,* vel *hanc animam,* dico suppositum: et cum dico *Angelum* vel *animam* dico naturam cujus est suppositum illud: et ideo in talibus et quod est et quo est praedicantur de supposito" (*ibid.*).

The text of Aristotle is as follows: "ἐπεὶ οὖν ἐστιν ὁ οὐρανός αἰσθητός, τῶν καθ' ἕκαστον ἄν εἴη· τὸ γὰρ αἰσθητὸν ἅπαν ἐν τῇ ὕλῃ ὑπῆρχεν. εἰ δὲ τῶν καθ' ἕκαστον, ἕτερον ἄν εἴη τῷδε τῷ οὐρανῷ εἶναι καὶ οὐρανῷ ἁπλῶς, καὶ τὸ μὲν ὡς εἶδος καὶ μορφή, τὸ δ' ὡς τῇ ὕλῃ μεμιγμένον" (*De Coelo et Mundo,* I, 9, 278a10-15).

The commentary of St. Thomas Aquinas is useful on this point: " . . . dicit quod, *cum coelum,* idest mundus, sit quoddam sensibile, necesse est quod sit de numero singularium: et hoc ideo, quia omne sensibile habet esse in materia. Id autem quod est forma non in materia, non est sensibile, sed intelligible tantum . . . Et dico quod si *caelum,* idest mundus, est de numero singularium, ut ostensum est, *alterum erit esse huic caelo* singulariter dicto, et *caelo simpliciter,* idest universaliter sumpto; idest alia erit ratio utriusque. Et sic sequitur quod alterum sit secundum considerationem *hoc caelum* singulariter dictum et *caelum* universaliter sumptum: ita scilicet

What is the significance of such a composition? It means that no creature is its own essence, and this, as we have seen, goes back to the *De Hebdomadibus* of Boethius. The *quod est* of itself does not imply existence, and it is only by the *quo est* that I am what I am. In a creature, the *quod est* is the subject of the act of being serving as the *fundamentum* or subject or ground on which this act of being is founded. There is thus a similarity between the *quod est* and matter, because both receive as subjects what they do not themselves include and what is therefore different from them. There is also a similarity between *quo est* and form.[79] In the case of

---

quod hoc caelum universaliter sumptum sit sicut species et forma; hoc autem scilicet caelum singulariter sumptum, sit sicut forma conjuncta materiae. Quod non est sic intelligendum quod in ratione rei naturalis universaliter sumptae nullo modo cadat materia; sed quod non cadat ibi materia signata" (*Comm. in hunc loc.*, cap. 9, lect. 19; ed. Leon., vol. 3, p. 77, no. 5-6).

79. "Secundum genus compositionis est, quando duo vel plura ita conveniunt ad unum constituendum, quod unum illorum est sicut cujus est actus et esse, et alterum sicut quo effective vel formaliter vel utroque modo est esse in illo: et haec vocatur *compositio ex quo est et quod est*: quod enim est, non est ex se in actu essendi, sed dependet ad aliud a quo effective vel formaliter vel utroque modo accipit esse. Et hoc est quod dicit Boethius in libro de *Hebdomadibus* sic: *Quod est* habere aliquid potest praeter id quod ipsum est: *esse* vero nihil admixtum habet. Sicut enim dicit Avicenna, *quod est* secundum seipsum et nihil, et ex nihilo est, sed esse sibi est ab eo quo est efficienter vel formaliter vel utroque modo: et ideo dicit Boethius quod 'in omni creato aliud est quod est, et aliud quo est'" (*Sum. Theol.*, P. II, tract. 1, q. 3, m. 3, a. 2; vol. 32, p. 29).—"Et sic bene concedimus, quod compositum sequitur creatum: in nullo enim creato verum est, quod creatum secundum id quod est sit sua essentia qua est: sed in solo primo principio hoc verum est: et ideo solum simplex est et in eo idem quod est et quo est: quod non est in aliis: in illis enim quod est, est subjectum esse: et quia hoc subjectum est quasi fundamentum in quo fundatur esse, et essentia est cujus actus est esse: et esse est actus essentiae in eo quod est: et haec inter se ponunt diversitatem" (*ibid.*, ad 2, p. 34-35).

the *quod est,* however, the receptivity is different from that
of matter, because the *quod est* is receptive of the act of
being which gives it real existence in a species.[80]

As these conclusions apply both to angels and souls as
complete substances, how are we to distinguish a soul from
an angel? Let us consider the angel. Following the *De
Hebdomadibus* of Boethius, St. Albert holds that angels are
composite and that this composition is of the *quod est* and
the *quo est.*[81] The angel is also a *hoc aliquid,* or individual
substance and a *suppositum* or subject of a certain kind of
being, common to many, by which it is placed in a particular
genus or species of that nature, and is called a *hoc aliquid,*
that is, a *signatum* or *stamped* individual that indicates by
its existence that it is a *this* of *such* a nature.   Incidentally,
this twofold aspect proves its composition.[82]   Furthermore,

---

80. "Ex hoc etiam patet, quod *quod est* ex hoc similitudinem
habet cum materia: quia recipit aliud quod est praeter ipsum et
differens ab ipso, sicut et genus materialiter dicitur, cum tamen
forma sit: *quo est* autem similitudinem habet cum forma: quamvis
nec quod est sit materia generaliter, nec quo est forma generaliter:
quia susceptio qua quod est suscipit, non est susceptio materiae,
sed est susceptio primi subjecti et primi formabilis in unoquoque
genere, sicut dictum est: et haec susceptio, ut dicit Avicenna in
primo *Philosophiae,* non est susceptio materiae, quia ex suscepto
non determinatur aliquod ad esse simpliciter, sicut materia determinatur et perficitur per formam ad esse simpliciter: sed est susceptio qua confusum suscipit actum differentiae determinantis ipsum ad esse distinctum in genere, specie, vel individuo" (*ibid.,* ad
quaest. 2; p. 37).—The text goes on to say that the *quod est—quo
est* composition is more universal than the matter and form composition, and in fact more universal than any other composition.
Matter has the same *quod est* and *quo est* because of itself it has
not an *esse,* except through a form. And in the form itself there is a
composition, because, as we have seen, in material things the substantial form is not coextensive with the *forma totius* or nature
(*ibid.*).

81. *Op. cit.,* tract. 4, q. 21, a. 1, *Solutio;* vol. 34, p. 463.
82. "*Solutio.*   Dicendum, quod Angelus substantia composita

all angels belong to one species, differing among themselves
only in their hierarchies and orders. It is interesting to
note that St. Albert states the opinion of St. Thomas as being
one of the three *opiniones solemnes* on this question.[83]   St.
Albert does not agree with his pupil.   For him the angels
are like soldiers, more akin to citizens in a great republic,

est, et est suppositum, et hoc aliquid. Suppositum autem et hoc
aliquid in ratione sui habent, quod sint compositum ad minus ex
quod est et quo est: omne enim suppositum alicui substat communi, scilicet naturae, qua est in genere vel specie illius naturae:
et omne quod substat, res naturae determinata est in illa natura
ad hoc quod est signatum hoc aliquid. Et per hoc patet, quod in
ratione suppositi est, quod compositum sit" (*Sum. Theol.*, P. II,
tract. 4, q. 13, mem. 1, *Solutio;* vol. 32, p. 160). We may note here,
too, the great influence of Boethius whose *De Hebdomadibus* is
used continually in the arguments of the *Sed contra* (p. 159). St.
Albert's notion of *hoc aliquid* is thus not fixed; for, whereas pre-
viously (cfr. *supra*, p. 110) he denied that the term could extend to
anything but matter, here he is applying it to spiritual substance.

83. The Thomistic position is clearly found in this text:
"Adhuc, Commune substantiale non contrahitur ad hoc vel illud,
nisi differentia constitutiva vel materia: constat autem, quod hoc
commune quod est substantia intellectualis in Angelis, ad hunc
non contrahitur per materiam: relinquitur ergo, quod contrahatur
per formam, quae est differentia constitutiva. Differentia autem
constitutiva cum genere facit speciem, ut dicit Porphyrius: ergo
videtur, quod singuli sint in singulis speciebus, et quod singuli a
se invicem differant specie" (*Sum. Theol.*, P. II, tract. 2, q. 8, obj.
2; p. 135). Cf. St. Thomas, *Sum. Theol.*, I, q. 50, a. 3, Resp.   St.
Thomas is clearly metaphysical in determining the status of the
angel, but St. Albert is not. In answering the first objection, whose
doctrine is similar to that of St. Thomas, he says that only in
logic and natural science will such an argument prove sound,
while "in civilibus non autem est verum. In civilibus enim multi-
plicatio est ad ministeria per ordinationem politici sapientis: *et
sicut saepe dictum, distributio regni coelestis magis similis est
politicis, et civilibus, quam sit logicis et naturalibus*: cujus signum est, quod regnum coelorum etiam *civitas* vocatur" (*ibid.*, ad
1; p. 138). The last part of this text is certainly personal, and is
no doubt intended for the benefit of some recalcitrant pupil such
as St. Thomas Aquinas.

than to beings whose nature has been metaphysically determined; for the kingdom of Heaven, observes the aged Albert,
is more akin to government than to logic and metaphysics.[84]

Now, how are we to conceive the difference between the
angels and rational souls? We may note, first of all, that the
difference between them is one not only of species, but also
of genus, and lies principally in this. The soul has an
inclination for the pleasures of the body, and is indeed
naturally capable of joining the body.[85] Beyond this inclination towards the body, there is no other indication in
St. Albert on the difference between the soul and an angel.
And this is all the more remarkable when we discover that
both angels and souls have the same metaphysical composition.[86]

---

84. *Ibid., Sed Contra*, 2-3; p. 136.

85. *Sum. Theol.*, P. II, tract. 2, q. 9, *Solutio;* p. 140-141. The
article is too long to quote. In any case, it reproduces arguments
we have already seen in determining the meaning of the Aristotelian definition of the soul. Here is the central text: "Nec potest
dici, quod id quod ordinativum est omnium aliorum, ad ea quae
ordinat, non se habeat ut forma: propter quod dicit Avicenna in VI
de *Naturalibus*, quod anima rationalis sola secundum esse est
actus et anima hominis: vegetabilis autem et sensibilis non se
habent, nisi ut potentiae ad illam. Et quamvis sic quoad esse sit
unibilis corpori, et sit actus corporis physici organici potentiam
vitam habentis, tamen, ut dicit Gregorius Nyssenus (i.e. Nemesius),
Platonem sequens in hoc vera dicentem, non est tantum actus corporis, sed etiam suppositum et subjectum in se perfectum, utens
corpore et regens corpus. Propter hoc separatur post mortem, et
est substantia vitae in seipsa: et in hoc principaliter differt ab
Angelo" (p. 141).—This difference continues even after death, because the separated soul still retains its "affectum et intentionem
. . . ad corpus, in tantum quod etiam a contemplatione retrahatur"
(*ibid.*).—The *ordinativum* mentioned above is only another form
of the governing attitude of the soul, and indeed in this very text
St. Albert speaks in language which reminds one of the pilot image:
cf. *ibid.*, ad *Per hoc patet.*

86. There is considerable fluctuation in the meaning of *quo
est* and *quod est* in St. Albert: cf. M-D. Roland-Gosselin, *Le "De*

Such, in its fundamental outline, is the doctrine of St. Albert on the nature of the soul and its relation to the body. This doctrine is characterized, above all, by a desire to safeguard the full substantiality of the soul and, at the same time, to explain its union with the body. Now, what St. Albert cannot understand is how the soul can be an immaterial substance and a form joined essentially to the body. Apparently, he never succeeded in considering the nature of the soul and its unibility to the body as more than two irreducible aspects of the soul; and, as we have seen, it is Avicenna who enables him to bridge the distance separating the Platonic conception of the soul from the Aristotelian. Nevertheless, in this synthesis Aristotle is assigned the somewhat questionable honor of defining only the external or accidental aspects of the soul. In the last analysis, the soul is not joined to the body in an essential way. But if such is the case, then it is difficult to see how soul and body form an essential unity. If we say with Avicenna that the term *soul* refers to the substance for which it stands not because of anything in its essence or substance which indicates the function of animating the body, but because, apart from its own essential aspects, the soul rules the body and has some relations to it,[87] then it is indeed difficult to defend the

---

Ente et Essentia" de s. Thomas d'Aquin (Bibliothèque thomiste, viii) Le Saulchoir, Kain, 1926, p. 172-184. As concerns the composition of spiritual substances, while St. Albert has eliminated the doctrine of their hylemorphic composition, it would appear that the *fundamentum* which he requires within the essence of these substances has functions and characteristics analogous to those of the matter posited by Ibn Gebirol: cf. A. Forest, *La structure métaphysique du concret selon saint Thomas d'Aquin,* p. 124-125.

87. "Et hoc nomen est nomen hujus rei, non ex ejus essentia . . . Hoc enim nomen *anima* non est indictum ei ex substantia sua, sed ex hoc quod regit corpora et refertur ad illa" (Avicenna, *Lib. VI Naturalium,* P. i, c. 1; quoted by E. Gilson, *Les sources gréco-arabes de l'augustinisme avicennisant (Archives d'hist. doctr. et litt. du moyen âge,* iv, 1929), p. 81, note 1.—On the problem of the

unity of man. And when St. Albert, along with Avicenna,[88] admits the doctrine of the plurality of forms,[89] it becomes very much a question as to whether he understood or accepted the Aristotelian doctrine of the soul as the substantial form of the body.

But apart from the fact that we may question the Avicennian. synthesis of St. Albert, we must say, apparently, that on this point, at least, his speculations belong to the Platonic-Augustinian direction of mediaeval thought, to which an Arabian Neoplatonic interpretation of Aristotle enabled him to add what appears to be the doctrine of the *De Anima* on the nature of the soul. When we turn to St. Thomas, it is to a new phase of the problem and to a new solution; and we may say, even now, that the influence of the master on the disciple is almost non-existent within the limits of the present problem. Such a fact, however, only serves to focus the attention of the historian more firmly and more consciously on the Angelic Doctor as a new point of departure in the history of ideas.

---

relation between soul and body in Avicenna, cf. M.-D. Roland-Gosselin, *Sur les relations de l'âme et du corps d'après Avicenne.* in *Mélanges Mandonnet (Bibliothèque thomiste*, xiii-xiv), Paris, 1930, vol. ii, p. 47-54.

88. Cf. M. deWulf, *Le traité* De Unitate Formae *de Gilles de Lessines*, p. 33; A. Forest, *La structure métaphysique du concret selon saint Thomas d'Aquin*, p. 197-198.

89. There are at least indications of pluralism in St. Albert: cf. A. Forest, *La structure métaphysique du concret selon saint Thomas d'Aquin*, p. 200-201. This point, however, has been recently denied by J. A. McWilliams, *St. Albert the Great and Plurality of Forms* (The Modern Schoolman, ix, 3, March, 1932, p. 43-44, 59-61). But this fact only serves to indicate more strongly that the metaphysical problem of the substantial form was not present as a whole to the mind of St. Albert, and that he did not feel its significance in discussing the nature of the soul; which, among other things, throws grave doubt on the theory that St. Albert was the predecessor of the Angelical Doctor.

IV. ST. THOMAS AND THE PROBLEM OF THE SOUL: HISTORICAL DEVELOPMENT.

A. Metaphysical Foundations.

One of the most significant features of the problem of the soul in the thirteenth century is the evidence it gives of the resistance of Christian thought to Aristotle. Behind such a resistance, as the experiences of St. Bonaventure and St. Albert clearly indicate, lies a Christian desire to insure the substantiality and the immortality of the soul. Nemesius is a good example of what the Christian feared in Aristotle. That intimate union between soul and body, which seemed to rob the soul of all its native glory and to reduce it to the status of the form of the body, was a doctrine which did not please Nemesius and which did not please the early as well as (for the most part) the late thirteenth century. Under such circumstances it was natural to turn to Plato, and St. Thomas himself has outlined the difficulties which led to such a solution. But in thus safeguarding the substantial character of the soul and its radical independence of the body, Christian thought was open to the charge of endangering the unity of man. St. Bonaventure and St. Albert leave nothing to be desired in their insistence on the unity of man, but the difficulties which they raise refer not to the doctrine of unity itself, but to the explanation of that doctrine.

As we have noted, Godfrey of Fontaines, profiting by the criticism of St. Thomas, has pointed out that there are really two problems involved in this question. The first is whether or not the doctrine of plurality of forms is compatible with the unity of man; the second, whether or not this doctrine is compatible with Aristotle. Answering both points negatively, Godfrey goes on to insist that a true explanation of the unity of man necessitates an entirely new metaphysics underlying the concepts of matter and form; and it is Aristotle who will be the guide in this reinterpretation of man. While it is possible to say, therefore, that the doctrine of plurality of forms is a problem which arises in an Aristotelian environment, it is also necessary to say that the Aristotelians themselves were agreed in rejecting the doctrine as having no place within the system of the Stagirite and as being a remnant of the older mediaeval thought which was finding expression in the revived Aristotle. They implied that it was impossible for St. Augustine to speak the language of Aristotle, and that it was equally impossible for Plato and Aristotle to be reconciled on the most fundamental problems of philosophy. At the center of this metaphysical conflict stands the figure of the Angelic Doctor.

Bernard Geyer observes that St. Thomas, much more than his teacher, undertook to make philosophy and theology Aristotelian.[1] The stream of Platonic thought, especially by way of the Arabians, was very strong in St. Albert, and his allegiance to Aristotle, however faithful, was only a graft

---

1. "Was am meisten zum Siege des Aristotelismus beitrug ist die allseitige Verwertung der aristotelischen Philosophie in den systematischen Schriften von Thomas, insbesondere in seinen beiden Summen. Er hat noch mehr als Albert die Philosophie und in gleichen Weise auch die Theologie mit durchschlagendem erfolge zu Aristotelisieren verstanden" (*Grundriss*, 11th ed., p. 428).—Cf. C. Baeumker, *Petrus von Hibernia* . . . (Sitzungsberichte der Bayer. Akad. des Wissenschaften, 1920, 8. Abhandl.), Müuchen, 1920, p. 36-37. For Avicenna and Albert, cf. *ibid.*, p. 31.

Apart from the Vivès and Leonine editions of the works of St. Thomas, the following editions of the separate treatises were used: i. *In IV Lib. Sententiarum*, ed. P. Mandonnet-M. F. Moos, Paris, 1929—(three volumes have appeared: vol. i-ii, ed. Mandonnet, 1929; vol. iii, ed. Moos, 1933). ii. *Opuscula Omnia*, ed. P. Mandonnet, 5 vols., Paris, 1927. iii. *De Ente et Essentia*, ed. M-. D. Roland-Gosselin (*Bibliothèque thomiste*, viii), Le Saulchoir, Kain, 1926. iv. *Quaestiones Disputatae* and *Quaestiones Quodlibetales*, Marietti edition, 5th ed., Taurini-Romae, 1927. v. *Contra Gentiles*, Marietti edition, Taurini, 1927.

upon a Platonic trunk. But St. Thomas, Geyer goes on to say, "wusste den Neoplatonismus möglichst fernzuhalten."[2] In the problem of the definition of the soul the transition from St. Albert to St. Thomas means not only the abandonment of any attempt to combine Plato and Aristotle but also, as will become abundantly clear, the systematic elimination of almost all the Platonism which had survived in Christian thought principally through St. Augustine.

In thus abandoning Plato and his followers, after giving

---

2. *Ibid.*, Cf. Baeumker, *op. cit.*, p. 38-39, who thinks that Petrus de Hibernia was in a measure responsible for this in St. Thomas: "Wieder liegt es hier nahe, für besondere Form des von Thomas verstretenen Aristotelismus, im Gegensatz zu dem von Albert gelehrten, an seinen Jugendlehrer Petrus von Hibernia als ersten Anstoss zu denken. Jene besonderen Sätze von der Einheit der Form, dem Individuationsprinzip usw. zwar konnen wir bei diesen nicht mehr nachweisen. Das sein Aristotelismus aber von dem, was Averroes bot, einen immerhin bemerkenswerten Gebrauch machte, das konnte uns selbst jenes kurze, dürftige Stück zeigen, . . . " (p. 39). Whence, Baeumker concludes, "In Thomas, so dürfen wir jetzt wohl sagen, lebt seinen nunmehr aus dem dunkel an das Licht gebrachten Jugendlehrer ein bescheidenes Plätzchen gönnen" (p. 40). Though still inconclusive, this current of thought, as adduced by Baeumker, is significant, because it would account somewhat for the almost inexplicable paradox that St. Thomas was for the thirteenth century. As against Baeumker's conclusion, cf. E. Gilson, *Le thomisme*, 3rd ed., (*Etudes de philosophie médiévale*, I) Paris, 1927, p. 15, n. 3. Gilson explains the anti-Avicennian attitude of Peter of Ireland as being really only a particular expression of the spread of Averroism between 1244 and 1260.— The traditional current of thought, a mixture of Avicenna and Aristotle, has been traced by Baeumker in his *Die Stellung des Alfred Sareshel (Alfredus Anglicus) und seiner Schrift de Motu Cordis in der Wissenschaft des beginnenden XIII Jahrhunderts* (Sitzungsberichte der Bayer. Akad. der Wissenschaften . . . 1913, 9. Abhandl.) by way of Gundissalinus and Alfred Sareshel. Alfred's definition of the soul which, as we have seen, passed into St. Albert, is a striking but impossible mixture of Neoplatonism and Aristotle. Cf. *ibid.*, p. 48-52, and also E. Gilson, *Sources grécoarabes de l'augustinisme avicennisant* (*Archives*, 4, 1929) p. 102 ff.

an illuminating analysis of the problem of the soul in this tradition,[3] St. Thomas adopts a new point of departure, namely, the *unity of man,* and consequently his concern will be to show the implications in the doctrine of the *soul as form.* He will never admit that man is, in any Platonic sense, a soul using a body, and this on account of purely philosophical reasons. What these reasons are we must leave for the conclusion of the present work.

Among the early writing of St. Thomas it is still impossible to determine an exact chronology.[4] For our problem, particularly, a chronological determination of texts would be somewhat difficult. We must therefore proceed in a twofold way, following chronology as far as it will permit, and, at the same time, correcting such a method by the logical procedure which the subject demands. The Commentary on Peter Lombard will be used to state the problem, and then quotations will be made freely from those works which have been dated before or contemporaneous with the *Contra Gentiles* (c. 1260). As it is known, the whole second book is an elaborate discussion of practically all the points involved in

---

3. *Contra Gentiles,* II, 57. Notice that the analysis in this chapter has been prepared by a careful argument in c. 56 on the difficulties of substantial union: i. the impossibility of either mixture or contact; ii. the nature of *contactus virtutis;* iii. the resulting question of unity *secundum esse;* iv. the means of such unity, namely, the substantial form, which five arguments deny; which leads directly into the Platonic position of c. 57. It is out of this discussion that the Thomistic polemic on the soul, extending to within about a dozen questions of the end of the second book of the *Contra Gentiles,* takes its origin.—On II, 56-57, cf. *infra,* p. 147 ff.

4. The authorities on the chronology of St. Thomas Aquinas are P. Mandonnet and M. Grabmann. The result of their work will be found in B. Geyer, *Grundriss,* p. 424-426. A convenient table of this comparative chronology is given by E. Gilson, *Le thomisme,* 3rd ed. (*Etudes de philosophie médiévale,* I), Paris, 1927, p. 20-21.

the problem of the soul. From here on, the arrangement is somewhat chaotic, and I must trust to the logic of the subject and the relevency of the questions raised as guide. At the same time, where repetition will inevitably result, some attempt will be made to use the idea of parallel texts suggested by Joseph de Guibert, with a view to seeing what nuances the problem of the soul had in the mind of St. Thomas.[5]

From the Commentary on the *Sentences* we may take the following texts as the starting point: *Deinde quaeritur de simplicitate ex parte creaturae.* The division of this question introduce us to problems we have already discussed:

i. utrum aliqua creatura sit simplex.

ii. *utrum anima sit simplex, quia hoc habet specialem difficultatem.*

iii. utrum sit tota in qualibet parte corporis.[6]

In the first article we are immediately plunged into a metaphysical discussion on the necessity of composition in creatures, and from what we have seen of the rôle of Boethius in such discussions, we are not surprised to find St. Thomas using Boethius to announce his position: ''Contra, Boethius, I *De Trinitate,* cap. II: 'In omni eo quod est citra primum, differt et quod est et quo est.' Sed omnis creatura est citra primum. Ergo est composita ex esse et quod est.'' Every creature is thus composite, because, as it need not be, existence is external to its essence. Only God *is* what He is: everything else *has* what it is, and this non-implication of existence in every finite essence binds the creature in an initial and universal composition, namely, the composition of its essence or *quidditas* (*natura, quod est*) with the existence or *esse* (*quo est*) which it receives from God.[7]

---

5. Joseph de Guibert, *Les doublets de s. Thomas d'Aquin,* Paris, 1926.

6. *In I Sent.* d. 8, q. 5. ,a. 1-3; (ed. Vivès) vol. 7, p. 119-124.

7. ''Respondeo dicendum, quod omne quod procedit a Deo in

In what relation does the soul stand to this analysis?
That is the problem of the next article, namely, *utrum anima
sit simplex*. The objectors will introduce us to the problem.
They hold (*a*) that as the soul according to Aristotle is the
form of the body, and as it is neither matter nor the composite resulting from the union of body and soul, it must be
simple; (*b*) that it must be simple because whatever is composite exists through its components. Now as the soul has
a definite *esse* of its own, and as its union with the body
will produce an *esse* which belongs to man, we must not endanger the unity of man by admitting in him the presence
of an *esse animae* and an *esse conjuncti*, or of the composite
man. The soul must therefore be simple. (*c*) Finally, it is
objected that, if a twofold *esse* in man is accepted, then it
must follow that every composition beyond the first, which
is indeed the one that introduces a being into the category of
substance, is accidental. In accepting, therefore, an *esse
animae*, we must also hold that the soul is joined to the body
accidentally, and that man is thus an accidental unity.[8]

As against these arguments for the simplicity of the soul,
we find three arguments put forth by those who uphold the
composition of the soul. (*a*) Quoting Boethius, this objector
to the simplicity of the soul says that no simple form can be
a subject. But the soul is the subject of faculties, habits
and intelligible species. Consequently, the soul must be composite.[9] (*b*) Furthermore, a simple form does not exist

diversitate essentiae, deficit a simplicitate ejus . . . Quaedam enim
est quae habet esse completum in se, sicut homo et hujusmodi, et
talis creatura ita deficit a simplicitate divina quod incidit in compositionem. Cum enim in solo Deo esse suum sit sua quidditas,
oportet quod in qualibet creatura, vel in corporali vel in spirituali,
inveniatur quidditas vel natura sua, et esse suum, quod est sibi
acquisitum a Deo, cujus essentia est suum esse; et ita componitur
ex esse, vel quo est, et quod est" (*In I Sent.*, d. 8, q. 5, a. 1; p. 120).

8. *Ibid.*, a. 2, obj. 1-3; p. 120.

9. The text of Boethius is *De Trinitate*, c. II; Patrologia Latina,

through itself, and under such circumstances the existence of this form will be dependent on its subject whose existence is required for the continuation of its own. There is the additional consequence that such a form cannot be the *motor* of the body in which it exists, because, though it can be a principle of motion, to be a *motor* it would have to be a perfect or subsistent being in itself. Thus, the form of fire is not a *motor*, though it is a principle of motion. The soul, however, actually does survive the body and is its *motor*. It cannot therefore be simple. (*c*) Since every form is common to many, no simple form can become individualized through itself. If the soul is a simple form, its individualization will come not through itself but through the body. The third objector to the simplicity of the soul, therefore, comes to this conclusion. If the body is the principle of individuation, then, on the removal of the body, souls will not exist differentiated as individuals. With the principle of individuation gone, all that will be left is one soul which is the nature of the soul itself.[10]

vol. 64, col. 1250 D: "Forma vero, quae est sine materia, non poterit esse subjectum . . ."; but Boethius is clearly speaking here of such a form as *humanity* which as such, of course, exists *praeter materiam* as an individuating principle. Hence, the relevancy of this quotation is doubtful. Cf. St. Thomas, *In Boetium De Trinitate*, Lectio II, a. 2. *Respondeo*, ad 1-2.

10. *Ibid.*, obj. 4-6; p. 120-121. The texts of objections five and six are useful, five for the appearance of the word "motor" so important in the history of our problem, and six for the problem of individuation. "5. Praeterea, forma simplex non habet esse per se, ut dictum est. Sed illud quod non habet esse nisi per hoc quod est in altero, non potest remanere post illud, nec etiam potest esse motor, quamvis possit esse principium motus, quod movens est ens perfectum in se; unde forma ignis non est motor, ut dicitur VIII *Physic.*, text. 40. Anima autem manet post corpus, et est motor corporis. Ergo non est forma simplex.—6. Praeterea, nulla forma simplex habet in se unde individuetur, cum omnis forma sit de se communis. Si igitur anima est forma simplex, non habebit in se unde individuetur; sed tantum individuabitur

The problem, then, is this. To say that the soul is composite is to render the human compound an accidental unity, because the soul as a complete substance could not enter into a further composition in an essential way.[11] But if we make the soul simple, then it must necessarily perish with the body. Here, then, is the old antithesis: the soul is either a substance or it is a purely material form.[12] Furthermore, the problem of individuation through the body presents a real difficulty, because there appears to be no reason why anything more than the common nature of the soul should remain after the removal of the body. This enumeration of alternatives need not necessarily be complete, nor need the alternatives, as the logician would say, be mutually exclusive. But that is the way in which the problem is presented to St. Thomas: either alternative has to be accepted at the expense of the other. Composition involves substantiality, and simplicity accounts for the unity of man and at the same time endangers the substantial character of the soul. It is not difficult to see why St. Bonaventure should be preoccupied especially with safeguarding the substantiality of the soul; nor is it difficult to see why St. Albert should make its aspect as the form of the body a characteristic external to the essence of the soul.

The problem, therefore, appears to St. Thomas in its ex-

---

per corpus. Remoto autem eo quod est causa individuationis, tollitur individuatio. Ergo, remoto corpore, non remanebunt animae diversae secundum individua; et ita non remanebit nisi anima quae erit ipsa natura animae."

11. We may note here, what we shall have to develop later on, that it was this difficulty, according to St. Thomas Aquinas, which led to the Platonic conception of soul and body. If indeed we cannot say of soul and body that they are *unum per se*, we must change our perspective and consider man to be a soul using a body. Cf. *infra*, ch. iv, B.

12. This is Avicennian, according to which conception, as we have seen (cf. *supra*, p. 90), the alternatives were exactly these.

treme form and his task is precisely that of uniting the extremes. He turns his attention first to the analysis of the
two positions involved in this problem. Those who hold the
first opinion say that the soul is composed of matter and
form. For St. Thomas the source of this doctrine is Ibn
Gebirol. Now, among those who hold this doctrine there
are some who go to the extent of saying that the matter in
the soul, and in other substances, both corporeal and incorporeal, is the same.[13] St. Thomas does not consider this doctrine as true, for if the condition on which rests the intelli-

---

13. Apparently, St. Thomas is here distinguishing between
those who held the doctrine of spiritual matter and those who
said that the matter of corporeal and spiritual substances was the
same. St. Bonaventure, as we have seen, held the latter; but it is
not by any means easy to see who held the doctrine of two basically different kinds of matter. J. Guttmann has attributed such a
doctrine to Alexander of Hales: cf. *Die Scholastik des Dreizehnten
Jahrhunderts in ihren Beziehungen zum Judenthum und zur Judi-
schen Literatur*, Breslau, 1902, p. 39-41. M. De Wulf, *Histoire de la
philosophie médiévale*, 3e ed., Louvain, 1924, vol. 1, p. 331, with
note 2, seems to follow Guttmann. But this attribution is not certain, because at least one of Alexander's texts suggests that he is
not thinking of matter *prior* to distinction through forms, which,
of course, has nothing to do with the problem of matter apart from
all determinations. Cf. Alexander of Hales, *Summa Theologica*,
Inq. iii, tract. i, quaest. 1, no. 249, *Solutio*, ad *Si vero dicatur;* ed.
Quaracchi, vol. ii, 1928, p. 310, where he indicates a difference to
be observed according as one considers matter from the standpoint
of an existing determination or from one prior to any determination.

As to what St. Thomas thought on the origins of the conflicting
doctrines of matter in his day, cf. *In II Sent.*, d. 3, q. 1, a. 1, *Solutio*, (Vivès) vol. 8, p. 46: "Respondeo dicendum, quod circa hanc
materiam tres sunt positiones. Quidam enim dicunt quod in omni
substantia creata est materia, et quod omnium est materia una;
et hujus positionis auctor videtur Avicebron, qui fecit librum *Fons
Vitae*, quem multi sequuntur. Secunda positio est quod materia
non est in substantiis incorporeis sed tamen est in omnibus corporibus, etiam una; et haec est positio Avicennae . . . Tertia positio
est quod corpora caelestia et elementa non communicant in ma-

gibility of a form is freedom from matter, then such a position
is clearly not true. Nor can we say that this is true only in
those cases where matter exists under a corporeal form, for the
corporeal form itself is intelligible when separated from matter. And that is why those substances that are intelligible by
nature do not appear to be material. Furthermore, prime
matter, considered apart from all forms, has no diversity in it
whatever. Consequently, the first substantial form which is
united to it will perfect the whole matter. As Averroes had
pointed out, this first substantial form is a corporeal form
which matter never loses. It appears, therefore, that the form
of corporeity exists in all matter, and that matter belongs
only to bodies. There can be no diversity in matter except
as corporeal and possessed of spatially distinct parts.[14]   In

---

teria, et haec est positio Averrois, . . . et Rabbi Moysis . . . et videtur magis dictis Aristotelis consonare; et ideo istam eligimus, quantum ad praesens pertinet . . ." A little later, St. Thomas, again
concerned with the question whether there is one matter for all
corporeal substances, mentions Averroes as the opponent of this
doctrine defended by Avicenna, and again sides against Avicenna:
"Et ideo ipse vult quod nullo modo in materia conveniant superiora
et inferiora corpora: et hoc videtur probabilius, et magis con-
sonum dictis Philosophi . ." *(In II Sent.,* d. 12, q. 1, a. 1, *Solutio;*
vol. 8, p. 157-158). The "ipse" is Averroes. Notice the comparison
of both Avicenna and Averroes with Aristotle as expressing the
anxiety of St. Thomas to establish the position of the historical
Aristotle.

14. On the *forma corporeitatis,* cf.: "Corporeitas autem dupliciter accipi potest:—Uno modo, secundum quod est forma substantialis corporis, prout in genere substantiae collocatur; *et sic corporeitas cujuscumque corporis nihil aliud est quam forma substantialis ejus,* secundum quam in genere et specie collocatur, ex
qua debetur rei corporali quod habeat tres dimensiones . . . Alio
modo accipitur corporeitas prout est forma accidentalis, secundum
quam dicitur corpus esse in genere quantitatis; et sic corporeitas
nihil aliud est quam tres dimensiones quae corporis rationam con-
stituunt." *(Contra Gentiles,* IV, 81). With this cp. an earlier text:
". . . sicut et forma quaelibet ex hoc ipso quod per essentiam suam
materiam informat, est origo proprietatum quae compositum na-

fact (taking up the argument of the *De Substantiis Separatis*), to suppose a common matter underlying both corporeal and spiritual substance is to require a principle of division and diversity. If this common matter is the subject of both spiritual and corporeal forms, then, *the diversity of matter itself* is the ground of the forms to be received in matter; and therefore the diversity which we require cannot be understood as coming from the forms. If, on the supposition of a common matter, the diversity must come from some forms, then it is through prior forms received throughout matter (for to suppose that these forms are received in part would imply an existing diversity, which contradicts the assumption of a common matter). Nor is this all. We now require the presence of some diversity in matter which will underlie this receptivity of more than one form. As a result, this requirement of a prior form must be unending, or we must say that the first diversity preceding the reception of the forms lies in the matter itself.[15]

----

turaliter consequuntur." *(In IV Sent.,* d. 44, q. 3, a. 3, quaestiuncula 3; vol. 11, p. 348).—Cf. *Summa Theologica,* I-II, q. 56, a. 1, ad 3, and III, q. 77, a. 2. It is the first of these two definitions of *corporeitas* which is important for us. The *forma corporeitatis* is the substantial form. St. Thomas never hesitated on this point.

15. "Quidam enim dicunt, quod anima est composita ex materia et forma; quorum etiam sunt quidam dicentes, eandem esse materiam animae et aliorum corporalium et spiritualium. Sed hoc non videtur esse verum, quia nulla forma efficitur intelligibilis, nisi per hoc quod separatur a materia et ab appendentiis materiae. Hoc autem non est inquantum est materia corporalis perfecta corporeitate, cum ipsa forma corporeitatis sit intelligibilis per separationem a materia. Unde illae substantiae quae sunt intelligibiles per naturam, non videntur esse materiales: alias species rerum in ipsis non essent secundum esse intelligibiles. Et propterea materia prima, prout consideratur nuda ab omni forma, non habet aliquam diversitatem, nec efficitur diversa per aliqua accidentia ante adventum formae substantialis, cum esse accidentale non praecedat substantiale. Uni autem perfectibili debetur una perfectio. Ergo oportet quod prima forma substantialis perfecit totam materiam.

The matter of reality, therefore, is not one. If there is
anything that distinguishes matter at all it is its potentiality,
and, as this potentiality is undistinguished, those who defend
the sameness of matter in spiritual and corporeal substances
have to account for the fact that this apparently undistinguished potentiality has different modes of reception. And
there is a difference in the mode of receiving forms between
corporeal and spiritual substances, for, while a spiritual substance receives a form according to the totality of its nature,
a material substance receives a form only as realized in its
particular representatives. However, therefore, we may consider the matter, the first conclusion that seems to follow is
this: *Relinquitur igitur quod materia, si sit in spiritualibus,
non est eadem cum materia corporalium rerum, sed multo*

Sed prima forma quae recipitur in materia, est corporeitas, a qua
nunquam denudatur, ut dicit Commemtator in I *Physic.*, text. com.
63. Ergo forma corporeitatis est in tota materia, et ita materia
non erit nisi in corporibus. Si enim diceres, quod quidditas substantiae esset prima forma recepta in materia, adhuc redibit in
idem; quia ex quidditate substantiae materia non habet divisionem,
sed ex corporeitate, quam consequuntur dimensiones quantitatis
in actu; et postea per divisionem materiae, secundum quod diversis sitibus, acquiruntur in ipsa diversae formae . . . ; et ideo
non videtur quod anima habeat materiam, nisi materia aequivoce
sumatur" (*In I Sent.*, d. 8, q. 5, a. 2, *Solutio;* vol. 7, p. 121).—Cp.
In II Sent., d. 3, q. 1, a. 1, *Solutio;* vol. 8, p. 46.

In the *De Substantiis Separatis*, c. IV, ad *Quarto, quia anti-
quis;* (ed. Mandonnet *Opuscula Omnia*, vol. 1, p. 89), St. Thomas
argues even more clearly against the *unity* and universality of
matter: "Si igitur ponatur universalis materia, quae est communis
omnium substantia, non habens in sui ratione quantitatem; ejus
divisio non potest intelligi nisi vel secundum formam, vel secundum materiam ipsam. Cum autem dicitur quod materia incorporea communis partim recipit formam hanc, et partim recipit
formam illam; divisio materiae praesupponitur diversitati formarum in materia receptarum. Non igitur illa divisio potest secundum has formas intelligi. Si ergo intelligatur secundum formas
aliquas, oportet quod intelligatur secundum formas priores; quas
neutra materia per totam recipit. Unde oportet iterum in materia

altior et sublimior, utpote recipiens formam secundum ejus totalitatem.[16]

The immediate result of such a difference is that the term matter loses its meaning when applied to spiritual substance. This is what St. Thomas now proceeds to show. Though all philosophers, he observes, admit the simplicity of the first cause, there are some who argue that matter and form enter as the component parts of intelligences and of souls. Now such a position does not agree with what philosophers have thought concerning these substances, because they have considered them to be separate from matter. The strongest argument they advanced in defense of this contention was based on the power of knowing possessed by these substances. The forms of things are not really intelligible

---

praeintelligere divisionem vel distinctionem quamcumque. Erit igitur et haec secundum aliquas formas in infinitum, vel oportet devenire ad hoc quod prima divisio sit secundum ipsam materiam. *Non est autem divisio·secundum materiam nisi quia materia secundum seipsam distinguitur*, non propter diversam dispositionem vel formam aut quantitatem . . . Oportet igitur quod finaliter deveniatur ad hoc quod non sit una omnium materia . . ."—Cp. *In II Sent.*, q. 1, a. 1, ad 1; vol. 8, p. 158.

The first point, therefore, to observe in the question of spiritual matter is that, if it exists at all, it is not the same basically as that of corporeal substances. Then we can proceed to the further question of determining whether or not spiritual matter exists. The greatest argument for it is that "non posset esse diversitas in spiritualibus substantiis, si non essent ex materia et forma compositae" (*De Sub. Sep.*, c. V; p. 92). For the present we can say that individuality does not come from this composition alone.

16. *De Sub. Sep.*, c. V; p. 91.—Cf. "Oportet igitur quod finaliter deveniatur ad hoc quod non sit una omnium materia, sed sint multae et distinctae secundum seipsas. Materiae autem proprium est in potentia esse. Hanc igitur materiae distinctionem accipere oportet non secundum quod est vestita diversis formis aut dispositionibus (hoc enim est praeter essentiam materiae), sed secundum distinctionem potentiae respectu diversitatis formarum" (*De Sub. Sep.*. c. V; p. 89).

unless separated from their matter by the power of the intellect in the act of knowing and at the moment when they are received in the intellect. The intellect must therefore be free from matter in the sense that neither is a part of it matter nor is it impressed in matter as are the material forms. In other words, we can admit neither the composition of matter and form in the soul nor the existence of the soul in the body as a material form.[17] Nor can we say that matter is unintelligible because of its corporeal form, since, as we have seen, the corporeal form is only the substantial form of the individual substance which is itself perfectly intelligible when separated from its individuating conditions. As a result, we

---

17. As a matter of fact, only a few years later (c. 1260) St. Thomas Aquinas will reduce these two positions to one, differing, according to him, only *secundum nomen*. On the general principle announced in *Contra Gentiles*, II, 50, ("Sicut homo non est sine hoc homine, ita materia non est sine hac materia. Quicquid igitur in rebus est subsistens ex materia et forma compositum, est compositum ex materia et forma individuali"), he proceeds to his analysis of our question: "Amplius, si intellectus esset forma in materia et non per se subsistens, sequeretur quod id quod recipitur in intellectu reciperetur in materia; hujusmodi enim formae quae habent esse in materia obligatum non recipiunt aliquid quod in materia non recipiatur. Quum igitur receptio formarum in intellectu non sit receptio in materia, impossibile est quod intellectus sit forma materialis. Praeterea, Dicere quod intellectus sit forma non subsistens, sed materiae immersa, idem est secundum rem ac si dicatur quod intellectus sit compositus ex materia et forma; differt autem solum secundum nomen; nam primo modo diceretur intellectus forma ipsa compositi, secundo vero modo diceretur intellectus ipsum compositum" (II, 51).

St. Bonaventure would come under this criticism: "Et ideo est tertius modus dicendi, tenens medium inter utrumque, scilicet quod anima rationalis, cum sit *hoc aliquid* et per se nata subsistere et agere et pati, movere et moveri, quod habet intra se *fundamentum* suae existentiae et *principium materiale*, a quo habet *existere* et *formale*, a quo habet *esse*. De brutali autem non oportet illud dicere cum ipsa fundatur in corpore" (*In II Sent.*, d. 17, q. 2, concl., op. 3; vol. 2, p. 414).

must place this repugnance to intelligibility in matter itself.[18]

Metaphysics supports the tradition of philosophers, as we may determine by noting what composition is to be admitted

18. "Nunc restat videre per quem modum sit essentia in sub-stantiis separatis, scilicet in anima et in intelligencia et in causa prima. Quamvis autem simplicitatem prime cause omnes conce-dant tamen compositionem forme et materie quidam nituntur in-ducere et in intelligencias et in animam; cujus positionis videtur auctor fuisse Avicebron, auctor libri *Fontis uitae.* Hoc enim dictis philosophorum communiter repugnat, quoniam eas substantias separatas a materia nominant et absque omni materia esse pro-bant. Cujus dicti ratio potissima est ex virtute intelligendi qui in eis est. Videmus enim formas non esse intelligibiles nisi secundum quod separantur a materia et a conditionibus eius, nec efficiuntur intelligibiles in actu nisi per virtutem substantie intelligentis, se-cundum quod aguntur per eam. Unde oportet quod in qualibet substantia intelligentie sit omnino immunitas a materia ita quod neque habeat materiam partem sui neque sit eciam sicut forma impressa in materia ut est de formis materialibus. Nec potest ali-quis dicere quod intelligibilitatem non impediat materia quelibet sed materia corporalis tantum. Si enim hoc esset ratione ma-terie corporalis tantum, cum materia non dicatur corporalis nisi secundum quod stat sub forma corporali, tunc oporteret quod hoc haberet materia, scilicet impedire intelligibilitatem, a forma corporali, et hoc non potest esse quia et ipsa forma eciam corpora-lis actu intelligibilis est, sicut et alie forme, secundum quod a materia abstrahitur. Unde in anima uel intelligentia nullo modo est compositio ex materia et forma ut hoc modo accipiatur essentia in eis sicut in substantiis corporalibus" (*De Ente et Essentia*, c. iv; ed. M.-D. Roland-Gosselin, *Bibliothèque thomiste*, viii, Le Saul-choir, 1926, p. 29-32). Cf. *ibid.*, p. 30, note 2, where references to mediaeval Augustinians who held the doctrine of spiritual matter will be found.—For the *forma corporalis* cf. *supra*, note 14; while the following text from St. Bonaventure will explain what St. Thomas is here opposing: "Ad illud quod obiicitur, quod substantia intellectiva nihil cognoscit, nisi quod abstrahitur a materia; dicen-dum, quod hoc non facit propter hoc, quod ipsa sit omnino imma-terialis, sed propter hoc, quod res non potest ei uniri secundum *veritatem.* Ideo oportet, quod uniatur secundum *similitudinem*, quam anima abstrahit a re.—Alia est etiam ratio, quia intellectus per similitudinem, per quam intelligit, debet fieri in actu intelli-

in spiritual substances. St. Thomas calls it the composition of *forma* and *esse,* or of *quod est* and *quo est*.[19] The pure intelligences of Proclus and of the *Liber de Causis* are composed of *forma* and *esse,* and *forma* here means the essence of simple quiddity of the intelligence. The first point to note in such a composition is that whatever gives existence to the composite can exist itself without the other component; and, as in the relation of matter and form it is the form which gives existence to the compound, the form can exist apart from the matter, as not depending on it, but the matter must always be with the form in order to exist.

Now, essences themselves are not composite, but simple. But, as the essences of composite substances are received in matter, they are individualized according to each subject, and are thus specifically alike, but numerically different.[20] In the case of the simple essence, however, which has no subject, but subsists by itself, such individuation is impossible; so

---

gendi; illud autem, quod facit, rem esse in actu, species est et forma. Ideo anima non cognoscit rem, nisi speciem eius et formam sibi imprimat: et hoc non potest esse nisi illa abstrahatur a materia. Nec ex hoc sequitur, quod anima careat materia; res enim abstracta a materia propria bene potest fieri in re alia, quae suam habet propriam materiam et formam, sicut similitudo coloris in speculo" (*In II Sent.,* d. 17, a. 1, q. 2, ad 4; vol. 2, p. 415).

19. His point of departure is a reference to the *Liber de Causis* to the effect that only the One is simple: cf. *In II Sent.,* d. 3, q. 1, a. 1, *Solutio*; vol. 8, p. 47, and *De Ente et Essentia,* c. 4; (ed. Roland-Gosselin) p. 32. This is how St. Thomas understands the *Liber De Causis* reference: "In tantum igitur intelligentia est composita in suo esse ex finito et infinito, inquantum natura intelligentiae dicitur secundum potentiam essendi, et ipsum esse quod recipit est finitum" (*In Lib. de Causis,* Lect. IV, Vivès ed., vol. 26, p. 525 (ed. Mandonnet, vol. 1, p. 216); cp. *De Sub. Sep.,* c. VI, p. 98, for the infinity of the essence. For the *Liber de Causis* and Proclus on the composition of essence (infinitum) and existence (finitum), cf. Roland-Gosselin, *op. cit.,* p. 146-149.

20. *De Ente et Essentia, ibid.;* p. 33; *In II Sent.,* d. 3, q. 1, a. 1, *Solutio,* ad *Et tamen aliquam;* vol. 8, p. 46-47.

that each angel exhausts the perfection of a whole species. Furthermore, an angel and an individual substance agree in this, that neither of them possesses necessary existence, and the composition of *quod est* and *quo est,* or potency and act, explains their separation from the necessary character of the divine essence. We are here concerned, therefore, with two types of receptivity. St. Thomas thus concludes that, if we wish to call by the name of matter the possibility of receiving existence, we may do so, remembering that such usage is only equivocal, and that, after all, *sapientis . . . est non curare de nominibus.*

Consequently, if we wish to say that the soul or an angel is simple, we may do so, if we mean that neither of them has any parts. At the same time, we must observe that, as derived substances, both suffer the limitation or, if you will, the composition of not necessarily implying existence *in rerum natura* by their own essence.[21] Briefly, then, as only

---

21. "Et quia omne quod non habet aliquid a se, est possibile respectu illius; huiusmodi quidditas cum habeat esse ab alio, erit possibilis respectu illius esse, et respectu ejus a quo esse habet, in quo nulla cadit potentia; et ita in tali quidditate invenietur potentia et actus, secundum quod ipsa quidditas est possibilis, et esse suum est actus ejus. Et hoc modo intelligo in angelis compositionem potentiae et actus, et de "quo est" et "quod est", et similiter in anima. Unde angelus vel anima potest dici quidditas vel natura vel forma simplex, inquantum eorum quidditas non componitur ex diversis; sed tamen advenit ibi compositio horum duorum, scilicet quidditatis et esse" (*In II Sent.,* d. 8, q. 5, a. 2, *Solutio,* vol. 7, p. 121-122).—"Et quia ut dictum est, intelligencie quiditas est ipsamet intelligentia, ideo quiditas vel essentia ejus est ipsum quod est ipsa, et esse suum, receptum a Deo, est id quo subsistit in rerum natura; et propter hoc a quibusdam dicuntur hujusmodi substantiae composite ex quo est ex quod est, vel ex quod est esse ut Boecius dicit" (*De Ente et Essentia,* c. IV, *ed. cit.,* p. 35-36). On the *aequivoce,* cf. *De Sub. Sep.* c. VI; ed. Mandonnet, p. 97-98; "Quia igitur materia recipit esse determinatum actuale per formam, et non e converso; nihil prohibet esse aliquam formam quae recipit esse in seipsa, non in aliquo subjecto; non enim causa dependet ab effectu,

the possibility to exist extends to creatures, we must note that there is a difference in the way in which this existence is realized in spiritual and material substances. Spiritual substances are the immediate subjects of the act of existence, while matter is the immediate subject of a form through which it will receive existence. The potentiality of a spiritual substance refers to existence alone; the potentiality of matter refers at once to a form and to existence. To extend the term matter to both spiritual and corporeal substances is to lose sight of the single composition present in spiritual substances and the twofold composition present in material

---

sed potius e converso. Ipsa igitur forma sic per se subsistens, esse participat in seipsa, sicut forma materialis in subjecto. Si igitur per hoc quod dico, *non ens*, removeatur solum esse in actu; ipsa forma secundum se considerata, est non ens, sed esse participans. Si autem *non ens* removeat non solum ipsum esse in actu, sed etiam actum seu formam, per quam aliquid participat esse; sic materia est non ens, forma vero subsistens non est non ens, sed est actus, quae est forma participativa ultimi actus, qui est esse. Patet igtiur in quo differt potentia quae est in substantiis spiritualibus, a potentia quae est in materia. Nam potentia substantiae spiritualis attenditur *solum* secundum ordinem ipsius ad esse; potentia vero materiae secundum ordinem *et* ad formam *et* ad esse. Si quis autem utrumque materiam esse dicat, manifestum est quod aequivoce materiam nominabit."—We must observe a further result on the basis of this *aequivoce;* "Unde eciam pati, recipere, *subiectum esse*, et omnia huiusmodi quae videntur rebus ratione materiae convenire, equivoce conveniant substantiis intellectualibus et corporalibus . . ." (*De Ente et Essentia*, c. IV., *ed. cit.*, p. 35).

Furthermore, the problem of individuation among the angels is to be seen in the light of the potency and act composition, according as there is more of one or the other depending on the position in the scale of being (p. 36). On the other hand, having once made this purely metaphysical determination, he will say quite readily enough, "quamvis earum *differentie* proprie nobis occulte sunt" (c. V; p. 40). The *differentie* is, of course, the specific character of each angel as a member of a genus; cf. *In II Sent.*, d. 3, q. 1, a. 5; vol. 8, p. 53, *Sed contra* and *Solutio*, where the name of Avicenna is quite significant.

substances. And that is why the term matter loses its significance when applied to spiritual substances.

Such considerations enable us to answer the question of the soul's simplicity. The soul is not composite if composition means matter and form; it is composite if composition means the derivation of its being from God. But if the composition of *quo est* and *quod est* reveals to us the subsistent yet derived nature of the soul, it does not reveal to us anything concerning the inner structure of its substance. We must see the soul in operation in order to discover what kind of substance it is. In other words, we must see the rôle played by the individual soul in the human composite. And this opens up, in fact, the problem of the soul as the form of man.

Now it is clear that the problem lies in this. Since the soul has a subsistent existence, what must be the manner of its union with the body to insure both the unity of man and the subsistence of the soul? The unity of man requires that there be a unique principle of existence in the composite, and as it is the soul which is the principle of man's existence, it must be through the soul that man exists. In other words, the existence which belongs to the soul as a subsistent form will become the existence of the being of which it is a form: *esse enim conjuncti non est nisi esse formae.*[22] Nor are we thereby endangering the substantiality of the soul, for if the soul gives being to its matter, it does not follow that therefore its own subsistence is lost and that now it is simply a principle whereby the composite exists. There is no incompatibility between saying that the soul is subsistent and that it is the principle of man's subsistence. It is an imperfection rather than a perfection for forms to be merely the principle whereby composites exist: *Sed verum est quod aliae formae materiales, propter earum imperfectionem, non subsistunt*

---

22. *In I Sent.*, d. 8, q. 5, a. 2, ad 2; vol. 7, p. 122.

per illud esse, sed sunt tantum principia essendi;[23] *sed quia anima est forma absoluta, non dependens a materia, quod convenit sibi propter assimilationem et propinquitatem ad Deum, ipsa habet esse per se quod non habent aliae formae corporales.*[24]

As soul and body share the *esse* of the soul in the unity of the individual man, the question of individuation has to be considered. We shall deal with it briefly, however, pointing out the principle that St. Thomas lays down and the source of his formulation of that principle, Avicenna. If the soul were a *hoc aliquid,* as St. Bonaventure held, then it would be individuated in itself;[25] and that is why, observes St. Thomas, those who denied the soul to be a *hoc aliquid* but affirmed its subsistence said that there was nothing in the soul to individuate it.[26] We must say, then, that the soul is

---

23. *Ibid.*

24. Ibid., ad 1.

25. In St Bonaventure, as we have seen, the soul was composed of matter and form, and therefore, as such a composition results, according to him, in individuality, the soul is an individual in itself.—Cf. the short discussion and especially the references to St. Bonaventure's texts in Roland-Gosselin, *op. cit.,* p. 80-81.

26. St. Thomas is clearly referring to a doctrine that could be found in his master:

St. Albert	St. Thomas
"Ad aliud dicendum, quod anima sit hoc aliquid, hoc est dictum a Magistris, non a Philosophis, nec a Sanctis: et puto, quod sit dictum falsum: quoniam in principio libri II de *Anima* habetur, quod materia non est hoc aliquid, nec etiam forma, et quod anima non est hoc aliquid: sed hoc bene concedo, quod anima est substantia composita:	"Ad sextum dicendum, quod, secundum praedicta, in anima non est aliquid quo individuetur, et hoc bene intellexerunt qui negaverunt eam esse hoc aliquid, et non quod non habeat per se absolutum esse" (*In I Sent.,* d. 8, q. 5, a. 2, ad 6; vol. 8, p. 122).

sed ipsa non est composita ut hoc aliquid; quia secundum naturam habet dependentiam ad corpus, licet posset esse sine illo. Sed bene concedo, quod perfectio sua non est omnino completa sine illo" (*In II Sent.,* d. 17, C, a. 2, ad 2; vol. 27, p. 299).

individuated *ex corpore,* and this logically rules out pre-existence, because plurality among souls exists according as they are infused into many bodies. But the real difficulty is concerned with the individuality of the soul after it leaves the body. It is still individual after its separation from the body, though ordinarily one might have thought that as individuation comes from the body, it ceases when the soul is separated from the body. St. Thomas rejects this, and his reason is as follows. Although the soul depends upon the body of which it is the form as the occasion of its own individuation, because when it comes into existence it is as the form of *this* body, nevertheless, with the removal of the body, it does not follow that individuation is lost, because the soul, in being subsistent, will naturally retain its individual perfection, just as it will retain its existence. There is no reason why, if it can exist by itself, it should not continue to be what it has become through the body, retaining all the dispositions that it has thus received.[27]

There is one more question in the early text of St. Thomas which we must discuss: *utrum anima sit tota in toto corpore*

---

27. "Et dico quod non individuatur nisi ex corpore. Unde impossibilis est error ponentium animas primo creatas, et postea incorporeatas: quia non efficiuntur plures nisi secundum quod iunguntur pluribus corporibus" (*ibid.*). "Et licet individuatio eius (*scil.* animae) ex corpore occasionaliter dependeat quantum ad sui inchoationem, quia non acquiritur sibi esse individuatum nisi in corpore cuius est actus, non tamen oportet quod, substracto corpore, individuatio pereat, quia cum habeat esse absolutum ex quo acquisitum est sibi esse individuatum ex hoc quod facta est forma huius corporis, illud esse semper remanet individuatum; et ideo dicit Avicenna quod individuatio animarum et multitudo dependet ex corpore quantum ad sui principium sed non quantum ad sui finem" (*De Ente et Essentia,* c. V; (*ed. Roland-Gosselin*) p. 39-40). In the text of the Commentary on the *Sentences* (*In I Sent.,* d. 8, q. 5, a. 2, ad 6; vol. 8, p. 123), after giving a similar solution, he writes even more clearly on his relation to Avicenna in this prob-

et tota in qualibet parte.[28]   The conclusion of St. Thomas is aimed largely at the doctrine to be found in the *De Motu Cordis* of Alfredus Anglicus and also accepted by St. Albert. St. Albert had argued that the soul is not *tota in qualibet parte.* Against the position that St. Albert[29] thus adopts

---

lem: *"Et haec est solutio Avicennae."* Here are the texts of Avicenna on the point:

"Impossibile est ut animae in ipso esse habeant multitudinem. Multitudo enim rerum aut est ex essentia et forma, aut est ex comparatione qua est ad materiam et originem multiplicatam ex locis quae circumdant unamquamque materiam secundum aliquid, aut ex temporibus propriis uniuscuiusque illarum quae accidunt illis accidentibus, aut ex causis dividentibus illam . . . Si anima autem esset tantum absque corpore, una anima non posset esse alia ab alia numero" (*De Anima*, V, 3, Venetiis, 1508, f. 24b B; quoted by Roland-Gosselin, *op. cit., p.* 61, n. 2).

"Singularitas ergo animarum est aliquid quod esse incipit, et non est aeterum quod fuerit semper. Sed incipit esse cum corpore tantum. Ergo jam manifestum est animas incipere esse cum incipit materia corporalis apta ad serviendum eis, et corpus creatum est regnum ejus et instrumentum. Sed in substantia animae quae incipit esse cum aliquo corpore, propter quod debuit creari, inest ex primis principiis affectio inclinationis naturalis ad occupandum se circa illud. . . Corpori autem singulari principium singularitatis suae accidit ex affectionibus quibus exprimitur singulare per quas affectiones illa anima fit propria illius corporis, quae sunt habitudines quibus unum fit dignum altero, quamvis non facile intelligatur a nobis illa affectio et illa comparatio" (*ibid.;* quoted by Roland-Gosselin, *op. cit.,* p. 66, n. 1).

"Postquam autem fit singularis per se est impossibile ut sit anima alia numero et ut sit una essentia" (*Op. cit.,* V. 3, f. 24va; quoted by Roland-Gosselin, *ibid.*). Conclusions: i. the soul is created in the body; ii. the individuality or singularity, once obtained, is not lost.—Finally, we may note that this theory passed into St. Albert the Great: *Sum. de Creat.,* P. II, tract. 1, q. 5, a. 1, *Sed contra,* 3; vol. 35, p. 78.

28. *In I Sent.,* d. 8, q. 5, a. 3; vol. 7, p. 123.

29 *De Anima,* lib. II, tract. 1, cap. 7; vol. 5, p. 203: *Utrum quaelibet virium animae sit anima, et utrum sit tota in toto?*

from the *De Motu Cordis* St. Bonaventure and St. Thomas both will hold that the soul is *tota in qualibet parte,* as St. Augustine had held. One of the arguments used was that the soul feels with equal readiness an injury in any part of the body. There is a much more serious objection, however, to St. Albert's doctrine. In fact, to think of the soul as

(a) The indivisibility of the soul would lead one to think that it was *tota in toto*: "Cum igitur anima sit indivisibilis, oportet quod sit tota in toto. Amplius constat quod quaelibet vis sua essentiae animae est immediata: ergo tota anima cum sit indivisibilis, adest cuilibet virtuti: sed virtutes diffusae sunt per totum corpus: ergo ipsa est in toto corpore tota" (p. 204).

(b) But against this position is the following curious difficulty: "Sed contrarium huic videtur esse, quia ex hoc sequitur quod sit in oculo tota: et si extrahatur oculus, videbitur tunc extrahi tota anima: quod non est verum". Whence followed the Platonic position: "et haec omnia moverunt Platonem ad dicendum quod in uno corpore sunt multae animae" (*ibid.*). This latter assertion St. Albert will, of course, deny: "Sed dicendum quod in uno corpore non est nisi anima una . . ." (*ibid.*).

(c) Here is the conclusion that St. Albert, therefore, reaches: "Dicimus quod anima est una et habet partes organicas, quae omnes continuationem habent ad unam quae est cor, et tunc dicendum quod anima est in corde, et inde influit potestates suas in totum corpus, et sic non est in toto tota, ita quod in qualibet parte sit tota, sed in qualibet parte est secundum aliquam suarum potentiarum: . . . et licet essentia ejus adsit cuilibet virtuti ejus, non tamen virtute separata separatur necessario essentia ejus: quia virtus illa affixa est illi organo et non essentia animae, sed potius illa est in corde, quod est organum essentiae animae deputatum: et ideo non separatur a corde essentia nisi secundum hanc operationem quam habet in membro separato et non simpliciter . . . Et haec est Peripateticorum sententia. Fuerunt tamen et *sunt quidam adhuc,* qui dixerunt quod anima est tota in toto corpore, quod non tamen fuit opinio *alicujus Philosophi*: et dixerunt quod non extrahitur tota in oculo, quia dicunt quod manet in alia parte principaliori secundum vitae operationem: et ideo corpus animatum remanet adhuc animatum et vivum. Non enim tota dicebatur in oculo, nisi secundum quod tota substat virtuti visivae: hoc autem

present only in the heart *secundum suam essentiam* is, according to St. Thomas, to think of the soul as occupying the body
spatially, as if it were only the *motor* and not the *forma* of
the body. According to such a spatial conception, the soul
would be in the body as a sailor is in a ship. Again, to think
of the soul as occupying only one part of the body essentially
is to conceive of its simplicity and indivisibility after the

---

est secundum quod per ipsam operatur visus: et hoc modo conce-
dunt eam separari totam, quia de ea postea visum operatur. Ego
autem multas dictarum opinionum non intelligens dicendum puto
esse cum Peripateticis, quod anima totalitatem non habet nisi
suorum organorum, et ideo in uno corpore non est nisi secundum
unam partem, et remanet in aliis potestatibus suis adhuc operans
in corpore: uniens autem has potestates est substantia quae est in
corde: et potestates omnes animae diriguntur ad cor, et sic substantiae animae adjacent tanquam ad eam directae, sicut organa
corporis omnia connectuntur cordi" (*ibid.*; p. 205). For the
opinion *alicujus Philosophi*, cf. Alfredus Anglicus, *De Motu Cordis*,
c. 2, 5-6 (ed. C. Baeumker, *Beiträge*, Band XXIII, Heft 1-2, Munster
i. W., 1923, p. 11-12); c. 7. 6-8 (p. 27-28); c. 8. 8-9 (p. 34-35).—Cf.
supra, chapter III, note 21.

St. Bonaventure has little respect for this doctrine of the heart
as the *domicilium vitae*, and he will say without reservation that
"ad hoc ponendum movit eos *experimentum* cum *defectu rationis.*"
That he is referring to the *De Motu Cordis* is clearly probable from
an interpolation by one of the scribes, (cod. K), who observes
"sicut dicitur in libro de *Motu cordis.*" St. Bonaventure will therefore follow St. Augustine and say that "anima in qualibet parte
corporis sit tota". His reasons we have seen already; cf. his discussion in *In I Sent.*, d. 8, p. 2, a. unicus, q. 3, *Respondeo* and ad
1-2; vol. 1, p. 171-172.

Though it is true that the *De Anima* of St. Albert the Great
was written after St. Thomas' Commentary on the *Sentences*, the
doctrine is still the one referred to by St. Thomas and can be seen,
for example, in his teacher's early work, the *Summa de Creaturis*:
cf. P. II, tract. 1, q. 78, *Solutio;* vol. 35, p. 636-637, where, however,
the name of Alfredus Anglicus or reference to the *De Motu Cordis*
is lacking. However, the implication of the whole *Solutio* is that
the soul is *tota in toto*, but *in qualibet parte* only *secundum potentiam.*

manner of a point, and thus to conceive it also to be something indivisible inhabiting an indivisible place.[30]

On the contrary, we must reject such foolish tricks of the imagination and say with St. Augustine[31]that the soul is essentially in every part of the body. The reason for this is that every part of the body has existence through the soul as its form. As to the powers of the soul, it is clear that they are in the various organs of the body according to the various dispositions of these organs. It is the first point in which St. Thomas is interested. Once he has pointed out that the soul is joined to the body immediately as a form, and therefore completely to each part, he will say, as all did say,

---

30. "Respondeo dicendum, quod quidam posuerunt animam dupliciter posse considerari: aut secundum suam essentiam, aut secundum quod est quoddam totum potentiale. Si primo modo, sic dicebant, ipsam non esse in toto corpore, sed in. aliqua parte ejus, scilicet corde, et per cor vivificare totum corpus per spiritus vitales procedentes a corde. Si secundo modo, sic anima consideratur ut quaedam potentia integrata ex omnibus particularibus potentiis, et sic tota animá est in toto corpore, et non tota in qualibet parte corporis . . . Hujus autem positionis causa fuit duplex falsa imaginatio: una est, quia imaginati sunt animam esse in corpore sicut in loco, ac si tantum esset motor, et non forma, sicut est nauta in navi; alia est, quia imaginati sunt simplicitatem animae esse ad modum puncti, ut sit aliquid indivisibile habens situm indivisibilem. Et utrumque horum stultum est" (*In I Sent.*, d. 8, q. 5, a. 3, *Respondeo;* vol. 7, p. 123).

31. "Creatura quoque spiritualis sicut est anima, est quidem in corporis comparatione simplicior: sine comparatione autem corporis multiplex est, etiam ipsa non simplex. Nam ideo simplicior est corpore, quia non mole diffunditur per spatium loci, sed in unoquoque corpore, et in toto tota est, et in qualibet ejus parte tota est; et ideo cum fit aliquid in quavis exigua particula corporis quod sentiat anima, quamvis non fiat in toto corpore, illa tamen tota sentit, quia totam non latet" (*De Trinitate*, VI, 6. 8; Pat. Lat. vol. 42, col. 929).—On the famous *"non latet"* theory of sensation, cf. *De Musica*, VI, 5. 10; P. L., vol. 32, col. 1169, and the analysis of E. Gilson, *Introduction à l'étude de saint Augustin* (*Etudes de philosophie médiévale*, XI), Paris, 1929, p. 71-86.

when it came to considering the operations of the soul, that the soul operates through the heart. But this does not refer to the *union* of soul and body; it refers rather to the operations of the soul in the body.[32]

Now these two questions of individuation by the body and of unity *secundum esse* between soul and body clearly involve a very intimate relation between the soul and the body, as well as a very distinctive conception of the soul as a substantial form. One of the implications already drawn by St. Thomas is, as we have seen, that a substantial form is by nature the *forma corporis*. Fearing for the soul's immortality, St. Bonaventure had denied this. St. Albert, following a different line of argument, had reached practically the same conclusion. St. Thomas, on the contrary, thinks it

---

32. "Et ideo dicendum cum Augustino, *VI De Trinitate*, cap. VI, quod anima secundum essentiam suam considerata, tota est in qualibet parte corporis. Non tamen tota, si accipiatur secundum totalitatem potentiarum, sic enim est tota in toto animali. Et ratio hujus est, quia nulli substantiae simplici debetur locus, nisi secundum relationem quam habet ad corpus. Anima autem comparatur ad corpus ut ejus forma a qua totum corpus et quaelibet pars ejus habet esse, sicut a forma substantiali. Sed tamen potentias ejus, non omnes partes corporis participant: immo sunt aliquae potentiae quibus non est possibile perfici aliquid corporeum, sicut potentiae intellectivae; aliae autem sunt quae possunt esse perfectiones corporum, non tamen omnes influit anima in qualibet parte corporis, cum non quaelibet pars corporis sit ejusdem harmoniae et commixtionis; et nihil recipitur in aliquo nisi secundum proportionem recipientis; et ideo non eandem perfectionem recipit ab anima auris et oculus, cum tamen quaelibet pars recipit esse. Unde si consideratur anima prout est forma et essentia, est in qualibet parte corporis tota; si autem prout est motor secundum potentias suas, sic est tota in toto, et in diversis partibus secundum diversas potentias" (*In I Sent.*, d. 8, q. 5, a. 3, *Respondeo;* vol. 7, p. 123-124).

Clearly, therefore, the use of *motor* in St. Thomas refers not to the relations between soul and body, but, given a unity *in essendo*, it refers to the administrations carried on by the soul in the body according to the various organs and their degree of complexity.

possible to safeguard both the real unity of man and the immortality of the soul. Not only is there no incompatibility between this unity and the substantiality of the soul, but there is also, according to St. Thomas, a definite need of relating them to each other; for, as he will show, there is a very deep sense in which the full substantiality of the soul cannot be realized apart from such a unity. These early texts of St. Thomas, therefore, lay the metaphysical foundations which his future works are destined only to strengthen. But in the pursuit of these problems St. Thomas was destined to meet so many theories which endangered, in different ways, the unity of man, that he was forced to go to the root of the whole difficulty involved in this problem and to make a searching analysis of Plato. The history of this conflict is contained largely in the second book of the *Summa Contra Gentiles.*

B. Historical Preparation: the Analysis of the Platonic Tradition.

To see the fundamental basis of the problem of the soul and the decisive rôle played by Plato, we shall begin by questioning the possibility of union between a spiritual substance and a material body.[33]. It is obvious that a union by

---

33. Here, again, St. Thomas first considers the metaphysical problem. Beginning with the divine simplicity, we observe that in spiritual substances there is a composition of *esse* and *quod est* (*Contra Gentiles*, II, 52). Here is the conclusion: "Ipsum igitur esse competit omnibus aliis a primo agente, per participationem quamdam. Quod autem competit alicui per participationem, non est substantia ejus. Impossibile est igitur quod substantia alicujus entis, praeter agens primum, sit ipsum esse" (*ibid.*). Whence it follows that in created intellectual substances there is a composition of potency and act, indicating their distinctive mark of being *derived* (II, 53). This does not imply a composition of matter and form, for the reasons we have already examined (II, 54). Finally, intellectual substances, as being free from matter, are in-

mixture is out of the question, because such a union clearly belongs to two substances both of which are material.   There is the further and equally obvious reason that in a mixture the component elements are not present as such, once the union has been effected; which could not be true in the union of soul and body.[34]   Likewise, a tactual union is impossible because such union exists only between bodies through some form of immediacy or continuity.[35]   In union through touch, changes of quantity and quality take place.   In some instances, as in the action of the heavenly bodies on the elements below the sphere of the moon, the relations established resulted in qualitative changes only.   This type of union can be called the union of agent and patient, and consists in a movement of influence set up from the agent to the patient without involving quantitative relations.[36] Perhaps the soul as a spiritual substance can be united to the body in this way.   Such a *contactus virtutis* has these points in its favor: it allows contact between the indivisible and the divisible, so that the soul can thus touch the body by acting upon it; it sets up a relation in which what is affected undergoes the influence of the agent not at its own physical limits, which would be true of physical touch, but as a whole, because it is in potency, or subject, to the agent completely; it allows, finally, a certain necessary indwelling

---

corruptible (II, 55). We are now ready for the further question: *Utrum substantia intellectualis possit uniri corpori, et per quem modum* (II, 56).—Notice that the sequence of ideas is the same as that of the Commentary on the *Sentences*.

For convenience, I am using the Marietti edition of the *Contra Gentiles*, Taurini, 1927.

34. *Contra Gentiles*, II, 56.

35. "Tactus enim nonnisi corporum est; sunt einm tangentia quorum ultima sunt simul, ut puncta vel lineae vel superficies, quae sunt corporum ultima.   Non igitur per modum contactus substantia intellectualis corpori uniri potest" (*ibid.*).

36. *Ibid.*

of the soul in the body, because, as being a non-physical relation, *facit substantiam tangentem esse intra id quod tangitur
et incedentum per ipsam absque impedimento.*[37]

In spite of the apparent plausibility of this last argument,
St. Thomas rejects it along with its predecessors, and this
for a reason with which we have been concerned for some
time. Such a union, he says, is not a real unity, but a unity
or concurrence in action—*in agendo et patiendo;* it is not
a unity in existence, expressing an undivided mode of existence. To be an agent is not the same as to be; and therefore
to be a unity in action is not the same as to be a unity in
being.[38]

In thus rejecting the unity of action as explaining the
union between soul and body, we are called upon to discover
a unity between soul and body which is as permanent as being itself. Let us see whether soul and body can be joined
to each other in such a way that they are absolutely one—
unum simpliciter. There are, however, three different meanings which the expression *unum simpliciter* can have. It
may refer to something that is one in the sense of being indivisible; or, to something that is one in the sense of being
a physical continuous whole; or, finally, to something that
is one in the sense of being the object of an essential defini-

---

37. *Ibid.*

38. "Quae autem uniuntur secundum talem contactum, non
sunt unum simpliciter; sic enim dicitur esse unum quodammodo
et ens; esse autem agens non significat esse simpliciter; unde nec
esse unum in agendo est esse unum simpliciter" (*ibid.*) Cf. the
locus classicus for the derivation of the transcendental attributes
of being, *De Veritate*, I, 1, *Respondeo*: " . . . secundum hoc aliqua
dicuntur addere supra ens, inquantum exprimunt ipsius modum,
qui nomine ipsius entis non exprimitur . . . ita quod modus ex-
pressus sit modus generaliter consequens omne ens. . . Negatio
autem, quae est consequens omne ens absolute est indivisio; et
hanc exprimit hoc nomen *unum*: nihil enim est aliud *unum* quam
ens indivisum".

tion. Soul and body are not an indivisible unity, since they are present in the unity of the composite as component parts; nor are they a unity in the sense of being a physical continuum, because the parts of a continuum are quantified. Can soul and body make a unity of definition? Such a unity cannot result from the union of two existing things, but it can result from the union of a substantial form and matter.[39] Is such a union between soul and body possible? The chapter of the *Contra Gentiles* which we are considering concludes with five arguments that can be brought forth against it.

Some of these arguments we have already seen. On the premises assumed, soul and body are existing substances: no unity can result from them.[40] Furthermore, though matter and form are in the same genus, an intellectual substance and a material body are not. Therefore, an intellectual substance cannot be the form of the body.[41] Then, if the *esse* of the soul is in matter, it ought to be material; and, in fact, St. Bonaventure and St. Albert, drawing such a conclusion, refuse to make the soul, in any essential way, the form of the body.[42] What is more, if the existence of the soul depended on the body, it could not be separated from the body. But, as an intellectual substance is admittedly neither a body nor a

---

39. "Unum autem simpliciter tripliciter dicitur: vel sicut indivisibile, vel sicut continuum, vel sicut quod est ratione unum. Ex substantia autem intellectuali et corpore non potest fieri unum quod sit indivisibile (oportet enim illud esse compositium ex duobus). Relinquitur igitur inquirendem utrum ex substantia intellectuali et corpore possit fieri unum sicut quod est ratione unum. Ex duobus autem permanentibus non fit ratione unum nisi sicut ex forma substantiali et materia; ex substantia enim et accidente non fit ratione unum; non enim est eadem ratio hominis et albi" (*Contra Gentiles*, *loc. cit.*).

40. *Ibid.*, ad *Ex duobus enim substantiis.*

41. *Ibid.*, ad *Adhuc, Forma et materia.*

42. *Ibid.*, ad *Amplius, Omne illud.*

power in a body, it cannot be the form of the body.[43] Finally, if soul and body have a common existence, they have a common operation, because the operations of a being do not exceed the capacities of its nature. Whence it follows that the soul is material; which contradicts the premises with which we began.[44]

The logical outcome of such arguments was the denial of any possibility of union between an intellectual substance and material body of which it was to be the form. But both experience and human nature refuted such logic. As a result, some way had to be found by which *natura hominis salveretur*. It is to none other than to Plato that St. Thomas points as a way out of these difficulties.[45] Faced by an impasse in the direction of substantial union, Plato and his followers held that the soul is not joined to the body as form to matter, but as a *motor* is joined to what is moved. In fact, the soul is in the body as a sailor is in a ship. In other words, the relation between soul and body becomes one of *contactus virtutis* or, according to another expression, of unity of action. But the difficulty with such a solution was that it did not make man a real unity.   Only, as we must hasten to add, this difficulty did not exist for Platonism; and this is true because Plato altered the conception of man.

To avoid the difficulty which the question of unity raises, Plato held, says St. Thomas, that man was not composed of soul and body, but that man was a soul using a body, just as an individual man is not composed of his humanity and the garments he wears, but is a man using those garments.[46]

---

43. *Ibid.*, ad *Item, Impossibile est.*

44. *Ibid.*, ad *Adhuc, Cujus esse.*

45. *Contra Gentiles*, II, 57: *Positio Platonis de unione animae intellectivae ad corpus.*

46. "Ad hoc autem evitandum, Plato posuit quod homo non sit aliquid compositum ex anima et corpore, sed quod ipsa anima utens corpore sit homo; sicut non est aliquid compositum ex ho-

Whatever may be thought of this well-known metaphor, St. Thomas considers Platonism one of the two fundamental traditions concerning the soul which affected the whole European tradition. Indeed, as we shall see, the Platonic alternative extends to the whole realm of metaphysics, and is radically different, as St. Thomas thinks, from the Aristotelian tradition which he accepted. To see, in fact, the depth to which the Platonic conception of soul and body penetrated into Christian thought, and to see as well St. Thomas' clear understanding of this influence we must return to two questions that he raises in his commentary on the third book of *Sentences*. These questions are concerned with the personality of the separated soul and with the problem of the humanity of our Lord during the three days when His body lay in the sepulchre. The first question is, *utrum anima separata sit persona?* [47] The second question seeks to discover whether Christ could have been called a man during the interval of these three days: *utrum Christus in triduo quo jacuit in sepulchro, potuerit dici homo?*[48]

In St. Thomas' discussion of these questions several points are observable. According to him, an affirmative answer to these questions is ultimately based on a Platonic conception of the soul. Furthermore, St. Thomas is aware not only of the deeply Platonic attitude prevalent before the coming of Aristotle into the west, but also of the different outlook current among the *moderni* since the coming of Aristotle. We may note, finally, that these texts indicate, what the *Contra Gentiles* does not, that St. Thomas' source for what he says here concerning Plato is the *De Natura Hominis* of Nemesius.

Now, how are we to answer the first question? Is the

---

mine et indumento, sed homo utens indumento. Hoc autem esse impossibile ostenditur" (*ibid.*). Cf. note 53.

47. *In III Sent.*, d. 5, q. 3, a. 2; vol. 9, p. 102.

48. *In III Sent.*, d. 22, q. 1, a. 1; vol. 9, p. 325.

separated soul a person? There are several arguments in favor
of an affirmative answer. It is generally granted, observes
the first defender, that the rational soul is a *hoc aliquid,* and,
as is the case of a rational nature a *hoc aliquid* is a person,
the separated soul is a person.[49]. The second defender points
out that the difference between a separated soul and an angel
is that the soul has affinities for the body which it has left.
But the separated soul will not be joined to its body at the
resurrection except through the power of God; and since a
union so produced is not natural, the separated soul is a person because whatever happens through the power of God does
not change the nature of a being.[50]. That is also the opinion
of the third defender of the personality of the separated
soul.[51].

St. Thomas does not agree. If the soul is a form, it is not
a person, because, while *person* has the nature of something
complete or whole, the soul as a form is only a part. It is
not therefore a person.[52] To understand this reasoning we
must examine two different traditions among the *antiqui* on
the union of soul and body. According to one of these traditions, the soul is joined to the body as one complete being
to another. Plato, therefore, as Nemesius says (St. Thomas
writes *Gregorius Nyssenus*), held that man was not constituted of body and soul, but was a soul possessing a body.[53]

---

49. "Praeterea, conceditur quod anima rationalis est hoc
aliquid. Sed hoc aliquid in natura rationali est persona. Ergo
anima separata est persona" (*In III Sent.*, d. 5, q. 3, a. 2, obj. 3;
loc. cit.).

50. *Obj.* 4; *ibid.*

51. *Obj.* 5; *ibid.*

52. Ad *Praeterea; ibid.*

53. The Vivès edition prints "corpore *inducta*". In the notes
there is the variant of the Parma edition, *induta*, which I think is
the right reading, in view of the text of the *Contra Gentiles* al-

According to this explanation, the whole personality of man
would be found in the soul, so that a separated soul could be
truly called a man. And this is, indeed, what Hugh of St.
Victor has done.[54] Peter Lombard, therefore, would be correct in saying that the separated soul is a person,[55] once such
a conception of man is granted. But it cannot be granted,
St. Thomas continues, because, in spite of the different attitude that it adopts towards man, Platonism, as we shall see

---

ready quoted (n. 46; cf. *indumento*) and the reading of Burgundio's translation ("sed animam corpore utentem et velut *indutam* corpus"; *De Natura Hominis*, c. 3, ed. S. Burkhard, Vindobonae, 1902, p. 47). "Indutam", of course, translates the ἐνδεδυμένην
of Nemesius (*loc cit.; Patrologia Graeca*, vol. 40, col. 595B).

54. "Si autem homo mortuus non est homo, ergo homo quando
vivere desinit homo esse desinit. . . Quid autem moritur, nisi
solum corpus quod ab anima deseritur. Anima enim non moritur,
nec vivere desinit, etiam quando vivificare desinit. Ergo solum
corpus moritur. Sed homo, inquit, id est ipsa persona moritur.
Quid est persona? Nonne individuum rationalis substantiae? Si
ergo individuum rationalis substantiae persona est; rationalis
utique spiritus, qui et simplicitate unus est, et natura rationis
capax, proprie personam esse habet; ex se quidem in quantum
spiritus rationalis est, per se autem quando sine corpore est.
Quando autem corpus illi unitum est in quantum cum corpore
unitum est; una cum corpore persona est. Quando vero a corpore
separatur; persona tamen esse non desinit; et ipsa eadem persona
quae prius fuit, quoniam corpus a societate spiritus decedens, eidem
spiritui personam esse non tollit, sicut prius quando jungebatur
ipsi ut persona esset non dedit. Remanet itaque separata anima
a carne, eadem persona spiritus rationalis. . ." (*De Sacramentis*,
Lib. II, P. 1, c. xii; *Patrologia Latina*, vol. 176, col. 410D-411B).

55. "Hic a quibusdam opponitur, quod personam assumpserit
persona. Persona enim est 'substantia rationalis individuae naturae'; hoc autem est anima; igitur si animam assumpsit (*scil.*
Christ, in the incarnation) et personam. Quod ideo non sequitur,
quia anima non est persona, quando alii rei est unita personaliter,
sed quando per se est: absoluta enim a corpore persona est, sicut
Angelus" (Petri Lombardi *Libri IV Sententiarum*, Quaracchi, 2nd
ed., 1916, Lib. III, d. 5, c. 3. 34; vol. 2, p. 572).

more fully when we return to the *Contra Gentiles,* continues
to violate the unity of man.[56]

The other opinion is that of Aristotle, *quam omnes moderni sequuntur,* according to which the soul is united to the

---

56. "*Solutio.* Respondeo dicendum, quod de unione animae ad
corpus apud antiquos fuit duplex opinio. Una quod anima unitur
corpori sicut ens completum enti completo, ut esset in corpore
sicut nauta in navi: unde sicut dicit Gregorius Nyssenus, Plato
posuit quod homo non est aliquid constitutum ex corpore et anima,
sed est anima corpore inducta (*read:* induta; cf. n. 53): et secundum hoc tota personalitas hominis consisteret in anima, adeo quod
anima separata posset dici homo vere, ut dicit Hugo de Sancto
Victore: et secundum hanc opinionem esset verum quod Magister
dicit, quod anima est persona quando est separata. Sed haec opinio
non potest stare: quia sic corpus animae accidentaliter adveniret;
unde, hoc nomen homo, de cujus intellectu est anima et corpus,
non significaret unum per se, sed per accidens; et ita non esset in
genere substantiae (*In III Sent.,* d. 5, q. 3, a. 2, *Solutio,* vol. 9, p.
102-103). For Nemesius, cf. *De Natura Hominis,* c. 3; P. G., vol.
40, col. 595B, where, in discussing Plato's position, Nemesius observes that it is not free from difficulties: "ἔχει δὲ καὶ οὗτος ὁ λόγος
ἄπορον τι" (*ibid.*) but accepts the solution of Ammonius Saccas;
cf. *ibid.,* especially col. 600A-B.

St. Bonaventure has the same condemnation of Hugh of St.
Victor and of Peter Lombard: "*Respondeo:* Dicendum, quod sicut
apparet ex textu, opinio Magistri fuit, quod anima separata sit
persona; et haec opinio fuit magistri Hugonis de sancto Victore.
Ratio autem, quae movit eos ad hoc ponendum, fuit actualis dis-
tinctio et completio reperta in anima separata, quoniam actus no-
biles liberius exerceat et perfectius, quam exerceat in corpore.
Haec tamen opinio non sustinetur communiter a doctoribus. . . .
Quamvis autem in anima separata sit reperire singularitatem et
dignitatem, non est tamen reperire incommunicabilitatem, quia
appetitum et aptitudinem habet, ut uniatur corpori ad constitutionem tertii. Et ideo necesse est, ipsam carere distinctione per-
sonalitatis; quoniam, si completior est anima, dum appetitus eius
terminatur, quem habet respectu corporis resumendi, sicut vult
Augustinus duodecimo super Genesim ad litteram, et tunc non
habet in se intentionem personae; necessario sequitur, quod per-
sonalitate careat, cum est separata a corpore. . . : Et ideo non
immerito in hac opinione communiter non sustinent Magistrum

body as form to matter. The soul now becomes a part of human nature, and is no longer a complete nature in itself. From this it follows that the separated soul, being only a part of man, is not a person, because, although it is not an actual part, since the whole man is no longer existent, it is its nature to be a part.[57]   As a result, we must say, in reply to the first objector, that the soul is a *hoc aliquid* because it is subsistent, not because it is a complete substance or nature. To the second objector we must say that if the union of soul and body at the resurrection requires the divine assistance, it is only because of bodily defects and does not in any way alter the natural character of that union.[58]   The reply to the last objection, finally, is distinctively Thomastic. The soul is undoubtedly more noble than the body, but, nevertheless, it is joined to the body as the constituent part of man.   In a sense, therefore, man is even more noble than the soul because he is more complete: *quamvis anima sit dignior corpore, tamen unitur ei ut pars totius hominis, quod quodammodo est*

. . . " (*In III Sent.*, d. 5, a. 2, q. 3, *Conclusio;* vol. 3, p. 136).   The reference to St. Augustine is *De Genesi ad Litteram, Lib. XIII*, c. 35, 68; Patrologia Latina, vol. 34, col. 483-484.—On certain points in which the opinion of Peter Lombard was rejected, cf. *Chartularium*, I, p. 220-221.

57. "Alia opinio est Aristotelis, II *De Anima*, cap. XI, quam omnes moderni sequuntur, quod anima unitur corpori sicut forma materiae: unde anima est pars humanae naturae, et non natura quaedam per se: et quia ratio partis contrariatur rationi personae, ut dictum est, ideo anima separata non potest dici persona: quia quamvis separata non sit pars actu, tamen habet naturam ut sit pars" (*In III Sent.*, d. 5, q. 3, a. 2, *Solutio;* vol. 9, p. 103).

58. *Ibid.*, ad. 3-4.   Cf. the reply to the third objection where it is important to notice the contrast between the soul as subsistent and as an incomplete nature: "Ad tertium dicendum, quod anima rationalis dicitur hoc aliquid per modum quo esse subsistens est hoc aliquid, etiam si habeat naturam partis; sed ad rationem personae exigitur ulterius quod sit totum et completum."

dignius anima, inquantum est completius.[59]. The spirit of
Christian humanism cannot hope to find better expression, for
the complement of this statement is another Thomistic text:
*Ad quintum dicendum, quod per visionem Dei non solum ipsa
ratio glorificatur, sed etiam totus homo; unde carentia divinae
visionis non est poena tantum rationis, sed totius hominis.*[60]

Let us now return to the *Contra Gentiles* and summarize
the difficulties which St. Thomas sees in the Platonic conception of soul and body. He repeats the argument that for
Plato the essence of man would be found in the soul and that
therefore the body could not be explained as in any sense a
part of man.[61] Furthermore, he objects that if soul and body
are not one in *esse*, they cannot possibly be one in operation.
Now, there do appear to be some operations that are common
to both, such as fear, anger, sensation, etc.; which leads us
to think that the Platonic position is impossible, for to be one
in operation, soul and body must be one in the principle of
their existence.[62] To avoid this difficulty, St. Thomas continues, Plato held that soul and body were one in operation in
the sense that during sensation, for example, the soul was
active and the body passive. But even this is impossible, for
an analysis of sensation will reveal that it is something purely
passive. The sense itself is the passive potency of the organ
affected by the external sensible object. During an act of
sensation, the sensitive soul is not active, because it has no

---

59. *Ibid.*, ad 5.
60. In II Sent., d. 31, q. 2, a. 1, ad 5. vol. II, p. 813. It is
unnecessary for our immediate purpose to give an analysis of the
other question in St. Thomas' Commentary cited above (for reference, cf. n. 48). We may observe in it that the same texts of Nemesius and Hugh of St. Victor are referred to, and the same Platonic
conception of the soul, by way of Nemesius' discussion, criticized.
Doctrinally, the conclusion of the article is a criticism of Peter
Lombard, as against whom. "omnes moderni tenent, quod Christus
in triduo non fuerit homo" (*ibid.*).
61. *Contra Gentiles*, II, 57, ad *Animal enim et homo.*
62. *Ibid.*, ad *Item, Impossibile est.*

other operation than to inform the body which is being affected through the senses. To attribute any activity to the soul in sensation would be equivalent to making the animal soul subsistent; and St. Thomas thinks that such a conclusion *a Platonis opinione non discordat.*[63]

Continuing his criticism of Plato, St. Thomas next turns to what he considered the basic difficulty in the whole discussion on the soul. He observes that the body as moved by the soul does not acquire its specifically human character from this relation to the soul as *motor,* because *ex hypothesi* the unity of being does not come from the soul, and consequently the body will have its specific character unchanged by the presence or absence of the soul. This is clearly not true, for upon the departure of the soul the parts of the body are no longer human, as not possessing a proper operation which is specifically human.[64] From the *motor-mobile* relation, furthermore, only the unity of motion can result, and not the unity of being; whence it would follow that the body did not have being from the soul, and, since life is a kind of being, it would follow also that the body did not have life from the soul.[65] Nor may we use the doctrine of plural souls as a means of offsetting these difficulties. For such a doctrine

---

63. Criticism of this doctrine was common. Cf. *Contra Gentiles,* II, 82; *Summa Theologica,* I, q. 75, a. 3, *Respondeo,* where we are told that Plato made of sensation an incorporeal function.— For St. Bonaventure, cf. *In II Sent.,* d. 17, a. 1, q. 2, *Conclusio* ad *Ideo fuerunt et alii;* vol. 2, p. 414.

64. "Amplius, Mobile non sortitur specimen a suo motore. Si igitur anima non conjungitur corpori nisi sicut motor mobili, corpus et partes ejus non consequuntur speciem ab anima. Abeunte igitur anima, remanebit corpus et partes ejus ejusdem speciei. Hoc autem est manifeste falsum, nam caro et os et manus et hujusmodi partes, post abscessum animae, non dicuntur nisi aequivoce, quum nulli harum partium propria operatio adsit quae speciem consequitur. Non igitur unitur anima corpori solum sicut motor mobili vel homo vestimento" (*Contra Gentiles,* II, 57).

65. *Ibid.,* ad *Adhuc, Mobile.*

says that the sensitive soul is the form of the body and that the intellect is thereby freed from any condition of materiality.[66] But this doctrine does not meet the difficulties, because it violates the unity of man, or, if it escapes violating this unity by placing the whole nature of man in the soul and saying that man is a soul using a body, then it meets the further difficulty of considering the functions of animal life, sensation, etc., as not included within the nature of man.[67]

These doctrines did not stop with Plato. There were others, says St. Thomas, who tried to show that an intellectual substance could not be joined to the body as its form. The argument is this. The intellect, in fact, the possible intellect of Aristotle, is a certain separate substance not joined to man as a form.[68] In order to know all things, the intellect must be free of all things; which would prevent, according to this argument, the relation of form and matter between the intellect and the body.[69] There is also the argument that if the intellect were the form of the body, its manner of reception would be of the same genus as the prime matter of which it is the form; and, as this must necessarily be individual for the intellect also, the knowledge of universals is thereby rendered impossible. Consequently, the intellect cannot be the form

---

66. *Ibid.*, II, 58, ad *Item ad haec;* cf. also ad *Adhuc ex duobus.*

67. *Ibid.*, ad *Amplius, Si homo.*

68. *Ibid.*, II, 59. An examination of the commentary of Averroes on the third book of Arstotle's *De Anima* will reveal that St. Thomas is here following the discussion of the Arabian commentator, and that the "alii" referred to are Theophrastus and Themistius. Cf. the commentary of Averroes on *De Anima, Lib. III*, Comm. 5, in the Venice edition of Aristotle (*Aristotelis Opera Omnia, Sextum Volumen, Aristotelis Stagiritae Libri Omnes, ad Animalium cognitionem attinentes, cum Averrois Cordubensis variis in eosdem Commentariis*, Venetiis apud Juntas, 1550) f. 160va-161ra.—A comparison with St. Thomas' Commentary on the *Sentences* will bring this parentage out very clearly (cf. *In II Sent.*, d. 17, q. 2, a. 1, *Solutio*, ad *Eorum autem qui ponunt;* vol. 8, p. 222).

69. *Contra Gentiles, loc cit.*, ad *Item, Per demonstrationem.*

of the body.[70]   These arguments, says St. Thomas, led Averroes to the conclusion that the possible intellect was not the form of the body.[71]   But Averroes fails by excess.   In placing the intellect outside of man, he makes it impossible for us to attribute an act of knowledge to the individual man, for it is the separate intellect that knows and not the individual. To be an action of the individual, knowledge must proceed

---

70. *Ibid.*, ad *Adhuc, Si esset forma*. This analysis is from Averroes, who writes as follows: "et ideo necesse est ut ista natura, quae dicitur intellectus, recipiat formas modo alio ab eo, secundum quem istae materiae recipiunt formas receptionis: quarum conclusio a materia est terminatio primae materiae in eis. Et ideo non est necesse ut sit de genere materiarum istarum, in quibus prima est inclusa, neque ipsa materia prima, quoniam, si ita esset, tunc receptio in eis esset ejusdem generis; diversitas enim naturae recepti facit diversitatem naturae recipientis. Hoc igitur movit Aristotelem ad imponendum hanc naturam, quae est alia a natura materiae, et a natura formae, et a natura congregati.

"Et hoc idem induxit Theophrastum, et Themistium, et plures expositores ad opinandum quod intellectus materialis est substantia, neque generabilis, neque corruptibilis; omne enim generabile et corruptibile est hoc: sed iam demonstratum est quod iste non est hoc, neque forma in corpore. Et induxit eos ad opinandum hoc, quod ista est sententia Aristotelis. Ista enim intentio, sive quod iste intellectus est talis, bene apparet intuentibus demonstrationem Aristotelis et sua verba. De demonstratione autem secundum quod exposuimus: de verbis vero, quia dicit ipsum esse non passivum, et dicit ipsum esse separabile, et simplex. Haec enim tria verba usitantur in eo ab Aristotele; et non est rectum, immo est remotum uti aliquo eorum in doctrina demonstrativa de generabili et corruptibili" . . . (*loc cit.*).—For knowledge by *continuation* or union which St. Thomas goes on to describe as being the doctrine of Averroes, cf. the text immediately after this, f. 161ra, ad *Et quia opinati sunt*.

Notice that Averroes is quite sure that he is following Aristotle. St. Thomas will disagree, and we shall find our discussion bound up immediately with the question of the status of the Aristotelian texts.

71. *Contra Gentiles*, II, 59, ad *Ex his autem motus.*

from a form that is intrinsically his.[72] That is why both
Plato and Averroes err in the same way. Both of them consider the union of soul and body as a union of operation.
But, whereas the position of Plato would lead us logically to
exclude animal life from the nature of man, that of Averroes would lead us to exclude intellectual life from the nature
of man. And the error in both cases is the same, for both
Plato and Averroes fail to explain the unity of man by not
making the intellect the form of the body.[73]

Averroes attempted to overcome these difficulties by showing that man derived his specific character as man not from
the separate possible intellect, but from the passive intellect
or imagination.[74] The difficulties in this position are obvious,
and, if pressed, really mean that in virtue of this passive
intellect we cannot be different from animals; while from the
standpoint of knowledge, St. Thomas argues that a theory
of continuation between the imagination and a separate intellect does not, as we have already noted, explain knowledge
as a human function.[75] Finally, we must mention here another Thomistic argument against Averroes. This argument
will become the cornerstone of the reconstruction of the doctrine of the soul that St. Thomas undertook. Can the separate intellect begin and complete its own operations? That

---

72. *Ibid.*, ad *Adhuc, omne cognoscens*, and ad *Amplius, Id quo
aliquid.*

73. "Amplius, quod consequitur ad operationem alicujus rei
non largitur alicui speciem, quia operatio est actus secundus,
forma autem per quam aliquid habet speciem est actus primus.
Unio autem intellectus possibilis ad hominem, secundum positionem
praedictam, consequitur hominis operationem; fit enim mediante
phantasia, quae, secundum philosophum est motus factus a sensu
secundum actum. Ex tali igitur unione non consequitur homo
speciem; non igitur differt homo specie a brutis animalibus per
hoc quod est intellectum habens" (*ibid.*).

74. *Contra Gentiles*, II, 60.

75. *Ibid.*, ad *Item, Sicut nihil est potens.*

is, if there are always present in the nature of a thing, whatever it be, those attributes by means of which that thing will carry out its proper function as the expression of its innermost nature, and if, consequently, there is set up in nature a strict relation between the nature of a being and its capacity for operation, what function is there in the separate possible intellect of Averroes which is the proper expression of its nature? Has it the power to initiate an act of knowledge? St. Thomas replies with a very decided negative,[76] and the point is important. We have broached, indeed, the problem of the relations between the definition of the soul and the nature and range of human knowledge. The unfolding of such a relation involves the question of the contribution of sensation to knowledge, and points to a further illustration of the fundamentally Thomistic conception that the composite man is or should be the starting point in an investigation of his parts. We must reserve this point for the conclusion.

The doctrine of Averroes, however, which St. Thomas is here concerned to refute, carries with it the apparent approval of Aristotelian authority. In other words, St. Thomas is faced by a conception of the soul which he considers to be essentially Platonic, but which is defended by an appeal to the authority of Aristotle. Thus it happens that the problem of defining the soul becomes one of interpreting Aristotle. Hitherto one of St. Thomas' main preoccupations has been to show the difficulties latent in Platonism; and in espousing an Aristotelian conception of the soul St. Thomas was concerned to avoid these difficulties by insisting that the soul is the form of the body. But here is Averroes enjoying the eminence of Aristotle's chief commentator and yet advancing a conception of the soul which to St. Thomas was not in the least Aristotelian. St. Thomas, therefore, must turn historian and begin that long exposition of Aristotle, directed

---

76. *Ibid*, ad *Adhuc Quaecumque.*

against his Greek and Arabian commentators, not to mention their Latin followers, in which an essentially Platonic separatism is attacked on all points and the unity of man defended.

In the *Contra Gentiles,* therefore, following the exposition of Averroes, we find a chapter with this significant title: *Quod praedicta positio est contra sententiam Aristotelis.*[77] The opening sentence of this chapter is couched in no ambiguous terms: *Sed quia huic positioni Averrhoes praestare robur auctoritatis nititur, propter hoc quod dicit Aristotelem ita sensisse, ostendemus manifeste quod praedicta positio est contra sententiam Aristotelis.* St. Thomas therefore challenges the Aristotelianism of Averroes. And this is not all. Aristotle's definition of the soul, the famous *actus primus physici corporis organici, potentia vitam habentis,*[78] is interpreted by Averroes incorrectly, because it is not given by Aristotle *sub dubitatione;* and this is clear, St. Thomas continues, *ex exemplaribus graecis et translatione Boetii.*[79] St.

---

77. II, 61, and cp. II, 70.

78. *De Anima,* II, 1, 412a27-28.

79. It was C. Baeumker who pointed out that a translation from the Greek text of the *De Anima* was used by Alfred Sareshel. The order, then, of the translations of the *De Anima* would be: about 1215, from a Greek original, by an unknown translator (called "translatio Boethii" by St. Thomas); before 1235, a translation from the Arabic by Michael Scottus; 1265-1268, the translation, Greek to Latin, by William of Moerbeke, on the basis of the first Greek-Latin translation. Cf. C. Baeumker, *Die Stellung des Alfred von Sareshel (Alfredus Anglicus) und seiner Schrift De motu cordis in der Wissenschaft des beginnenden XIII. Jahrhunderts,* München, 1913, p. 35-40; M. Grabmann, *Forschungen über die lateinischen Aristotelesübersetzungen des XIII. Jahrhunderts (Beiträge . . . Band XVII, Heft 5-6,* Münster, i. W., 1916, p. 190-198).—M. Grabmann has dated the *De Anima* commentary 1270-1272, on account of a reference in the third book (lectio 7, ed. Pirotta, no. 695) to a more elaborate attack on the Averroistic separation of the possible intellect ("quae alibi diligentius pertractavimus"); cf. his *Mittelalterliches Geistesleben,* München, 1926, p. 273. Finally, in the second edition of his *Die Werke des Hl. Thomas von*

Thomas then points out what the *textus vetus* reading should be, and what the interpretation of this text is. It is then he adds that, if Aristotle had really argued as Averroes thinks he did, he would have introduced a distinction into an argument which threatened to become an equivocation. Such is, indeed, Aristotle's custom—*sicut est consuetudo sua.*[80] St.

Aquin (Beiträge, XX, 1-2) Münster, 1931, p. 265-266, M. Grabmann repeats his arguments and holds to the date 1270-1272. This is expressly against Mandonnet whose date is 1266 cf. *Biblioghaphie thomiste (Bibliothèque thomiste,* 1) Le Saulchoir, 1921, p. xiii). M. Grabmann is not conclusively right, and the non-polemical character of the discussion combined with an express reference to Averroes (*"auctor hujus positionis"; De Anima, loc. cit.,* no. 693) makes it at least probable that the reference is to *Contra Gentiles,* II, 60-61, 73, etc. Consequently, there is no real reason for departing from Mandonnet's chronology. As concerns our discussion, the point is of little importance.

80. "Nec est intentio Aristotelis, ut Commentator praedictus fingit, dicere quod nondum est manifestum de intellectu utrum intellectus sit anima, sicut de aliis principiis. Non enim textus vetus habet *Nihil est declaratum* sive nihil est dictum, sed *Nihil est manifestum;* quod intelligendum est quantum ad id quod est proprium ei, non quantum ad communem diffinitionem. Si autem, ut ipse dicit, anima aequivoce dicitur de intellectu et aliis, primo distinxisset aequivocationem, postea diffinivisset, sicut est consuetudo sua; alias procederet in aequivoco, quod non est in scientiis demonstrativis" (*Contra Gentiles,* II, 61).

The text of Aristotle referred to is the following: "περὶ δὲ τοῦ νοῦ καὶ τῆς θεωρητικῆς δυνάμεως οὐδὲν πωφανερόν, ἀλλ' ἔοικε ψυχῆς γένος ἕτερον εἶναι, καὶ τοῦτο μόνον ἐνδέχεται χωρίζεσθαι, καθάπερ τὸ ἀΐδιον τοῦ φθαρτοῦ." (*De Anima,* II, 2, 413b24-27). Averroes comments on this as follows: "Cum dixit quod quaerendum est in unoquoque istorum principiorum utrum sit anima, aut non, incoepit declarare virtutem, quae non videtur esse anima, sed manifestius de ea ut sit non anima (*ad loc.,* Comm. 21, *ed. cit.,* f. 130va). . . . et dicit, 'sed tamen videtur esse aliquid genus animae' etc., id est, sed tamen melius est dicere, et magis videtur esse verum post perscrutationem, ut istud sit aliud genus animae; et si dicatur anima, erit secundum aequivocationem; et, si dispositio intellectus sit talis, necesse est ut ille solus inter omnes virtutes animae sit possibilis ut abstrahatur a corpore, et non cor-

Thomas questions, therefore, the reading and authenticity of the translations of Aristotle; which is evidence that he was consulting, no doubt with William of Moerbeke, as Grabmann supposes,[81] on the Greek texts of Aristotle in order to settle the questions of translation and interpretation. It is thus clear that at the time of the *Contra Gentiles* St. Thomas was faced with the problem of disentangling the historical Aristotle from the inaccuracies of the Arabian translators and commentators.

Averroes is not the only one to bear the burden of the Thomistic attack. Indeed, we find St. Thomas weighing carefully the interpretation of various commentators and then showing their impossibility either as philosophical theories or as interpretations of Aristotle. At the conclusion of his analysis of Averroes as an interpreter, St. Thomas quotes various texts from the *De Anima*[82] and shows that the intellect must be part of man, serving as the principle by which the human soul knows.[83] Here follows the historical criticism which we may note briefly. Alexander of Aphrodisias, reflecting on these texts of Aristotle, concluded that the possible intellect is a power residing in man; but as he could not see how an intellectual substance was the form of the body, he decided that the possible intellect was not founded in an intellectual substance but was the result of the mixture of the elements in the human body. Knowledge would then be produced by conjunction with the separate active intellect.[84] St.

---

rumpatur per suam corruptionem, quemadmodum sempiternum abstrahitur; et hoc erit, cum quandoque copulatur cum illo, et quandoque non copulatur cum illo" (*ibid.*, f. 130vb).

From this text the point of St. Thomas' criticism is quite clear, as is Averroes' anxiety to insure the immortality of the soul.

81. *Die lateinischen Aristotelesübersetzungen des XIII. Jahnhunderts*, p. 193-194.

82. *De Anima*, II, 2, 413b24-27; 3, 414a31-32; III, 4, 429a10ff; *ibid.*, a23.

83. *Contra Gentiles*, II, 61, *ad fin.*

84. *Ibid.*, II, 62.

Thomas then shows that the opinion of Alexander is similar to that of Gelen[85] who made of the soul a complexion or mean composed of contrary qualities. The complexion theory itself is then assimilated to the old Pythagorean harmony theory.[86] On this point St. Thomas' sources, as he admits, are Aristotle and Nemesius.[87]   St. Thomas then stops to examine

---

85. *Ibid.*   Cf. e.g., "Non igitur positio praedicta Alexandri potest stare cum verbis et demonstratione Aristotelis, ut videtur." —For the philosophical criticism, in which we may observe some similarities to the arguments against Averroes, cf. *ibid.*, ad *Item*, *Intelligere est.*

86. *Ibid.*, II, 63. "Praedicta autem opinio Alexandri de intellectu possibili propinqua est Galeni medici (opinio) de anima; dicit enim animam esse complexionem. . . Complexio . . . sit quoddam constitutum ex contrariis qualitatibus quasi medium inter eas . . . "

87. *Contra Gentiles*, II, 64. Cf. Aristotle, *De Anima;* I, 4, 407b27ff., and on Empedocles, *ibid.*, 408a18ff.; Nemesius, *De Natura Hominis*, c. II; Patrologia Graeca, vol. 40, col. 537A, and, especially, 552A ff., where, however, the complexion doctrine is attributed to Galen only as a tentative argument (ἔοικε δὲ ἐξ ὧν λέγει δοκιμάζειν μᾶλλον, τὸ κρᾶσιν εἶναι τὴν ψυχήν": 553B-556A).   In col. 552A, Nemesius couples the names of Dicaearchus and Simmias the Pythagorean interlocutor of Socrates in the *Phaedo*, which is cited here, and from which arguments against the soul-harmony doctrine are drawn: cf., e.g. col. 557A, and cp. Plato, *Phaedo*, p. 94b7-95a3.—By way of Nemesius, the Platonic attack on the harmony doctrine passed into St. Thomas:

Plato:	Nemesius:	St. Thomas:
"ἡγεμονεύουσά (*scil:* ψυχὴ) τε ἐκείνων πάντων ἐξ ὧν φησί τις αὐτὴν εἶναι, καὶ ἐναντεουμένη ὀλίγου πάντα . . . ταῖς ἐπιθυμίαις καὶ ὀργαῖς καὶ φόβοις ὡς ἄλλη οὖσα ἄλλῳ πράγματι διαλεγομένη." (*Phaedo*, p. 94c10-d6).	"ἔτι, ἡ κρᾶσις οὐκ ἐναντιοῦται ταῖς ἐπιθυμίαις τοῦ σώματος, ἀλλὰ καὶ συνεργεῖ· αὕτη γάρ ἐστιν ἡ κινοῦσα· ἡ δὲ ψυχὴ ἐναντιοῦται· οὐκ ἄρα ἡ κρᾶσις ἐστι ψυχή." (*De Natura Hominis*, c. II; P.G., vol. 40, col. 557A).	"Omne enim corpus mixtum harmoniam habet et complexionem: nec harmonia potest movere corpus aut regere ipsum vel repugnare passionibus, sicut et complexio" (*Contra Gentiles*, II, 64).

and refute the doctrine that the soul is a body, which is a doctrine, he says, held by many under many forms.[88] We find, finally, a criticism of those who identify sense and intellect,[89] and of those whose doctrine committed the same error by identifying the possible intellect with the imagination.[90] St. Thomas does not spend much time with either of these.

The impossibility of accepting any of these conclusions on the nature of the soul and its manner of union with the body now leads St. Thomas to give at once his own solution to the

---

88. *Contra Gentiles*, II, 65. One of the arguments apparently used was "per hoc quod filius generatur a patre per decisionem corporalem: — et quia anima compatitur corpori; — et quia separatur a corpore; separari autem est corporum tangentium" *(ibid.)*. —On the *tactus*, cf. *supra* p. 121.—St. Thomas passes judgment on them as follows: "Movit etiam ad hanc positionem multos, qui crediderunt quod non est corpus non esse, imaginationem transcendere non valentes, quae solum circa corpora versatur" *(ibid.)*.—A few years later in the *De Substantiis Separatis* (c. 1272, according to Mandonnet, or, at least, after 1260, according to Grabmann), he will accuse the ancient Greek cosmologists of this materialism: "his omnibus et eorum sequacibus nullas substantias incorporeas esse videbatur"; and thus the Epicureans, "ex Democriti doctrinis originem sumentes", make their gods after human proportions. He concludes, "Unde haec opinio intantum invaluit ut usque ad Judaeos Dei cultores perveniret, quorum Sadducaei dicebant non esse Angelum neque spiritum" (c. 1; ed. Mandonnet, vol. 1, p. 71).

89. *Contra Gentiles*, II, 66. These were "quidam antiquorum philosophorum", of whose doctrines Aristotle is undoubtedly the source. Cf. *De Anima*, III, 3, 427a 17ff., where Aristotle, in speaking of this confusion between intellect and sense, refers to Empedocles and Homer as typical of the ancients: "οἱ ἀρχαῖοι" who "τὸ φρονεῖν καὶ τὸ αἰσθάνεσθαι ταὐτὸν εἶναί φασιν" *(ibid.*, a21-22). For a longer list, and a reference to a similar criticism by Plato, cf. the edition of the *De Anima* by R. D. Hicks (Cambridge, 1907), note on 428a21, p. 454.

90. *Contra Gentiles*, II, 67. He uses the same kind of argument for this doctrine as for that in II, 66, that "intellectus universalium est" (II, 67).

problem and his interpretation of the Aristotelian position.[91]
Through this historical excursus of St. Thomas we have ar-
rived again at the problem of the substantial form as the
only means of uniting the soul to the body; and we have
reached at the same time the problem of separating Aristotle
from his commentators. St. Thomas stands eminently on
both grounds of argument.

C. The Historical Rehabilitation of Aristotle.

The substantial union between soul and body requires two
things. It is necessary, in the first place, that the soul, joined
to the body as its form, should in this union give the body its
substantial existence, and be to the body that principle by
which it is called a being. The second point follows from the
first. The principle of existence must be one for both component parts, and must be that by which the composite substance exists as a unit.[92]   Whether or not the form in question

---

91. "Ex praemissis igitur rationibus concludere possumus quod
intellectualis substantia potest corpori uniri ut forma" (*Contra
Gentiles*, II, 68).

Notice, here again, the reference to Averroes: "Et quia Averrhoes maxime nititur suam opinionem confirmare per verba et
demonstrationem Aristotelis, ostendendum restat quod necessarium est dicere, secundum opinionem Aristotelis, intellectum secundum suam substantiam alicui corpori uniri ut formam" (*ibid.*,
II, 70).

92. "Ad hoc enim quod aliquid sit forma substantialis alterius
duo requiruntur. Quorum unum est ut forma sit principium essendi substantialiter ei cujus est forma; principium autem dico
non effectivum, sed formale, *quo aliquid est et denominatur ens.*
Unde sequitur aliud, scilicet quod forma et materia conveniant in
uno esse; quod non contingit de principio effectivo cum eo cui dat
esse; et hoc esse est in quo subsistit substantia composita, quae
est una secundum esse ex materia et forma constans. Non autem
impeditur substantia intellectualis, per hoc quod est subsistens, ut
probatum est, esse formale principium essendi materiae, quasi esse

is more than the form of the compound substance depends not upon its being the form of that substance, but upon what kind of form it is. Substantial union governs all natural objects in the same way: it signifies that the component elements converge in one act of existence, for otherwise the unity of the compound would be destroyed. From this point of view, man is not privileged in the least, and in fact has to observe this general law of composite beings on the penalty of not being a unity at all. These are the implications of a substantial form.

Now, while the problem of the immortality of the soul is not involved directly in the analysis of substantial union, it arises, however, just as soon as the conditions of unity have been satisfied. For if we have thus guaranteed the unity of man, we may have thereby endangered the immortality of the soul. In a doctrine such as that of St. Bonaventure or of St. Albert, such a question could not arise. The soul, whatever inclinations it may have towards the body, is a complete substance in itself, and its substantiality is a clear guarantee that it will continue to exist after its separation from the body. If the position of St. Thomas on the immortality of the soul is much the same, nevertheless, it presents differences which are the necessary consequence of his interpretation of the function of the soul as form of the body. In fact, the real problem from the standpoint of St. Thomas is not how the soul can be immortal if it is the form of the body, but what it is that requires this union with the body. Clearly, if the soul is a subsistent form and the principle of the subsistence of the body, there can be no question concerning immortality, for it is the body which owes its existence to

suum communicans materiae; non est enim inconveniens quod idem sit esse in quo subsistit compositum et forma ipsa, quum compositum non sit nisi per formam, nec seorsum utrumque subsistat" (*Contra Gentiles*, II, 68). The *utrumque*, of course, is the composite and the matter.

the soul and not the soul to the body. And that is why St.
Thomas can make his own the often repeated statement that
the intellectual soul in being at once an incorporeal substance and the form of a body, is a kind of horizon between
the corporeal and incorporeal worlds.[93] Only, here as elsewhere, St. Thomas pours new wine into old bottles. The
following analysis of Aristotle will prepare the way for this
distinctive interpretation of the soul.[94]

Since soul and body are not two existing substances, we
may see this all the more clearly by noting the Thomistic
criticism of the arguments against substantial unity which
we have already met.[95] Both soul and body have a common
principle of existence or *esse*, that given by the soul as form.[93]
Furthermore, as the soul is subsistent, it does not exist in
matter as its subject, even though in giving existence to matter it is true to say that the soul is, in a certain sense, in
matter.[97] In fact, we must consider not only the essence but
also the powers of the soul. The soul is united essentially to
a body to which it gives existence. But the soul has also
certain powers that flow from its essence. Now, the power in
operation, or, more accurately, the soul in operation through
the power, will complete its action either by means of the
body or without it. If the operation is accomplished without
the body, then the power is not founded in matter. It is in
this sense that we must conceive the separation of the intel-

---

93. *Ibid.*

94. For a brief statement of this question, cf. *ibid.*, ad *Unde
oportet quod.*

95. *Contra Gentiles*, II, 56, ad *videtur autem rationabiliter* ff.,
and cf. *supra* p. 148 ff. for an analysis of these texts. In notes 40-44
will be found the *incipit* of each reference.

96. *Contra Gentiles*, II, 69, ad *In prima enim ratione*, and cf.
no. 40. The next objection is the logical formulation of this; cf.
ad *Quod autem secundo*, and *supra*, no. 41.

97. *Ibid.*, ad *Non autem oportet;* cf. *supra*, no. 42.

lect. The intellect is a separate power in the sense that its activity is realized through itself and not through the body.[98]

We may use the same kind of argument against Averroes. The soul is joined to the body as its form. Given such a union, the separation of the possible intellect is to be understood as a separation from a bodily organ, and not as a separation from the soul. We may note throughout this criticism the frequent appearance of Aristotle's name and the insistence of St. Thomas that the texts of Aristotle do not lead to, or permit, an Averroistic conclusion.[99] Here the relations of St. Thomas to Averroes are quite clear, and indeed point very naturally to the subject of the next chapter in his *Contra Gentiles*. In fact, to remove every doubt as to what his intentions are, he tells us in the very first sentence the starting point of his reconstruction: it is because of these attempts on the part of Averroes to use Aristotle for the confirmation of his opinions that the time has come when the meaning of Aristotle himself in the problem of the relations between soul and body has to be established. This chapter, then, is concerned to show that *secundum opinionem Aristotelis, intellectum secundum suam substantiam alicui corpori uniri ut formam.*[100] In this way we reach the Thomistic

---

98. *Ibid.*, ad *Nec tamen per hoc;* cf. no. 43. The next argument (*ibid.*, ad *Non est autem;* cf. no. 44) follows the same procedure.

99. Thus, St. Thomas will write, "Verba enim Aristotelis . . . non cogunt confiteri quod substantia intellectiva non sit unita corpori ut forma dans esse. . . Unde patet quod nec demonstratio Aristotelis hoc concludit. . . Quod autem, per hoc quod Aristoteles dicit . . . non intendat excludere. . . " etc. (*ibid.*).

100. *Contra Gentiles*, II, 70. We cannot here enter into an analysis of this chapter. St. Thomas questions the Aristotelianism of Averroes on the ground that the theory of union by continuation through phantasms breaks down when applied to the soul of the heavens. St. Thomas is sure of at least this point of Aristotelian interpretation, namely, that there is a parallel between the manner of union between the soul of the heavens and the heavens

commentary on Aristotle's *De Anima*. It is in this work, naturally, which followed the *Contra Gentiles* by only a few years,[101] that we shall find St. Thomas' direct analysis of the text of Aristotle.

St. Thomas begins his discussion of the definition of the soul by showing the difference between the definition of substance and that of accident. The difference lies in this, that whereas in the definition of substance only the constitutive principles are posited, in the definition of an accident something is given as subject apart from the essence of the thing defined; and the reason for this addition of a subject is, clearly, that the accident has existence and being only in that subject.[102] Furthermore, in the definition of a form, matter must be posited as the subject. Hence, in the definition of the soul, matter is posited as the subject.[103] Within the unity of substance, we may distinguish matter as the purely determinable element, and form as the determining and actualizing element. Through their combination is produced the *hoc aliquid*, of substance, complete in its existence and in its

---

and between soul and body. He adds, however, quoting St. Augustine (*Enchiridion*, c. 58; Patrologia Latina, vol. 40, col. 260) that "hoc autem quod dictum est de animatione coeli non diximus quasi asserendo secundum fidei doctrinam, ad quam nihil pertinet sive sic, sive aliter dicatur . . ."

101. For the Mandonnet-Grabmann dispute on the date, cf. *supra*, n. 79.—I shall use the edition of Father Angeli M. Pirotta, Marietti, Taurini, 1925.

102. In *Aristotelis Librum De Anima Commentum*, Lib. II, lect. 1, ed. Pirotta, N. 213. For this, St. Thomas refers to *Metaph.* VI, 4, 1029b, where cf. especially 1, 19-21: "ἐν ᾧ ἄρα μὴ ἐνέσται λόγῳ λέγοντι αὐτό, οὗτος ὁ λόγος τοῦ τί ἦν εἶναι ἑκάστῳ."
Aristotle then proceeds to ask whether or not substances and accidents are capable of definition in the same sense, and concludes in the negative, after showing that definition belongs properly to substances: *ibid.*, 5, 1031a11-14, for which cf. St. Thomas, *In Metaph.* VII, lect. IV, ed. Cathala (Taurini, 1926). N. 1338-39.

103. *In De Anima, ibid.*, ad *Unde substantia composita*.

nature. Such an analysis is characteristic only of material substances. The separate substances, while not composed of matter and form, are, nevertheless, each of them *a hoc aliquid* as being subsistent and complete in their natures. The soul, however, can be called a *hoc aliquid* in that it is subsistent. But since it is not a complete species, being only a part of man, the term *hoc aliquid* is not proper to the soul in a complete sense. It is subsistent, but it is incomplete in its being.[104] As we shall see, it is this incompleteness which is the basis of the contribution of the body to the complete perfection of the soul.

Substances are natural or artificial. Among the natural substances there is the further division of living and non-living.[105] That by which the living body lives is the soul. The body, then, is not the soul but the subject of the soul. More accurately, this subject is matter, or, in the more specific interpretation of St. Thomas, prime matter.[106] The soul, therefore, being neither the compound nor the subject, is the form or species of the body. To repeat the famous definition, the soul is the form of a physical body possessing life in potency—*corporis physici potentia vitam habentis.*[107]

In this definition St. Thomas draws our attention to the term *potentia.* If Aristotle had said only "having life", that would be understood as indicating a perfection belong-

---

104. *Ibid.*, n. 215, especially, "Anima autem rationalis, quantum ad aliquid potest dici hoc aliquid, secundum hoc quod potest esse per se subsistens. Sed quia non habet speciem completam, sed magis est pars speciei, non omnino convenit ei quod sit hoc aliquid."—This is a commentary on *De Anima*, II, 1, 412a6-9. Immediately after there follows the distinction between *actus primus* and *actus secundus* (1. 10-11), which, as Hicks observes (*ad loc.; ed. cit.*, p. 307), in modern times would be relegated to a footnote.

105. *Ibid.*, n. 218-219. St. Thomas observes (no. 219) that the definition of life given here is 'per modum exempli'.

106. *Ibid.*, n. 220.

107. *De Anima*, II. 1, 412a1921; St. Thomas *ad loc.* n. 221.

ing to the composite living substance. But as we know already from the discussion in the *Metaphysics*,[108] the composite is not given in the definition of the form. The matter of the body, however, is compared to life as potency to act. This act is the soul through which the compound body is living. In other words, the subject of life is not the living body, but prime matter.[109]

It is the function of the soul as form that will explain what has just preceded. The soul is a substantial form, not an accidental form. An accidental form enables a thing to be large or white, etc. The substantial form enables it to be in an absolute sense. That is, the substantial form is not a qualifying predicate but an essential and constitutive part— that part from which the individual thing of which it is the form derives its existence. If, therefore, the substantial form is the principle of existence, its immediate subject is not an already existing being, but a being which exists potentially and to which the substantial form will give an actual existence. Such a potential being is prime matter. A substance can thus have only one substantial form, and the reason for this is obvious. Since, in fact, it is the first form which gives existence to the compound, every succeeding form will be received in an already existing subject and therefore be an accidental modification of that subject.[110]

Referring to the *Fons Vitae* of Ibn Gebirol, St. Thomas

---

108. N. 102.

109. *De Anima, ibid.*, n. 222. He illustrates as follows: "Sicut si dicerem quod figura est actus, non quidem corporis figurati in actu, hoc enim est compositum ex figura et corpore, sed corporis quod est subjectum figurae, quod comparatur ad figuram sicut potentia ad actum" (*ibid.*).

110. *Ibid.*, n. 224. Here in a sentence is the Thomistic position: "Forma autem substantialis non advenit subjecto jam praeexistenti in actu, sed existenti in potentia tantum, scilicet materiae primae"; and the following is the immediate consequence: "Ex quo

takes this opportunity to attack the doctrine of plural forms. According to Ibn Gebirol, an individual *A* is constituted a substance by one form, a body by another, a living body by a third. The Aristotelian theory of substantial forms does not permit such a conception. It is one and the same form, says St. Thomas, through which *A* is a *hoc aliquid,* a body and a living body. The soul, then, is not the form of the body in the sense that there is an already constituted body which becomes its subject; it is the form of the body in the sense that the soul is the principle through which the body exists and is living.[111] We may note, furthermore, that in considering the soul as the form or *actus* of the body, Aristotle refers to the soul not as operative but as continually present. That is why the soul is called the *actus primus*.[112]

One more point in Aristotle's definition of the soul has still to be explained. In that definition he has called the body organic. This refers to the variety of organs that the body possesses because of the many functions of the soul. We may illustrate this diversity of organs by means of plants whose different parts serve as organs having different operations to perform in the life of the plant.[113] That is why it is possible to consider as universal a definition of the soul which embraces the whole realm of living and organized substances. And it is possible from this also to solve a difficulty which

---

patet, quod impossibile est unius rei esse plures formas substantiales. . . " (*ibid.*).

111. "Oportet enim secundum praemissa dicere, quod una et eadem forma substantialis sit, per quam hoc individuum est hoc aliquid, sive substantia, et per quam est corpus et animatum corpus, et sic de aliis" (*ibid.*).

That is why, when the soul leaves, the body cannot be said to be the same specifically. A clear text on the point will be found in *In Metaph.* VII, lect. X, (ed. Cathala) n. 1485, with which cf. Aristotle, *Metaph.* VI, 10, 1035b23-25.

112. *In De Anima,* II, lect. 1, n. 227-229.

113. *De Anima,* II, 1, 412b1-3; St. Thomas *ad loc.* n. 230-32.

presented itself to Aristotle. Given such a definition, it is
not necessary to ask whether soul and body make a unity,
because there can be no problem of matter and form if for
matter to be actual is the same as to be united to form: *idem
est materiam uniri formae, quod materiam esse in actu.*[114]

After this general definition of the soul, Aristotle proceeds to elaborate some of the implications contained in the
doctrine of the soul as the substantial form of the body.[115] As
a substantial form, the soul is an essential component of the
animate body of which it is the form; as *form*, it is that
which gives essence to the body in the sense of effecting its
existence in a species.[116] To clarify this point, Aristotle considers two examples. If an axe were a living being, its essence would be axeity. This axeity would also be the soul
or substantial form of the axe upon whose separation the axe
would no longer exist, except equivocally. As a matter of
fact, however, that this piece of iron shoould be an axe is
purely accidental, and, once the axe is broken, the iron still
survives, because the substantial form which makes it iron

---

114. *De Anima, ibid.,* b4-6; St. Thomas *ad loc.* n. 233.

115. *De Anima, ibid.,* b8-9: "τὸ γὰρ ἕν καὶ τὸ εἶναι ἐπεὶ πλεο-
ναχῶς λέγεται, τὸ κυρίως ἡ ἐντελέχειά ἐστι; cf. St. Thomas *ad loc.,*
n. 234, with his reference to the meaning of unity and actuality in
Metaph. VII, 6, 1045b16-23. St. Thomas comments as follows: "Sed
sicut dictum est ultima materia, quae scilicet est appropriata ad
formam, et ipsa forma, sunt idem. Aliud enim eorum est sicut potentia, aliud sicut actus. Unde simile est quaerere quae est causa
alicujus rei, et quae est causa quod illa sit res una; quia unumquodque inquantum est, unum est, et potentia et actus quodammodo unum sunt. Et sic non oportet ea uniri per aliquod vinculum
sicut ea quae sunt penitus diversa. Unde nulla causa est faciens
unum ea quae sunt composita ex materia et forma, nisi quod movet
potentiam in actum" (*In Metaph.* VIII. Lect. V, (ed. Cathala) n.
1767).

116. *De Anima,* II, 1, 412b10-11; St. Thomas, *ad loc.,* n. 236.
For a grammatical analysis of the τὸ τί ἦν εἶναι, cf. R. D. Hicks,
ad. b11; p. 315.

has not been affected.[117]   Again, if the eye were a living being, sight would be its soul, or substantial form, precisely because it is sight which is the definitive essence of the eye.[118] The eye would be the matter of sight, and when the sight is gone there would no longer be an eye, except equivocally.[119]

We may apply this discussion of the eye and its ''soul'' to the whole animate body.   The capacity for life does not belong to a body that has lost its soul; it belongs to a body which still is in possession of its soul.   Correspondingly, the soul is united to the body to give it this life.   In the execution of the functions of life there will be a variety of powers expressed, all of which are necessarily bound up with specific organs.   In such cases, there is no separation in the function of the soul from the organ.   However, should there be parts of the soul which do not operate in this way, that is, by being joined to specific organs, these parts can be called separate in the execution of their functions.[120]

Having thus given the definition of the soul, Aristotle is now concerned to give it a causal formation.   What he means is illustrated by an example from geometry which he applies to the soul.[121]   The living is distinguished from the non-living by the possession of life.   This life may be manifested in any

---

117. *De Anima, ibid.*, b11-15; St. Thomas, *ad loc.* n. 237.

118. *De Anima, ibid.*, b19-20; St. Thomas, *ad loc.*, n. 239.

119. *Ibid.*

120. *De Anima, II*, 1, 413a1-7; St. Thomas, *ad loc.*, n. 240-242.

121. According to this procedure, a geometrical figure may be explained in two ways: (a) one way states a fact: thus τετραγων-ισμὸς or quadrature is the construction of a square (lit. an equilateral rectangle) equal in area to a given figure of unequal sides (τὸ ἴσον ἑτερομήκει ὀρθογόνειον εἶναι ἰσόπλευρον : *De Anīma*, II, 2, 413a17-18, and cf. Hicks on a17 for a discussion of Euclid on this point); (b) we may state the fact in a causal way by defining quadrature as finding a mean proportional (ὁ δὲ λέγων ὅτι ἐστὶν ὁ τετραγωνισμὸς μέσης εὕρεσις, τοῦ πράγματος λέγει το αἴτιον'' *ibid.*, a17-20, and cf. Hicks on a14; p. 322, for references to Aristotle on the causal definition).

one of several ways—intellection, sensation, local motion and rest, motion in the assimilation of food or nutrition, decay and growth.[122]   This inner principle, beginning with nutrition in plants,[123] becomes distinctively characteristic of animals through sensation.[124]   In some forms of life it is apparently true that the soul is one and yet potentially many because when the parts of plants are broken off they are able to keep on living; which is also true of some insects.[125]   This is not universally true because as organization increases, local differentiation takes place.   Thus, sight is in one part of the body and hearing in another, while touch, as a generic form of sensation, is distributed throughout.[126]   The case of the intellect is not yet clear, says Aristotle.   It appears to be another kind of soul, because it alone is capable of being separated as is the eternal from the perishable.[127]   We may consider the soul, therefore, as that by which we live, have sensation and think.   It is the form and not the subject of the compound.   More technically, it is the entelechy of the

---

122. *De Anima*, II, 2, 413a20-25. — The inclusion of νοῦς under the generic name of ζῆν apparently ought to decide the question of separation in the negative, following the interpretation of St. Thomas as against the interpretation of Averroes.

123. *De Anima, ibid.*, a. 30-34.

124. *Ibid.*, 413b2: "τὸ δὲ ζῶον διὰ τὴν αἴσθησιν πρώτως," which in its most universal aspects is connected with the sense of touch (*ibid.*, b4-5).

125. *Ibid.*, b16-21; St. Thomas, *In De Anima*, II, lect. IV, n. 262-265.

126. *De Anima*, II, 2, 414a2-3; St. Thomas, *ad loc.*, n. 266.

127. *De Anima*, II, 2, 413b24-27. As we have seen, it was on the occasion of this text that Averroes decided that soul was applied to νοῦς only in an equivocal sense, and held for real separation. Cf. *supra*, p. 164, n. 80, where St. Thomas points out that χωρίζεσθαι refers only to separation from any localized organ, and not from the soul: *ad loc.*, n. 268.—Cf. also *In II Sent.*, d. 19, q. 1, a. 1, ad 3; ed. Mandonnet, vol. ii, p. 483.

body, residing in a body equipped for the functions for which the compound is destined.[128]

While it is difficult to grasp the thought of Aristotle here, the meaning of St. Thomas is quite clear. According to his interpretation, Aristotle's aim is to give a strictly biological definition of the soul, to make it the form of matter in a strict sense and in this way to insure the metaphysical unity of the living compound. For St. Thomas to hold the soul as the *forma corporis,* a view so distasteful to his contemporaries, was required not only by substantial unity, as we have seen from the Commentary on the *Sentences,* but also by Aristotle's express intention. The reason in both cases is the same.

If Plato and his disciples, therefore, had succeeded in insuring the substantiality of the soul, they had succeeded also in destroying the unity of man. In separating his conception of the soul from what he considers to be the extreme position of Platonism, St. Thomas not only championed the cause of Aristotle; he also undertook to show why the very nature of the soul required its union with the body. Whereas with St. Bonaventure we found that the soul was a substance and certainly not an Aristotelian form, for the reason that it was a substance, here with St. Thomas we find something quite different. Within the essence of the soul itself there is a lack, a gap, an incompleteness. There is a sense in which it is true to say that man is more natural than the soul and that the body adds to the essential perfection of the soul. It is possible to show that the indispensable condition presupposed in the operations of the soul is realized only through the presence of the body. If that is true, then it is easy to understand why soul and body are joined together in such an intimate unity as St. Thomas has described. We shall turn

---

128. *De Anima, ibid.* b12-22; St. Thomas, *ad loc.* n. 272-278, especially n. 275.

to this point after a brief consideration of the definitive thought of St. Thomas in the *De Spiritualibus Creaturis,* the *Summa Theologica,* and the *Quaestio Disputata De Anima.*[129]

D. The Thomistic Synthesis.

The repetition which an historical treatment of the Thomistic texts has forced upon us shows quite clearly, in spite of a certain diffusiveness, how from the beginning there was no hesitation in the mind of St. Thomas on the question of the soul. A brief survey of the remaining texts will reveal the same unwavering attitude at a time when the stress of philosophical and theological controversy could force less firm spirits, such as Godfrey of Fontaines, to qualify their decisions with doubts and hesitations.[130] But there is no-

---

129. The chronology is here somewhat uncertain. For the *Quaestiones Disputatae,* cf. P. Glorieux, *Les Questions Disputées de s. Thomas et leur suite chronologique,* Recherches de théologie ancienne et médiévale, IV (1932), p. 5-33.

130. Cf. *supra,* p. 67, for the hesitations of Godfrey of Fontaines.

It is interesting to note that his own doctrinal hesitations did not prevent Godfrey from looking upon the inclusion of St. Thomas in the condemnation of 1277 with distinct disfavor. He recognizes that some of the doctrines condemned at that time were taken from the works of St. Thomas; and that is partly why he considers it necessary that the list of condemned articles be amended: *concedo quod praedicti articuli essent merito corrigendi* (*Quodl.* XII, q. v; ed. J. Hoffmans, *Les quodlibets onze et douze de Godfroid de Fontaines* (*Les philosophes belges,* v, 1-2), Louvain, 1932, p. 103). This quodlibet is dated after the year 1290: cf. M. de Wulf, *History of Mediaeval Philosophy,* vol. ii, p. 56.

With reference to St. Thomas, the correction is necessary because the condemnation may prevent students from becoming acquainted with a doctrine which is not only *perutilis,* but also, and this more than any other, a model of thought to be used in the correction and guidance of all others: "Sunt etiam (i.e., the articles of condemnation) in detrimentum non modicum doctrinae

thing in St. Thomas which even suggests the need or possibility of change and retraction in the fundamental points of his doctrine. In the *Summa Theologica,* where St. Thomas follows quite closely the discussion of the *De Anima* which we have just left, we begin naturally with the distinction that the soul is not a body but the principle of life in a body.[131] Having made this distinction, we must avoid two extremes in developing the definition of the soul. In other words, we must avoid making the soul either a purely material form

studentibus perutilis reverendissimi et excellentissimi doctoris scilicet Fratris Thomae, quae ex praedictis articulis minus iuste aliqualiter diffamatur. Quia articuli supra positi et quam plures alii videntur sumpti esse ex his, quae tantus doctor scripsit in doctrina tam utili et solemni. Et ideo in hoc quod tales articuli tanquam erronei reprobantur, dicta doctrina etiam suspecta a simplicionibus habetur, quia tanquam erronea et reprobabilis innuitur.

"Propter quod plures possent habere occasionem retrahendi se a studio in tali doctrina, in quo non solum ipsa doctrina caederetur, sed ipsi studentes vere damnum maximum sustinerent, quia, salva reverentia aliquorum doctorum, excepta doctrina sanctorum, et eorum quorum dicta pro auctoritatibus allegantur, praedicta doctrina inter ceteros videtur utilior et laudabilior reputanda, ut vere doctori qui hanc doctrinam scripsit, possit dici in singulari illud quod Dominus dixit in plurali apostolis, Matth. quinto (*Matthew*, V, 13): 'Vos estis sal terrae'; et cetera, sub hac forma: 'Tu es sal terrae, quod si sal evanuerit, in quo salietur'? Quia per ea quae in hac doctrina continentur quasi omnium doctorum aliorum doctrinae corriguntur, sapidae redduntur et condiuntur; et ideo si ista doctrina de medio auferretur studentes in doctrinis aliorum saporem modicum invenirent" (Quodl. XII, q. v; ed. cit., p. 102-103).

Godfrey has considered elsewhere the problem which presented itself to those theologians who accepted as true some articles condemned as false by the archbishop of Paris: cf. Godfrey of Fontaines, Quold. VII, q. xviii; ed. M. de Wulf J. Hoffmans, *Les quodlibets cinq, six et sept de Godefroid de Fontaines* (*Les philosophes belges*, III), Louvain, 1914, p. 402-405.

131. *Sum. Theol.*, I, q. 75, a. 1; cp. Aristotle, *De Anima*, II, 1, 412b15-22.—For a similar criticism of the early Greek cosmogonies as the one contained here in the *Summa*, cf. *De Substantiis Separatis*, c. 1.

or, in opposition to this materialistic interpretation, so separate from man that it can no longer properly be called a constituent form of his being.[132]   As we may well suspect, St.
Thomas has in mind here those who, in their anxiety to save
the immortality of the soul, place the intellect outside the
soul.   Out of the question as now presented arises the problem of correlating the conceptions of the soul as form and
as substance.[133]   St. Thomas sees quite clearly the breach
which exists for a Platonist between saying that the soul is
a substance and that it is the form of the body; he sees also
how it is precisely this breach which causes all the difficulties
and leads ultimately to the excessive separatism so characteristic, on this point, of the whole Platonic tradition.   If, in
order to bridge the gap which now separates soul and body,
we try to establish certain external relations between the
individual and his intellect, we find neither the continuation
theory of Averroes[134] nor the *motor-mobile* theory of Plato[135]

---

132. *Quaest. disp. De Anima*, a. 2, *Respondeo;* cp. ad *Sed hoc
quidam fugientes.*   Whenever St. Thomas meets this type of separation, as here with Averroes, he proceeds to show that the operations which follow from such a union of body and intellect are not
human.

133. *Quaest. disp. De Anima*, a. 1: "Utrum anima humana possit esse forma et hoc aliquid".—St. Thomas has marked quite clearly how the difficulty arises in the conception of the question by
Nemesius and how on the basis of his Platonic outlook he could
think of Aristotle as a materialist. Cf. *Quaest. disp. De Spirit.
Creat.*, a 2, *Respondeo;* B. Geyer, *Grundriss*, 11th ed., p. 120.

134. *De Spirit. Creat.*, a. 2, ad *Quidam vero concedentes.*

135. *Ibid.*, ad *Hac igitur opinione.*—As before, Nemesius is
the source of St. Thomas' knowledge on this point.—St. Thomas'
respect for Plato is brought out at times in such statements as the
following: "considerandum est quod Plato *efficacius* posuit hunc
hominem intelligere, nec tamen substantiam spiritualem uniri corpori ut formam" (*ibid.*). In fact, St. Thomas will make the same
sort of comparison between Plato and Avicenna and he will show
how Plato is the more consistent Platonist: Cf. *infra*, ch. V, p. 191.
St. Thomas was distinctly aware that there are some ideas which

satisfactory. As concerns Plato, St. Thomas, still following the discussion of Nemesius, repeats his analysis of the soul-pilot image from the *Contra Gentiles* and goes on to support this imputation to Plato from the *De Anima* of Aristotle.[136] However, he deals with Plato's position quite briefly, relying entirely on Aristotle for his criticism.[137] Here, as in the *Contra Gentiles*, the argument then turns to its real issue: the necessity of the soul as the substantial form of the body and the manner and means of such a union.[138]

The question may begin with Plato, and the substantiality of the soul will thus be assured; but from the subsistence of the soul we cannot go on to argue that it is complete as a substance. It is here that St. Thomas departs from the Platonic tradition.[139] If this second conclusion were true, man could not be a unity: that, in brief, is the sum and substance of the Thomistic criticism. That is why we must note two conditions which every substance must fulfil. In order to be a substance, a being must be both subsistent and

---

Platonism will not be able to assimilate, and he will tell Avicenna this in so many words.

136. Cf. *Contra Gentiles*, II, 57, and *supra*, p. 157-158, for the analysis of these texts.—The text of Aristotle is *De Anima*, II, 1, 413a8-9.

137. "Sed ad hujus rationis improbationem unum sufficiat quod Aristoteles in II de *Anima* inducit *directe contra hanc positionem*. Si enim anima non uniretur corpori ut forma, sequeretur quod corpus et partes ejus non haberent esse specificum per animam; quod manifeste falsum apparet; quia recedente anima non dicitur oculus aut caro et os nisi aequivoce" etc. *De Spirit. Creat.*, a. 2, ad *Hac igitur opinione; Quaest. disp. De Anima*, a. 1, ad *Sed ulterius posuit Plato*. Cp. Aristotle, *De Anima*, II, 1. 412b13-15, 20-21.

138. *De Spirit. Creat.*, *ibid.*

139. "Sed ulterius posuit Plato quod anima humana non solum per se subsisteret, *sed quod etiam haberet in se completam naturam speciei*". Why this last conclusion? St. Thomas continues: "Ponebat enim totam naturam speciei in anima esse . . ." (*Quaest. disp. De Anima*, a. 1, *loc. cit.*).

complete.[140]   The soul fulfils only one of these requirements.
It is subsistent, being capable of acting within itself, and to
this extent can be called a *hoc aliquid*.[141]   But the soul is not
the complete nature of man, and therefore man cannot be
called a soul.[142]   Furthermore, since the soul, though subsistent, is nevertheless an incomplete nature, it is not composed of matter and form.[143]   To consider the soul as the

---

140. *Ibid.*, ad *Respondeo.*   When applied to the soul, this doctrine gives St. Thomas the opportunity to review history and show
how the complexion or harmony theory destroys the soul's subsistence and its completeness alike; while the reaction to this materialism guarantees both of these points and fails by excess.

141. *Sum. Theol.*, I, q. 75, a. 2, ad 1: "Sic igitur, cum anima
humana sit pars speciei humanae, potest dici *hoc aliquid* primo
modo, quasi subsistens, sed non secundo modo: sic enim compositum ex anima et corpore dicitur hoc aliquid".

142. *Sum. Theol.*, I, q. 75, a. 4, *Respondeo,* where two interpretations of this statement will be found, that of Averroes and
that of Plato.   For Averroes' conception, according to which man
in general would be a soul, as possessing no matter, while *this
man*, being individual, would have matter and would thus not be a
soul, cf. St. Thomas, *In Metaph.* VII, lect. IX, n. 1467-1469, where
notice that St. Thomas accepts the interpretation of Avicenna.

143. *Sum Theol.*, I, q. 75, a. 5; *De Spirit. Creat.*, a. 1, *Respondeo,* the last part of which is the argument about the twofold composition in material things that we have already examined in the
De Substantiis Separatis.   We may note here the names of Avicenna, Algazel, Aristotle and St. Augustine in the *Sed Contra* of
St. Thomas (n. 5, 6, 9, 14) as opponents of spiritual matter.   He
defines matter according to Augustine and Aristotle as pure subject, receptive of forms and privations, and then argues that on
this definition ("quae est propria ejus acceptio et communis";
ibid.) it cannot exist in spiritual substances.   The reason is that
the gradation in the being of these substances does not come
from matter but results from their operation.   As this is of an
intellectual nature, and as it is impossible to receive intelligible
species into prime matter without individualizing them, it is impossible to have matter in purely intellectual substances *(ibid.).*

The *Quaestio disputata De Anima* (a. 6) is quite severe on Ibn

complete nature of man or to hold that it is composed of matter and form is really to leave unexplained the union of soul and body. In other words, if the completeness of human nature cannot be found in the soul alone, and if to explain human nature as implying both body and soul becomes impossible when the soul is considered to be complete even by those who defend the unity of soul and body, then the solution must lie in viewing the soul as joined naturally to the body, as part to part, for the completion of the nature of man. The intellectual soul must become the form of the body in one act of existence from which will be derived all the operations of life, from the lowest to the highest.[144]

As we know from his commentary on the *De Anima*, this is the position that St. Thomas considers to be authentically Aristotelian. It will not be necessary to repeat the analysis of the *De Anima* or the criticism that St. Thomas directs against Averroes. This much, however, is historically important. As it is clear from the *De Unitate Intellectus*, St. Thomas will not even countenance the current Averroism of his day, and this for two reasons. The unity of the possible intellect held by the Averroists was opposed not only to Christianity, because it removed the possibility of the just distribution of rewards and punishments, but also to philo-

---

Gebirol. Its argument is (a) that if the soul is composed of matter and form then it is a complete species and union with the body would be purely accidental *(ibid., ad Quod etiam positio)*; (b) the double composition of material things *(ibid., ad In substantiis enim ex materia)*, which destroys the unity and universality of matter.

144. *Sum. Theol.*, I, q. 76, a. 1, *Respondeo*. This question is very compact. It deals chiefly with three types of union which he rejects: Plato, Averroes and "quidam" who hold the *motor-mobile* doctrine. He rejects Plato because *sensation* requires the body as its subject; Averroes, because, as we have seen, continuation does not explain knowledge; and the "quidam" because the body is then accidental to the soul. Cf. an identical method in the controversial *De Unitate Intellectus* (ed. Mandonnet) vol. 1, p. 51-52.

sophy itself. Furthermore, it was not even Aristotelian.
And it was in answer to those who claimed to be following
Peripatetic teaching in holding this doctrine that St. Thomas
began the *De Unitate Intellectus* with a lengthy exposition of
Aristotle's doctrine on the soul and its faculties.[145] This
discussion is not directly pertinent to our problem. It illustrates, however, the defense of the unity of man and the rehabilitation of Aristotle as the single cause to which St.
Thomas gave his unfailing support.

Now it would be possible to analyze at length the Thomistic texts on this point of substantial union: how the soul
is the one substantial form of the body;[146] how it is joined
to the body immediately, becoming one with it;[147] how, as
the substantial form, it is *tota* in the whole body and in its
parts;[148]—but such an analysis would only repeat what St.
Thomas has already made abundantly clear, namely, his
unwavering and unvarying conception of the soul and of the
unity of man.

---

145. *De Unitate Intellectus, ed. cit.,* p. 33. cp. p. 41: "Et ne
alicui videatur quod hoc ex nostro sensu dicamus praeter Aristotelis intentionem, inducenda sunt verba Aristotelis expresse hoc
dicentis";—cf. also p. 61.—The appeal of the Averroists to Greek
and Arabian sources will force St. Thomas to quote Avicenna and
Algazel (p. 67) for an interpretation that is not *Latin* but does
not uphold the numerical unity of the possible intellect, and the
interpretation of Themistius among the Greek commentators
(p. 55).—The exposition of Aristotle covers p. 31-41, and repeats
systematically the doctrines we have touched upon, especially the
separation of the intellect only with respect to an organ, and the
need of making the soul the *forma corporis.*

146. *Sum. Theol.,* I, q. 76, a. 4; *Quaest. disp. De Anima,* a. 9.

147. *Sum. Theol.,* I, q. 76, a. 6; *De Spirit. Creat.,* a. 3; *Quaest.
disp. De Anima, ibid.*

148. *Sum. Theol.,* I, q. 76, a. 8. The argument is that the soul
is united to the body essentially, and not through its powers:
"quia non secundum quamlibet suam potentiam est in qualibet
parte corporis"; but as the soul *operates differently* according to
the difference in the bodily organs, the soul will be said to be

But the Thomistic defense of Aristotle is so clear and un-
compromising not only in the face of an Augustinian tradition, but also in the face of discordant interpretations of
Aristotle, that it is natural to look for the principles and
motives guiding his decisions. Not that his attitude came
about through the intervention of the Aristotelian texts. It
was present from the very beginning and appears to have
found in the language of Aristotle a more natural channel
of expression. The Thomistic synthesis is a purely metaphysical one and finds in Aristotle what is most significant in
itself. The new conception of man and of the soul which
St. Thomas elaborates has as its foundation a new interpretation of the causality of creatures and, more particularly,
of the range and efficacy of the human intellect in the acquisition of knowledge. To understand this point, we must
outline briefly the Thomistic answer to the problem of human knowledge in relation to the definition of the soul as
the form of the body.[149]

"tota . . in qualibet parte corporis secundum totalitatem perfectionis et essentiae; non autem secundum totalitatem virtutis"
(ibid.). Cf. *Quaest. disp. De Anima,* a. 10, *Respondeo,* ad *Si autem
quaeratur; De Spirit. Creat.,* a. 4, *Respondeo,* ad *Relinquitur ergo
quod.*

149. For the present I must refrain from burdening any further this discussion on the soul with the idea of parallel texts suggested by Father de Guibert. It is quite clear that the variations
which such a method is intended to show are not present in the
outlines of our problem, and that those variations which have appeared are not a matter of doctrine but of method. I have tried to
take into account this latter point by the four movements of chapter IV.

V. Conclusion.

If Averroes was in the eyes of St. Thomas neither a correct interpreter of Aristotle nor acceptable as a philosopher, because he made impossible the explanation of knowledge as a human function, Avicenna stood in a more favorable, even though unacceptable, position. Behind Avicenna rises the figure of Plato, and in Plato St. Thomas sees the parent of all doctrines incompatible with Aristotelianism. That this is so we may see clearly by examining some texts of the *Contra Gentiles* in which Avicenna and Plato are compared.[1] Now the transition to Avicenna meant for St. Thomas a definite turning away from any doctrine which held that the possible intellect was not part of the soul as form of the body, but was, as Averroes had held, one for all men. There might be some reason, doubtless, in saying that there is one active intellect for all men because no contradiction seems to follow if one and the same agent accomplishes many actions, just as all the powers of sight in animals are perfected by one sun. Plato, indeed (and St. Thomas is here referring to the well-known simile of the sun in the *Republic*[2] to illustrate the function of the Idea of Good in the universe) posited one separate in-

---

1. On this point the central text of Avicenna will be found in E. Gilson, *Pourquoi saint Thomas a critiqué saint Augustin*, Archives . . . I (1926-1927), p. 43, note 1. This text will also be found to be faithfully analyzed by St. Thomas, *Contra Gentiles*, II, 74.

2. *Republic*, VI, 508E29-509B15. Cf. the edition of James Adam (Cambridge, 1921) *ad loc.*, vol. 2, p. 60-62 for a technical analysis, and his third appendix to Book vii, vol. 2, p. 168-179, for the general interpretation of the Idea of Good, especially as concerns the relations with the *Timaeus* doctrine of the δεμιουργός (p. 170). Adam's ideas on this point are far from being unanimously accepted.

tellect, according to the testimony of Themistius,[3] and compared it to the sun. There is one sun, but there are many *lumina* diffused by the sun for the purpose of sight. This doctrine has at least some appearance of truth, but the doctrine of a separate possible intellect is untenable.[4]

Avicenna, therefore, and Platonism which, as this text implies and as the *Contra Gentiles* expressly affirms, is his source, while contrary to Aristotle, are a probable and alternative solution, and have as their center of gravity the activity

---

3. This discussion of St. Thomas (cf. the text of the following note) follows Themistius' analysis of *De Anima* III, 5: cf. *Themistii Paraphrases Aristotelis Librorum Quae Supersunt*, edidit L. Spengel, vol. 2, Lipsiae, 1866, p. 190, ad 'Αλλὰ ταῦτα μεν.

The *direct* use of Themistius in this connection, as compared with the *indirect* use of his ideas in the *Contra Gentiles* (cf. *supra*, ch. iv, note 68), indicates that the commentary of Themistius on the *De Anima* did not exist in a Latin translation until after the year 1260. M. Grabmann places the date of translation "kurz vor 1270": cf. his *Mittelalterliche lateinische Uebersetzungen von Schriften der Aristoteles-Kommentatoren Johannes Philoponos, Alexander von Aphrodisias und Themistios* (Sitzungsberichte der Bayerischen Akademie der Wissenschaften, Phil.-hist. Abteilung, 1929, Heft 7), München, 1929, p. 64.

4. "His igitur consideratis quantum ad id quod ponunt, intellectum non esse animam, quae est nostri corporis forma, neque partem ipsius, sed aliquid secundum substantiam separatum; considerandum restat de hoc quod dicunt, intellectum possibilem esse unum in omnibus. Forte enim de agente hoc dicere, aliquam rationem haberet, et multi philosophi hoc posuerunt; nihil enim videtur inconveniens sequi, si ab uno agente multa perficiantur, quemadmodum ab uno sole perficiuntur omnes potentiae visivae animalium ad videndum; *quamvis etiam hoc non sit secundum intentionem Aristotelis*, qui ponit intellectum agentem esse aliquid in anima, unde comparat ipsum lumini. Plato autem, ponens intellectum unum separatum, comparavit ipsum soli, ut Themistius dicit: est enim unus sol sed plura lumina diffusa a sole ad videndum. Sed quicquid sit de intellectu agente, dicere intellectum possibilem esse unum omnium hominum, multipliciter impossibile apparet" (*De Unitate Intellectus;* ed. Mandonnet, vol. 1, p. 57).

of a universal light proceeding from a separate active intellect. In the question of knowledge, this does not affect the completeness of man as man, because there is a power in him which knows, namely, the possible intellect; but it does affect the manner of his operation. We may see this point illustrated by a brief examination of the Avicennian system.[5] Avicenna explains the universe by a series of successive emanations from pure unity, and the sublunar world, consisting of the four elements and of rational beings, is only an instance of this universal emanation. Thus, the question of knowledge and its origin would be treated by Avicenna in the same way as the generation of physical substance.[6] That is, both substantial forms and intelligible species come from the separate intellect or *dator formarum,* after the way has been *prepared*[7] by inferior agents. The production of knowledge would take place in the same way. The imagination, in which sensible forms exist, serves as the starting point. The reason observes or *considers* these sensibles in the imagination, and after such an activity the soul is rendered able to receive

---

5. The necessary texts and analysis will be found in E. Gilson, *loc cit.,* p. 35-45.

6. Cf. St. Thomas, *Contra Gentiles,* II, 76. "Est autem haec positio Avicennae consona his quae de generatione rerum naturalium dicit . . ." He proceeds to discuss the similarity, and later assimilates this whole trend in Avicenna to the *Mutakallimim* who reduced the efficacy of second causes to a minimum: *Contra Gentiles,* III, 69, ad *Quia enim omne.* The Aristotelianism of this chapter is quite strong, and aims at the rehabilitation of the physical world.

7. E. Gilson, *loc cit.,* p. 39-40, especially the example on p. 40, note 2: "Medicus enim non dat sanitatem, sed praeparat ad eam materiam et instrumentum; non enim attribuit sanitatem nisi principium quod est excellentius sanitate; et hoc est quod dat materiae omnes suas formas, cujus essentia est nobilior materia" (Avicenna, *Metaphysica,* tract. IX, cap. 3; ed. Venetiis, 1495, f. 103v). According to Avicenna, then, the doctor prepares the way, and the active intelligence gives the health.

the abstract ideas from the active intelligence: *ex considera-tione eorum aptatur anima ut emanet in eam ab intelligentia agente abstractio.*[8] However, we may explain knowledge, therefore, sensible objects are not its origin; they are merely its occasion.

From this brief statement of the doctrine of Avicenna we can understand quite readily why St. Thomas thinks that Avicenna differs very little from Plato. For in either case it would follow that our knowledge would not be caused by sensible objects: *utrobique enim sequetur quod scientia nostra non causetur a sensibilibus.*[9] But if Avicenna is a Platonist, he is not a consistent one. It is something of an innovation, observes St. Thomas, to say that by inspecting the individual sensibles in the imagination the possible in-tellect is illumined by the light of the active intellect to see the universal, and that the activities of inferior powers, such as the imagination, render the soul capable of receiving the emanation from the active intelligence.[10] In fact, such a doctrine is not only an innovation but also an improbability because it would seem that Avicenna leads one directly into saying that the nearer the soul is to material objects the more is it disposed to come under the influence of separate sub-stances; while the truth of the matter seems to be that for this purpose our souls must be removed as much as possible from the influence of material objects.[11] And that is why the Platonism of Avicenna is inconsistent, and why Plato

---

8. Avicenna, *De Anima*, V, 5; quoted by E. Gilson, *loc cit.*, p. 41, note 1. Notice that the *consideratio* precedes *abstractio*, which itself has an entirely new meaning.

9. *Contra Gentiles*, II, 74; *Sum. Theol.*, I, q. 84, a. 4, *Respondeo*, ad *Sed secundum hanc positionem*.

10. *Contra Gentiles, ibid.*

11. "Videmus enim quod anima nostra tanto magis disponitur ad recipiendum a substantiis separatis, quanto magis a corporali-bus et sensibilibus removetur; per recessum enim ab eo quod infra est, acceditur ad id quod supra est. Non igitur est verisimile quod,

was the better Platonist in the development of the central point of his system: *Plato autem radicem suae positionis melius est prosecutus.* For according to Plato, in the interpretation of St. Thomas, sensible objects do not *dispose* the soul to receive the influence of the separate forms, but merely rouse the intellect to consider those things the knowledge of which the soul possessed from the very beginning.[12] Indeed, the knowledge of all knowable things was produced in the soul from the very beginning by the ideas, and therefore Plato *addiscere dixit esse quoddam reminisci.*[13] The implication to be drawn is that in a consistent Platonism sensible objects play no part in the actual *acquisition* of knowledge.

In fact, according to the Platonic allegory of preëxistence, the soul is possessed of all knowledge before it enters the body. Upon its entrance, it is clouded by the body, and it is only after the discipline of study has removed these hindrances that the soul is enabled to use the knowledge that it already possesses. Now, if such a doctrine were true there would be no difference between an angel and a soul; nor would there be any reason to account for the union of soul and body.[14]

---

per hoc quod anima respicit ad phantasmata corporalia, disponatur ad recipiendum influentiam intelligentiae separatae" (*ibid.*).

12. " . . . posuit enim quod sensibilia non sunt disponentia animam ad recipiendum influentiam formarum separatarum, sed solum *expergescentia* intellectum ad considerandum ea quorum scientiam habebat ab exteriori causatam" *(ibid.).*

13. *Ibid.*

14. "Initium autem naturalis perfectionis quoad cognitionem secundum duas opiniones diversimode assignatur. Quidam enim, ut Platonici, posuerunt quod anima ad corpus venit plena omnibus scientiis, sed nube corporis opprimitur, et impeditur ne scientia habita libere uti possit nisi tantum quaedam universalia; sed postmodum per exercitium studii et sensuum, hujusmodi impedimenta tolluntur; ut libere sua scientia uti possit: et sic discere dicunt esse idem quod reminisci. Quod si haec opinio vera esset, tunc oporteret dicere, quod pueri mox nati in statu innocentiae

But behind this allegory lies a much deeper difficulty. According to the Heraclitean conception of the physical world as a flux of becoming, which Plato had accepted, certitude was rendered impossible because there was no constant element in the object of knowledge. In order, therefore, to avoid scepticism or relativism (such as is drawn by the Protagoras of Plato's *Theaetetus*), Plato posited a world of being, the Ideas, free from matter and motion. It was by participation in these ideas that material objects existed, just as it was by participation in these ideas that knowledge was produced. In this way, the theory of Ideas explains the existence of things and the certitude of knowledge. The soul does not know material objects; it knows their separate essences in the world of Ideas.[15]

---

omnium scientiam habuissent, quia corpus illud in statu innocentiae illo erat omnino subditum animae, quia per molem corporis non potuisset anima ita opprimi ut suam perfectionem omnino amitteret. Sed quia haec opinio procedere videtur ex hoc quod eadem ponitur natura angeli et animae, ut sic anima in sui creatione plenam scientiam habeat, sicut et intelligentia dicitur esse plena formis creata; ratione cujus Platonici dicebant animas fuisse ante corpus, et post corpus redire ad compares stellas, quasi quasdam intelligentias: quae quidem opinio non est consona catholicae veritati. . . ."(*De Veritate*, Quaest. XVIII, a. 7).

15. "Respondeo dicendum, ad evidentiam huius quaestionis, quod primi philosophi qui de naturis rerum inquisiverunt putaverunt nihil esse in mundo praeter corpus. Et quia videbant omnia corpora mobilia esse, et putabant ea in continuo fluxo esse, aestimaverunt quod nulla certitudo de rerum veritate haberi posset a nobis. Quod enim est in continuo fluxu, per certitudinem apprehendi non potest, quia prius labitur quam mente diiudicetur: sicut Heraclitus dixit quod *non est possibile aquam fluvii currentis bis tangere*, ut recitat Philosophus in IV *Metaphysicorum*.

"His autem superveniens Plato, ut posset salvare certam cognitionem veritatis a nobis per intellectum haberi, posuit praeter ista corporalia aliud genus entium a materia et motu separatum, quod nominabat *species* sive *ideas*, per quarum participationem unumquodque istorum singularium et sensibilium dicitur vel homo vel equus vel aliquod huiusmodi. Sic ergo dicebat scientias et

This excessive dualism in Plato St. Thomas will not accept. The first point to note in his Aristotelianism, therefore, is the rehabilitation of the sensible world. Aristotle, says St. Thomas, shows in many ways that there is some stability present in the physical world; that our senses tell us the truth about their proper objects; and that we have an intellectual power above the senses which renders our experience intelligible.[16] In other words there are two changes that St. Thomas is introducing into the question of the origin of knowledge. First, he is reconstructing and redefining

---

definitiones et quicquid ad actum intellectus pertinet, non referri ad ista corpora sensibilia, sed ad illa immaterialia et separata; ut sic anima non intelligat ista corporalia, sed intelligat horum corporalium species separatas" (*Sum. Theol.*, I, q. 84, a. 1). Cf. *De Spirit. Creat.*, a. 10, ad 8*um*, for a similar text, where, however, it is further specified that the knowledge of ideas is not a *direct* perception of them but is a guide according to which we have knowledge of things. There is no contradiction in this. St. Thomas means that just as a stone would exist by participation in the idea of stone, so I would know a stone by participating in the same idea. In this way, knowledge would refer to the ideas as its normative principles. Cf. *Sum. Theol.*, I, q. 84, a. 4, *Respondeo*. Indeed in the next article of this question in the *Summa*, St. Thomas touches upon the problem of knowing material things in the eternal ideas, and shows how St. Augustine (*De Diversis Quaestionibus* 83, q. 46) modified the transcendental pluralism of Plato to meet the demands of Christianity.

16. "Aristoteles autem per aliam viam processit. Primo enim, multipliciter ostendit, in sensibilibus esse aliquid stabile. Secundo, quod judicium sensus verum est de sensibilibus propriis, sed decipitur circa sensibilia communia, magis autem circa sensibilia per accidens. Tertio, quod supra sensum est virtus intellectiva, quae judicat de veritate, non per aliqua intelligibilia extra existentia, sed per lumen intellectus agentis, quod facit intelligibilia" (*De Spirit. Creat.*, a 10, ad 8*um.*).

This point of Aristotelian criticism appeared decisive to Duns Scotus as well. Cf. E. Gilson, *Avicenne et le point de départ de Duns Scot (Archives d'hist. doctr. et litt. du moyen âge*, ii, 1927), p. 117 ff. and Aristotle, *Metaphysics*, III, 5, 1010a 15-25.

the nature of the physical world in such a way as to avoid
the extreme dualism of Plato. Indeed, he thinks that Plato
sought for the kind of stability in the physical world which
belongs only to the formal unity of a concept; or, what is
the same thing, that Plato made the mistake of thinking
that the necessary correspondence between thought and being required also that the mode of thought be as well the
mode of being.[17] Secondly, since there is no incompatibility
between the universality of knowledge and the concrete unity
of things, the ideas are transformed into substantial forms.
Such a change in the physical world guarantees the possibility of natural science[18] and changes the field of human
knowledge. As with Plato, so with Aristotle, knowledge is
of being, but with Aristotle there is the definite implication
that knowledge is of material being. Furthermore, with
St. Thomas Aquinas this implication becomes an important
part in a consciously developed doctrine that, in this life,
material being is the only proper object of human knowledge.[19] There are two important consequences of this doc-

17. "Neque tamen oportet quod, si scientiae sunt de univer-
salibus, universalia sint extra animam per se subsistentia, sicut
Plato posuit. Quamvis enim ad veritatem cognitionis necesse sit
ut cognito rei respondeat, non tamen oportet quod idem sit modus
cognitionis et rei; quae enim conjuncta sunt in re, interdum di-
visim cognoscuntur; simul enim una res est alba et dulcis; visus
tamen cognoscit solam albedinem, gustus solam dulcedinem. . .
Et sic haec duo non repugnant, quod universalia non subsistant
extra animam et quod intellectus, intelligens universalia, intelligat
res quae sunt extra animam" *(Contra Gentiles,* II, 85).

18. *Sum. Theol.,* I, q. 84, a. 8, *Respondeo,* ad *Sed hoc dupliciter.*

19. "Et ideo hic ostendit, quod intellectus indiget sensu. . .
Dicit ergo primo, quod quia *nulla* res intellecta a nobis, est praeter
magnitudines sensibiles, quasi ab eis separata secundum esse, sicut
sensibilia videntur ab invicem separata: necesse est quod intelligibilia intellectus nostri sint in speciebus sensibilibus secundum
esse, tam illae quae dicuntur per abstractionem, scilicet mathema-
tica, quam naturalia, quae sunt habitus et passiones sensibilium.
Et propter hoc sine sensu non potest aliquis homo addiscere quasi

trine. The first is that, as the direct object of the intellect, essence, is always found in an individual concrete being, the senses and the imagination become *necessary* parts of man in the fulfilment of this intellectual activity. In this way, an intelligible reason is assigned for the union of soul and body. The second consequence is that the soul of itself has no knowledge whatever and cannot gain any actual knowledge without the assistance of sensation.[20]

---

de novo acquirens scientiam, neque intelligere, quasi utens scientia habita. Sed oportet, cum aliquis speculatur in actu, quod simul formet aliquod phantasma. Phantasmata enim sunt similitudines sensibilium" (*In De Anima*, III, lect. XIII, ed. Pirotta, no. 791). On the relations between intellect and phantasm, cf. *Sum. Theol.*, I, q. 84, a. 7, *Respondeo*, especially, "Intellectus autem humani, qui est conjunctus corpori, proprium objectum est quidditas natura in materia corporali existens; et per huiusmodi naturas visibilium rerum in invisibilium rerum aliqualem cognitionem ascendit. De ratione huius naturae est, quod in aliquo individuo existat. . . Particulare autem apprehendimus per sensum et imaginationem. Et ideo necesse est ad hoc quod intellectus actu intelligat suum objectum proprium, quod convertat se ad phantasmata, ut speculetur naturam universalem in particulari existentem".

20. The significance of this doctrine is perhaps nowhere more apparent than in the Thomistic theory on the self-knowledge of the soul. The *Contra Gentiles* (II, 83 and III, 45-46) and the *De Veritate* (q. x, *De Mente*) present very clear texts on this question. If we consider these texts briefly, the following points of doctrine appear: Rejecting the Platonic explanation of the nature of the soul and its knowledge (because it forces us to say that the union of soul and body is a hindrance to the intellectual operations of the soul), and admitting the necessity of sensation in the acquisition of knowledge (*Contra Gentiles*, II, 83, ad *Item, Necesse est dicere*), we must determine whether the soul has any knowledge of those substances that are not the object of the senses, i.e., separate substances and itself. Here it is necessary to note immediately that the intelligibility of a substance in itself is no guarantee of its intelligibility to the possible intellect. On the contrary, we must interpret the range of the possible intellect according to the condition of its existence and its relation to the active intellect. For, if we suppose that soul and body are essentially

As against the Platonic tradition, St. Thomas will say that in the order of intelligent substances the soul is last, just as prime matter is last in the order of sensible substances.

---

united, then we must admit also an essential and necessary relation between the possible intellect and material substances; and from this it follows that the possible intellect cannot know separate substances. This conclusion is enforced by the relation of the possible intellect to the active intellect. Now, a passive power—and the possible intellect is, in some sense, a passive power—is capable of receiving only those modifications which the corresponding active power is capable of effecting; so that the possible intellect will be capable of understanding those things which the light of the active intellect has made actually intelligible. Since it is only material substances that fall under this power of the active intellect, it is only material substances that the possible intellect can know in its present condition: *Sic ergo intellectus possibilis, si ponitur corpori unitus secundum esse, non potest intelligere substantias separatas (Contra Gentiles, III, 45).*

This analysis, however, appears to differ radically from what St. Augustine had held on the same question, for he appears to have said that the soul knows separate substances through itself and material substances through the senses of the body; which seems to mean that for St. Augustine the soul has a direct knowledge of itself. We must consider, therefore, in what sense it is true to say that the soul knows itself through itself (*Contra Gentiles*, III, 46, ad in.). At this point we may follow the discussion of the *De Veritate*, where, as in the *Contra Gentiles*, the point of departure is the elimination of a Platonic theory of knowledge and the adoption of the Aristotelian position as one which is *prae omnibus praedictis positionibus rationabilior (De Veritate*, q. x, a. 6). We may note, first of all, that *mens* refers to the highest power or faculty of the soul or to the soul as possessing that faculty (*De Veritate*, q. x, a. 1). The question now is this: does the *mens* know itself through its essence or through some species? How is the phrase *through its essence* to be interpreted? It may simply mean that a thing is known through its essence when the essence itself of the thing is known. But it may mean also that the essence itself of the thing is the *means* of knowing that thing. It is this second interpretation of the phrase which is here in question. Now, the knowledge of the soul may be individual or general. If it is individual, it will include what a man may know

Both the human intellect and prime matter are absolutely un-
determined by any forms.   The human intellect begins its

---

of his own soul, e.g., its existence, when he perceives that he has
a soul; if it is general, it will include the essence as well as the
proper accident of the soul.   Individual knowledge is either actual
or habitual.   Actual individual knowledge of the soul includes the
actual observation that we have a soul, and this is possible only
through the acts of the soul.   We must understand something before we understand that we are understanding: the soul arrives at
an actual perception of its own existence through its activities.   In
the case of habitual knowledge, the soul knows itself through its
essence.   This means that since the soul is present to itself, it is
able to pass to an actual knowledge of itself, just as any one,
through possessing the habit of knowledge, is able, through the
presence of that habit, to perceive those things which fall within
the province of the habit.   For the soul to perceive that it exists
and to observe what is taking place within it no habit is required.
For this purpose, the essence alone of the soul, which is present
to the mind, is sufficient, for from this essence proceed the activities in which the essence of the soul is actually perceived.   To
conclude: the soul perceives itself actually through its operations;
it perceives itself habitually through its essence in the sense that
its essence is present to it and can therefore become actually
known by operating.   Habitual knowledge, therefore, refers simply
to the *presence* of the soul to itself.

If we turn now to the knowledge of the soul that is included
in its definition, we pass from the question of knowing *that* the
soul exists to the question of knowing *what* it is.   In what way
does the soul know what it is?   To answer this question we must
recall what St. Thomas has already said on the nature of the
possible intellect.   It is a power that is in potency to all intelligible forms; and since, for actual knowledge, the possible intellect
must be informed, the possible intellect becomes knowable in the
way and to the extent that it is informed.   In other words, the
possible intellect as informed is the means the soul has of knowing its own nature.   Now, the possible intellect is informed, as we
have seen, by the species abstracted by the active intellect.   Consequently, we must say that the *mens* cannot know itself in such a
way that it apprehends its own nature immediately; it knows its
own nature through apprehending the natures of other things, just
as the nature of prime matter is known by way of its information:

life by being merely capable of knowing all knowable things.[21]
There is a gap and a radical need in the perfection of its
substance; it is not, in a complete sense, fully substantial.
The reason for this affects the most vital aspect of the soul,
for the question resolves itself into this form: why is the
definition of the soul as the form of the body the essential
definition of the very substance of the soul itself? The answer is that if the function of an intellectual substance is to
know, the soul, while being such a substance, finds itself incapable of exercising the functions proper to its substance
until certain conditions have been fulfilled. It is clear that
the soul can know, but does not know unless an object is
present to it. Such an object is the physical world. But
since the material objects of our experience are only potentially intelligible, they cannot as such be the object of the
intellect. But they can be the object of the senses. Sensation thus becomes not a mere occasion as with Avicenna, nor

---

*Unde mens nostra non potest seipsam intelligere, ita quod seipsam
immediate apprehendat, sed ex hoc quod apprehendit alia, devenit
in suam cognitionem; sicut et natura materiae primae cognoscitur
ex hoc ipso quod est talium formarum receptiva (De Veritate,* q. x,
a. 8).

It is scarcely necessary to remark how this range in the field
of knowledge which St. Thomas assigns to the possible intellect
is only the expression of the metaphysical definition of the soul as
a form which completes its own nature by being the form of the
body.

21. " . . . ideo secundum opinionem Aristotelis alii dicunt,
quod intellectus humanus est ultimus in ordine intelligibilium,
sicut materia prima in ordine sensibilium: et sicut materia secundum suam essentiam considerata nullam formam habet, ita intellectus humanus in sui principio est sicut tabula in qua nihil
scriptum est, sed postmodum in eo scientia per sensus acquiritur
virtute intellectus agentis. Sic igitur principium naturale humanae cognitionis est esse quidem in potentia ad omnia cognos-
cibilia, non habere autem a principio notitiam nisi eorum quae
statim per lumen intellectus agentis cognoscuntur, sicut principia
universalia" (De Veritate, Quaest. XVIII, a. 7).

a means of awakening as with Plato, but a real and direct contribution to the content of knowledge itself. In this way, the body becomes necessary to the operations of the soul as an intelligent being; and this is the only reason that can be advanced to explain *why* the soul should be joined to the body: such an economy in the field of action only reflects the economy in metaphysics that is involved in the unity of man. From the standpoint of operation, the soul is helpless *until* there is something for it to grasp, an object to perfect and fulfil its capacities. It is not sufficient to say that the soul is joined to the body for the good of the body, because no form is joined to matter for the sake of the matter. It is the exact opposite that is true. The soul is joined to the body for the sake of the soul. *Man* exists for the sake of the soul, but man is more important than the soul for the simple but decisive reason that the soul can do what it is its nature to do only as the form of the body.[22]

This need of union was explained neither by Plato nor by Avicenna. And the crucial point in both instances was the origin of knowledge. Plato rendered the body useless,[23] while

---

22. "Sed secundum hanc positionem sufficiens ratio assignari non posset quare anima nostra corpori uniretur. Non enim potest dici quod anima intellectiva corpori uniatur propter mobile, sed potius e converso. Maxime autem videtur corpus esse necessarium animae intellectivae ad eius propriam operationem, quae est intelligere: quia secundum esse suum a corpore non dependet" (*Sum. Theol.*, I, q. 84, a. 4).—Cp. *Comm. in Anal. Post.*, II, c. 9, lect. 8, no. 3; ed. Leon., vol. i, p. 356.

23. "Si autem dicatur quod indiget anima nostra sensibus ad intelligendum, quibus quodammodo excitetur ad consideranda ea quorum species intelligibiles a principiis separatis recipit: hoc non videtur sufficere. Quia huiusmodi excitatio non videtur necessaria animae nisi inquantum est consopita, secundum Platonicos, quodammodo et obliviosa propter unionem ad corpus: et sic sensus non proficeret animae intellectivae nisi ad tollendum impedimentum quod animae provenit ex corporis unione. Remanet igitur quaerendum quae sit causa unionis animae ad corpus" (*ibid.*). That

the Platonism of Avicenna was inconsequent. This difficulty within the Avicennian system was really the product of an attempt to graft Aristotelian ideas onto a fundamentally Platonic psychology. As concerns Plato, St. Thomas says that not only does he leave the union of soul and body unexplained, but that he also leaves sensation unexplained. For sensation cannot be considered as an act of the soul alone, but must be explained as belonging to the composite man, for otherwise even animal souls would be subsistent.[24] Rather, following Aristotle, it is necessary to say that there are real physical changes of which the composite man is the subject through the body.[25] Now as we may remember from the Thomistic criticism of the Platonic conception of soul and body, it is impossible to explain sensation as a human activity if it takes place in a body which is joined to the soul only after the fashion of *motor-mobile*. If soul and body are not one in existence, they are not one in operation: *illud autem est unaquaeque res, quod operatur operationes illius rei. Unde illud est homo, quod operatur operationes hominis.*[26] This is the foundation upon which the definition of the soul must be built. We must take into account the distinctive activity of the soul and the origin of this activity; while it is necessary to safeguard, as St. Thomas constantly insists, the unity of the human substance. With this in mind, we are not surprised to find the following statement in the commentary on the Sentences of Peter Lombard concerning the unity of man: *intellectus non negatur esse forma ma-*

---

is, following the Platonic analysis of sensation, the cause of union would still remain a problem.

24. "Plato autem distinxit inter intellectum et sensum; utrumque tamen attribuit principio incorporeo, ponens quod, sicut intelligere ita et sentire convenit animae secundum seipsam. Et ex hoc sequebatur quod etiam animae brutorum animalium sint subsistentes" (*Sum. Theol.*, I, q. 75, a. 3).

25. *Ibid.*

26. *Sum. Theol.*, I, q. 75, a. 4, *Respondeo.*

*terialis, cum det esse materiae, sicut forma substantialis, quan-
tum ad esse primum.*   Only after this unity is established
may we proceed to say: *sed dicitur immaterialis respectu actus
secundi, qui est operatio: quia intelligere non expletur mediante organo corporali, et hoc contingit quia ab essentia animae non exit operatio nisi mediante virtute ejus vel potentia:
unde cum habeat quasdam virtutes quae non sunt actus aliquorum organorum corporis, oportet quod quaedam operationes animae sint non mediante corpore.*[27]

The firmness of this conclusion at so early a date did not
go unnoticed.   After stating the *novitas* of St. Thomas in a
passage so well known that it does not need quotation, William of Tocco remarks of St. Thomas that *statim tam certe
esse judicii coepisset.*   Indeed, the direction that the Thomistic synthesis took did not in the least escape this biographer.
In the eyes of William of Tocco the thought of St. Thomas
Aquinas was not only new, it was also pregnant with the rehabilitation of man and his dignity as a creature in the service
of God: *nec absurdum videatur aliquibus, quod in Sapientiae
divinae sententiis, secularibus quis utatur scientiis, cum ab
eodem intellectu divino objecta omnium scientiarum prodeant,
a quo divinae Sapientiae veritates emanent, cui omnes scientiae
juris deserviunt, a qua et humanitus acquisita procedunt.*[28]
The spirit of Christian humanism that pervades the writings
of the Angelic Doctor could not be more fittingly expressed.

---

27. *In II Sent.*, d. 17, q. 2, a. 1, ad 1; vol. 8, p. 224-225.   Cf.
Godfrey of Fontaines, *Quodl.* II, 7; p. 130, for a similar, if hesi-
tant, conclusion. The completeness of Godfrey's Thomism, however, is to be qualified: cf. *Quodl. VIII*, 9; p. 369-375.

28. *Vita S. Thomae Aquinatis*, Acta Sanctorum, March 7 (vol.
21), cap. iii, no. 15, p. 661F 662A.

VI. BIBLIOGRAPHY.

A. *Principal Sources.*

1. ST. ALBERT THE GREAT.—*Opera Omnia*, ed. A. Borgnet, Paris, Vivès, 38 vols., 1890-1899.

2. ALFRED OF SARESHEL.—*De Motu Cordis*, ed. C. Baeumker, *(Beiträge*, xxiii, 1-2), Münster i. W., 1923.

3. ARISTOTLE.—*Opera Omnia*, 5 vols., Paris (Didot), 1873 (vols. ii, v), 1878 (vol. iv), 1927 (vols. i, iii).

4. ST. AUGUSTINE.—*Opera Omnia*, in Migne, P.L., vol. 32-47.

5. AVERROES.—*Aristotelis Stagiritae Libri Omnes . . . . cum Averrois Cordubensis variis in eosdem Commentariis*, vol. vi, Venetiis apud Juntas, 1550.

6. AVICENNA. *Metaphysices Compendium* ex arabo in latinum reddidit et adnotationibus adornavit N. Carame, Roma, 1926.

7. BOETHIUS.—*Opera Omnia*, in Migne, P.L., vol. 63-64.

8. ST. BONAVENTURE.—*Opera Omnia*, Quaracchi, 1882-1902.

9. COSTA-BEN-LUCA.—*De Differentia Spiritus et Animae*, ed. C. S. Barach, Innsbruck, 1878.

10. DOMINICUS GUNDISSALINUS.—*De Immortalitate Animae*, ed. G. Bülow, in *Des Dominicus Gundissalinus Schrift "Von der Unsterblichkeit der Seele,"*....*(Beiträge*, ii, 3), Münster i. W., 1897.

11. —*De Processione Mundi*, ed. G. Bülow, *Des Dominicus Gundissalinus Schrift "Von dem Hervorgange der Welt" (De Processione Mundi) (Beiträge*, xxiv, 3), Münster i. W., 1925.

12. GILES OF LESSINES.—*De Unitate Formae*, ed. M. de Wulf (*Les philosophes belges*, i), Louvain, 1901.

13. GODFREY OF FONTAINES.—*Quodlibetum II*, ed. M. de Wulf-A. Pelzer in *Les quatres premiers Quodlibets de Godfroid de Fontaines (Les philosophes belges*, ii); Louvain, 1904; *Quodlibetum X*, ed. J. Hoffmans, *Le dixième Quodlibet de Godfroid de Fontaines (Les philosophes belges*, iv, 3), Louvain, 1931.

14. IBN GEBIROL.—*Fons Vitae*, ed. C. Baeumker (*Beiträge*, i, 2-4), Münster i. W., 1892-1897.

15. MATTHEW OF AQUASPARTA.—*Quaestiones Disputatae Selectae*, II. *Quaestiones de Christo*, Quaracchi, 1914.

16. NEMESIUS.—*De Natura Hominis*, in Migne, P.G., vol. 40.

17. —*De Natura Hominis*, in the tr. of Burgundio of Pisa, ed. C. Burkhard, Vindobonae, 1902.

18. PLATO.—*Opera Omnia*, ed. J. Burnet, Clarendon, Oxford U. Press, 1899-1905.

19. POMPONATIUS.—*Tractatus de Immortalitate Animae*, ed. C. G. Bardili, Tubingae, 1791.

20. SIGER OF BRABANT.—*Quaestiones de Anima Intellectiva*, ed. P. Mandonnet in *Siger de Brabant et l'avérroisme latin au XIIIe siècle*, 2e ed., P. II (*Les philosophes belges*, vii), Louvain, 1908, p. 143-171.

21. —*Quaestiones de Anima*, ed. F. Van Steenberghen in *Siger de Brabant d'après ses oeuvres inédites*, I. *Les oeuvres inédites* (*Les philosophes belges*, xii), Louvain, 1931, p. 1-160.

22. ST. THOMAS AQUINAS.—*Opera Omnia*, ed. E. Fretté and P. Maré, Paris, Vivès, 34 vols., 1872-1880.

23. —*Opera Omnia*, iussu impensaque Leonis XIII edita, Romae, 1882—(15 vols. have appeared).

24. CHARTULARIUM UNIVERSITATIS PARISIENSIS, ed. H. Denifle and E. Chatelain, 4 vols., Paris, 1889-1897.

B. *References.*

25. BAEUMKER, C.—*Petrus de Hibernia der Jugendlehrer der Thomas von Aquino und seine Disputation vor König Manfred* (*Sitzungsberichte der Bayerischen Akademie der Wissenschaften*, Philosophisch-philologische und historische Klasse, 1920, 8. Abhandlung), München, 1920.

26. —*Die Stellung des Alfred von Sareshel (Alfredus Anglicus) und seiner Schrift De Motu Cordis in der Wissenschaft des beginnenden XIII. Jahrhunderts* (*Sitzungsberichte der Bayerischen Akademie der Wissenschaften*, Phil.-phil. Klasse, 1913, 9. Abhandlung), München, 1913.

27. —*Les écrits philosophiques de Dominicus Gundissalinus*, Revue thomiste, V (1897), p. 723-745.

28. CARR, H.—*The Function of the Phantasm in St. Thomas Aquinas,* in *Philosophical Essays Presented to John Watson,* p. 179-203.

29. COADY, Sr. M. A.—*The Phantasm according to the Teaching of St. Thomas,* The Catholic U. of America, Washington, D.C., 1932.

30. CHRIST, P. S.—*The Psychology of the Active Intellect of Averroes,* Philadelphia, 1926.

31. FOREST, A.—*La structure métaphysique du concret selon saint Thomas d'Aquin (Etudes de philosophie médiévale,* xiv), Paris, 1931.

32. GARDEIL, A.—*La perception expérimentelle de l'âme par elle-même d'après saint Thomas,* in *Mélanges thomistes (Bibliothèque thomiste,* iii), Le Saulchoir, Kain, 1923, 219-236.

33. GAUL, L.—*Alberts des Grossen Verhältnis zu Plato (Beiträge,* xii, 1), Munster i. W., 1913.

34. GEYER, B. (ed.)—*Friedrich Ueberwegs Grundriss der Geschichte der Philosophie,* II. *Die Patristische und Scholastische Philosophie,* Elfte Auflage, Berlin, 1928.

35. —*Divi Thomae Aqinatis de essentia et potentiis animae in generali Quaest. Sum. Theol.,* I, 75-77 *una cum Guilelmi de la Mare Correctorii articulo* 28 *(Florilegium Patristicum,* xiv), Bonnae, 1920.

36. GILSON, E.—*La philosophie de saint Bonaventure (Etudes de philosophie médiévale,* iv), Paris, 1924.

37. —*La philosophie au moyen âge,* Paris, 1925.

38. —*Pourquoi saint Thomas a critiqué saint Augustin (Archives d'hist. doctr. et litt. du moyen âge,* i, 1926-1927), p. 5-127.

39. —*Avicenne et le point de départ de Duns Scot (Archives d'hist. doctr. et litt. du moyen âge,* ii, 1927), p. 89-149.

40. —*Le thomisme,* 3e ed. *(Etudes de philosophie médiévale,* i), Paris, 1927.

41. —*Introduction à l'étude de saint Augustin (Etudes de philosophie médiévale,* xi), Paris, 1929.

42. —*Les sources gréco-arabes de l'augustinisme avicennisant (Archives d'hist. doctr. et litt. du moyen âge,* iv, 1929, p. 5-149.

43. —*Réflexions sur la controverse s. Thomas - s. Augustin,* in *Mélanges Mandonnet,* I *(Bibliothèque thomiste,* xiii), Paris, 1930, p. 371-382.

44. —*Etudes sur le rôle de la pensée médiévale dans la formation du système cartésien* (*Etudes de philosophie médiévale,* xiii), Paris, 1930, Part I, ch. i: *L'innéisme cartésien et la théologie* (p. 9-50); Part II, ch. i: *De la critique des formes substantielles au doute méthodique* (p. 141-190).

45. —*L'idée de philosophie chez saint Augustin et chez saint Thomas d'Aquin* in *Acta Hebdomadae Augustinanae-Thomisticae,* Taurini-Romae, 1931, p. 75-87.

46. —*L'esprit de la philosophie médiévale,* 2 vols., Paris, 1932.

47. GLORIEUX, P.—*Les premières polémiques thomistes: I. Le Correctorium Corruptorii "Quare"* (*Bibliothèque thomiste,* ix), Le Saulchoir, Kain, 1927.

48. —*Les Questions Disputées de s. Thomas et leur suite chronologique,* Recherches de théologie ancienne et médiévale, iv (1932), p. 5-33.

49. GRABMANN, M.—*Forschungen über die lateinische Aristoteles-übersetzungen des XIII. Jahrhunderts (Beiträge,* xvii, 5-6), Münster i. W., 1916.

50. —*Geschichte der Philosophie, III. Die Philosophie des Mittelalters* (Sammlung Goschen), Berlin, 1921.

51. —*Mittelalterliches Geistesleben,* München, 1926, ch. vii-viii (p. 249-313), on Peter of Ireland and on St. Thomas' commentaries on Aristotle.

52. —*Mittelalterliche lateinische Uebersetzungen von Schriften der Aristoteles-Kommentatoren Johannes Philoponos, Alexander von Aphrodisias und Themistios* (*Sitzungsberichte der Bayerischen Akademie der Wissenschaften,* Phil.-hist. Abteilung, 1929, Heft 7), München, 1929.

53. —*Der lateinische Averroismus des 13. Jahrhunderts und seine Stellung zur christlichen Weltanschauung* (*Sitzungberichte der Bayerischen Akademie der Wissenschaften,* Phil.-hist. Abteilung, 1933, Heft 2)), München, 1931.

54. —*Die Werke des Hl. Thomas von Aquin,* (*Beiträge,* xx, 1-2), Münster i. W., 1931.

55. —*Der Hl. Albert des Grosse,* München, 1932.

56. GUILLET, J.—*La "lumière intellectuelle" d'après saint Thomas* (*Archives d'hist. doctr. et litt. du moyen âge,* ii, 1927), p. 77-88.

57. HASKINS, C. H.—*Studies in the History of Mediaeval Science,* Cambridge, Harvard U. Press, 1st ed., 1924, 2nd ed., 1927.

58. HAUREAU, J. B.—*Histoire de la philosophie scolastique*, 3 vols., Paris, 1872-1880.

59. HUSIK, I.—*A History of Medieval Jewish Philosophy*, New York, 1916 (reprinted, 1930).

60 LONGPRE, E.—*La philosophie du b. Duns Scot*, Paris, 1924.

61. LUTZ, E.—*Die Psychologie Bonaventuras (Beiträge*, vi. 4-5), Münster, i. W., 1909.

62. MANDONNET, P.—*Des écrits authentiques de s. Thomas d'Aquin*, 2e ed., Fribourg (Suisse), 1910.

63. —*Siger de Brabant et l'avérroisme latin au XIIIe siècle*, 2e ed., P.I.: *Etude critique (Les philosophes belges*, vi), Louvain, 1911.

64. —*Chronologie des questions disputées de saint Thomas d'Aquin*, Revue thomiste, nouvelle série, I (1918), p. 266-287, 340-371.

65. —*Albert le Grand*, in *Dictionnaire de théologie catholique*, I (1923), col. 666-674.

66. —*Thomas d'Aquin lecteur à la curie romaine. Chronologie du séjour* (1259-1268), in *Xenia Thomistica*, Roma, 1925, vol. iii, p. 9-40.

67. McWILLIAMS, J. A.—*St. Albert the Great and Plurality of Forms* (The Modern Schoolman, ix, 3, March, 1932, p. 43-44, 59-61).

68. O'LEARY, C. J.—*The Substantial Composition of Man according to St. Bonaventure*, The Catholic U. of America, Washington, D.C., 1931.

69. O'LEARY, De L.—*Arabic Thought and its Place in History*, London, 1922.

70. O'NEIL, J.—*Cosmology. An Introduction to the Philosophy of Matter*, I. *The Greeks and the Aristotelian Schoolmen*, London, 1923.

71. ROHMER, J.—*La théorie de l'abstraction dans l'école franciscaine d'Alexandre de Halès à Jean Peckam (Archives d'hist. doctr. et litt. du moyen âge*, iii, 1928), p. 105-184.

72. ROLAND-GOSSELIN, M.-D.—*Le "De Ente et Essentia" de s. Thomas d'Aquin (Bibliothèque thomiste*, viii), Le Saulchoir, Kain, 1926.

73. —*Sur les relations de l'âme et du corps d'après Avicenne*, in *Mélanges Mandonnet*, II *(Bibliothèque thomiste*, xiv), Paris, 1930, p. 47-54.

74. SCHNEIDER, A.—*Die Psychologie Alberts des Grossen* (*Beiträge*, iv, 5-6), Münster i. W., 1903-1906.

75. SERTILLANGES, A.-D.—*S. Thomas d'Aquin*, 2 vols., 4e ed., Paris, 1925.

76. TAYLOR, A. E.—*St. Thomas as a Philosopher* (in *St. Thomas Aquinas*, a collection of papers read at Manchester, 1924, and published by B. Herder, St. Louis, 1925, p. 33-62).

77. THERY, G.—*Autour du décret de* 1210: *I. David de Dinant* (*Bibliothèque thomiste*, vi), Le Saulchoir, Kain, 1925.

78. —*Autour du décret de* 1210: *II. Alexandre d'Aphrodise* (*Bibliothèque thomiste*, vii), Le Saulchoir, Kain, 1926.

79. —*L'augustinisme médiéval et le problème de l'unité de la forme substantielle*, in *Acta Hebdomadae Augustinianae-Thomisticae*, Taurini-Romae, 1931, p. 140-200.

80. THORNDYKE, L.—*A History of Magic and Experimental Science*, 2 vols., New York, 1923.

81. DE WULF, M.—*Le traité De Unitate Formae de Gilles de Lessines* (*Les philosophes belges*, i), Louvain, 1901, p. 3-122 (an historical introduction to the doctrine of plural forms in the thirteenth century).

82. *Histoire de la philosophie médiévale*, 2 vols., 3e ed., Louvain, 1924-1925. English tr. by E. Messenger under the title *History of Medieval Philosophy*, 5th ed., New York and London, 1926.

83. ZIESCHE, K.—*Die Naturlehre Bonaventuras*, In Philosophisches Jahrbuch, xxi, 2, Fulda, 1908, p. 156-189.

ADDENDA.

1. FESTUGIERE, A. M.—*La place du De Anima dans le système aristotélicien d'après saint Thomas*, in *Archives d'hist. doct. et litt. du moyen âge*, iv, 1931, p. 25-47.

2. GRABMANN, M.—*Neu aufgefundene Werke des Siger von Brabant und Boetius von Dacien* (Sitzungsberichte der Bayer. Akad. der Wissenschaften, Phil.-phil. und hist. Klasse, 1924, 2. Abhandlung), München, 1924.

3. —*Die Opuscula de Summo Bono sive de Vita Philosophi und de Sompniis des Boetius von Dacien*, in *Archives d'hist. doctr. et litt. du moyen âge*, iv, 1931, p. 287-317.

4. McCORMICK, J. F.—*Suarez on Matter and Form*, in *Proceedings of the Tenth Annual Convention* of the Jesuit Educational Association, Chicago, Loyola U. Press, 1931, p. 172-183.

5. SHARP, D. E.—*Franciscan Philosophy at Oxford in the Thirteenth Century*, Oxford Press, 1930.

6. DeGUIBERT, JOSEPH.—*Les doublets de s. Thomas d'Aquin*, Paris, 1926.

INDEX TO PROPER NAMES.